I0824272

NIRENBERG

NIRENBERG

The Education of a Texas Public Servant

RON NIRENBERG
AND DAVID W. LESCH

MAVERICK BOOKS / TRINITY UNIVERSITY PRESS
San Antonio, Texas

Maverick Books, an imprint of Trinity University Press
San Antonio, Texas 78212

Jacket design by John Andrade, AND/COM
Book design by BookMatters, Berkeley
Cover photo by David Teran, originally published in *San Antonio Woman*
Author photo of Ron Nirenberg by Siggi Ragnar
Author photo of David W. Lesch by Trinity University

ISBN 978-1-59534-330-7 paper
ISBN 978-1-59534-331-4 ebook

Trinity University Press strives to produce its books using methods and materials in an environmentally sensitive manner. We favor working with manufacturers that practice sustainable management of all natural resources, produce paper using recycled stock, and manage forests with the best possible practices for people, biodiversity, and sustainability. The press is a member of the Green Press Initiative, a nonprofit program dedicated to supporting publishers in their efforts to reduce their impacts on endangered forests, climate change, and forest-dependent communities.

The paper used in this publication meets the minimum requirements of the American National Standard for Information Sciences—Permanence of Paper for Printed Library Materials, ANSI 39.48–1992.

CIP data on file at the Library of Congress
30 29 28 27 26 | 5 4 3 2 1

PRINTED IN CANADA

To my wife Erika and my son Jonah,

and my beloved city of San Antonio

CONTENTS

SOPHIA

She lived for two hours. Sophia was her name. She was my daughter. Her mother—my wife, Erika Prosper—and I were able to hold her for a short time before the doctors came in to take her away, and she soon passed. She was so small. Erika remembers her almost fitting in my hand. Sophia was our first child. We still think about her every day.

We still don't know what happened that day in February 2007. Sophia was born prematurely at twenty-nine weeks. Erika had something called PUPPP, or pruritic urticarial papules and plaques of pregnancy. She recalls it being a really weird type of inflammation around the stretch marks during her pregnancy. It was a severe itchy rash for which she could not take normal steroids or antihistamines. She had to take some sort of special steroidal medicine. But PUPPP is not a threat to the mother or child during pregnancy, just annoying, and other than that, there was really no indication of anything out of the ordinary. A normal pregnancy is about forty weeks, and a premature baby is defined as one who is born before thirty-seven weeks—or about three weeks prior to the expected day of birth.

Premature babies do not have enough time to grow and develop as much as full-term babies. Every week, even every day, counts. Premature babies, particularly those born in the thirty-three- to thirty-seven-week period, can live long healthy lives, especially with the technology that exists today in many hospitals' neonatal intensive care units. The prognosis for a baby born before thirty weeks, however, was not good in 2007, and even today, with Sophia born at only twenty-nine weeks, it would have been a challenge for her to survive, much less live a healthy life.

I remember Erika coming down the stairs that morning to the garage, where I was getting in a quick workout, and saying that we had to go to the hospital immediately. She said it felt like her water was breaking, and of course, that alarmed us both. We got in my car and took off for the hospital, less than ten minutes away.

The next couple of hours were a blur. Erika was panicked, and I recall the doctors giving us medical information in real time while they were checking out what was wrong. I couldn't really understand it all; I think Erika did. But mixed up in this stream of sentences from the doctors were the words we knew were coming but didn't want to hear: Sophia was not going to survive. From then on it seemed like both of us were going through shock and stages of grief in fast-forward.

I remember that several hours later, after the intensity of the morning was gone and the doctors took Sophia away, I stared into a mirror above the sink in the hospital room. Erika's ob-gyn was just walking out, but she stopped and put her hand on my shoulder for a second—as if to absorb some of the grief that she knew was coming for us. I fell apart.

We were devastated. It is a wrenching thing to go through. Erika's boss in San Antonio at the time, Luis Garcia, still gave her the full maternity leave, but in Erika's words she was "a mess" for the next year. She would tell me that her body would still sometimes feel pregnant for a while afterward—phantom kicks, skin reactions. But the emptiness was overwhelming for us. The hardest part was hearing Erika have to answer when someone asked when her baby was due. It was like having to go through that awful day again and again.

We went through a host of tests afterward to try to figure out what had gone wrong, and there was nothing conclusive. Pregnancy complications happen, and they happen a lot to some people, we were told. But we could still keep trying, the doctor said. Cold comfort as we were still trying to overcome the lost dreams of Sophia.

Erika began to wonder if something was particularly wrong with her. Had she done something wrong? You go through life, graduate from college, get a job, find the love of your life, get married. Everything seems to be going well, as planned even—and then this. It really makes you question what's it all for. Why did this happen to us? What did we do wrong?

Still, we wanted nothing more than to be parents. Erika was thirty-three, and I was thirty-one. We had spent almost a decade together as a married couple without that responsibility. We were ready for the next phase of our lives. In some ways, the tragedy of losing Sophia tested our relationship. We made it through scarred but stronger and more connected, and we weren't going to shy away from having another child.

But such a loss makes a person sit back and rethink things. At the time of the pregnancy, I was traveling a lot for work. And I began to regret that, especially when Erika, who was already into her second trimester, slipped on our iced-over back porch and landed on her back. I was not there to help. So when we found out Erika was pregnant again in 2008 I began to cut back on travel. At the time I was working for the Annenberg Public Policy Center, based in Philadelphia, directing civic engagement and municipal policy research projects. I worked out of my home office in San Antonio but traveled frequently—one of our projects had sites in twenty-two cities.

Now, with this second pregnancy, my paternal instincts went into overdrive. As I saw it, my main job was to take care of Erika: I prepped all of her prenatal vitamins, did all the coconut oil belly rubs she wanted, and attended every medical appointment from the moment we found out she was expecting. It felt like nine months of waiting to exhale. We prayed to reach the milestone when we had lost Sophia, and we braced ourselves and prayed every moment after.

We were extra careful about every aspect of the pregnancy. Without knowing what went wrong the first time, we were on pins and needles at every step of the way—so paranoid!

Jonah was born in June, less than a year and a half after his sister. We probably would not have tried to have another child so soon if Sophia had lived. So, in a way, the miracle that became Jonah was a kind of gift from her.

Jonah's birth was a miracle in and of itself. He went full term, but during extended labor we watched—horrified—as the baby's heartrate sped into the red zone when Erika pushed and then dropped to the low fifties when she relaxed. It sent the doctors scrambling for an answer.

Ultimately, Erika's obstetrician, Dr. Parke Hedges, decided to do an emergency C-section, and when Jonah was delivered, he confirmed that, indeed, Jonah's birth was a miracle. He was breech, and the umbilical cord was wrapped around his neck several times. Every time Erika pushed, Jonah was getting choked. Dr. Hedges, was great—he acted quickly and decisively.

We were ecstatic about our son. I remember those first moments like they were yesterday. They were moments I had imagined and prayed for since we learned Erika was pregnant the first time. Jonah Bernard Nirenberg was named after Erika's adopted father, Jonah French Gray III, and my grandfather, Bernard Israel Nirenberg, who I called Papa Bernie. If you're wondering, had our child been a girl, she would have been named Julia Klein Prosper. Erika and I agreed ahead of time that a girl would carry on Erika's family legacy and a boy would carry on mine.

After we brought Jonah home, I was a focused parent to say the least, admittedly uptight, still paranoid that something could go wrong. I tend to be super focused about stuff anyway, like my work. Circumstances at the time didn't help; swine flu was gripping American cities, so we were even more vigilant. For six weeks I would not let mother and child even go for a walk outside. Erika accuses me of "kidnapping" them for a couple of months. I just did not want to take any chances.

A few years later we tried one more time to have a child, but about twelve weeks in, during a normal checkup on the fetus, there was no heartbeat. The embryo had passed away—something about it attaching itself improperly to the uterus. After the D&C procedure to keep Erika from getting an infection, the doctor told us that we could not have any more kids. It was another trauma, and for a brief time we felt like we were reliving 2007 all over again. This time it was having to face three-year-old Jonah and tell him he wasn't going to be a big brother. The three of us, including a toddler who could barely comprehend the situation, pulled together, though, and we refused to let the fear and sadness grip us as it had before.

As parents, Erika and I resolved to count our blessings and thanked God for the miracle of Jonah. He's now a teenager, and we still count those blessings, even while we scold him for using all of the hot water or not cleaning up after Tenshi, our precocious Shiba Inu–husky rescue.

Incidentally, on our early dates as a young couple, Erika and I talked quite a bit about being parents and how we would raise kids. We found out that on important matters, we were compatible. We both wanted two kids, no more and no less. We both agreed that we wanted to honor family in their names. And (Erika's idea) that if we could teach our kids good grammar and good manners, we'd be 99 percent of the way there. Agreed.

As life turns out, most people wouldn't know that we did have two kids. Other than friends, family, and some of Erika's coworkers, there weren't any announcements. But it happened. And it has shaped much of our support for women's health care.

I choose to honor Sophia in my own ways too. In 2017, when I was elected mayor, some readers were shocked that a *San Antonio*

Express-News article about my workout regimen featured a photo of me doing pull-ups in a short-sleeve shirt at the gym. (Prior to that, as an elected official, I rarely wore short sleeves in public places.) They were shocked because I had two visible tattoos, one of an open can of spinach on my left forearm (more on that later) and one of an owl—the Greek goddess Athena's owl, to be precise—on my right.

The meaning of the Greek word *sophia* is "wisdom." In fact, one of the great architectural structures from the early medieval world is the Hagia Sophia in Istanbul. It is a mosque now and still known as Holy Wisdom, or Aya Sofya in Turkish. Athena, the virgin goddess of wisdom in Greek mythology, was often accompanied by an owl—hence the owl of Athena, which appeared on Greek coinage. I had that image tattooed on my right arm in memory of our Sophia, our bringer of wisdom so early in our lives.

Sophia was an apt name to give our daughter. Despite the feeling of loss and thoughts of what could have been, she forced me to learn about myself, Erika and me to deepen the bonds of our marriage, and me to become much more cognizant of sacrifice and gratitude. Perseverance and resiliency through pain have been part of becoming the person I am, and are part of the public servant I am today. Accumulated wisdom helped and guided me through it all. Thank you, Sophia.

WELCOME TO TEXAS

Before I ever met Erika or held a newborn child in my hands, true love for me was the Boston Red Sox. I was three years old when my dad's job moved us from Massachusetts to Texas, and while I've been a Texan ever since, if you're born into a Boston sports family, Fenway stays in your blood. Roger "the Rocket" Clemens was my favorite player, and the 1986 World Series collapse was a seminal childhood experience—no less powerful than watching your first crush slip away.

It was also my first Wall Street experience. My group of friends and I created as many side hustles as necessary to add to a growing baseball card collection, sitting in the back of the class and trading them based on whatever value we nine-year-olds assigned. In fact, before I began my professional life—and even now—my dream job was to be the beat writer for the Red Sox. I have always fantasized about spending every day in the Fenway Park press box, tracking every play on a scorecard and telling the world how it happened. I'll count winning over quite a few Yankees fans (they're everywhere!) among my proudest accomplishments in politics. Who says people can't cross divides and come together on shared goals?

The bottom line is I am a Texas-raised San Antonian by choice, but I am a Bostonian by birth. Arlington, Massachusetts, to be exact, where my mom, dad, brother, and I lived until we moved to Austin in 1980. Arlington is a town in Middlesex County, about six miles northwest of Boston, and falls within the Boston metropolitan area. Today its population is about fifty thousand, where the count has generally remained for the past fifty years. Arlington was—and remains—a typical mix of urban-suburban, a mostly working-class community that, like many towns in the area, played a prominent role in the fighting during the Revolutionary War.

The images of playing baseball in the yard and seeing the Green Monster as my family walked up the steps of the first base grandstands are burned into my memory. From what my parents told me, we lived in a modest basement apartment in the middle of town. It looked like the $162.50 a month, all-expenses-paid flat I was renting in San Antonio during college (a good deal in 1998 for a place that probably had a couple of years left before demolition). Mine was a typical New England immigrant nuclear family. According to my father, my great-grandfather Charles Nirenberg was born in Ukraine, and during World War I he immigrated to the United States by himself because he could not afford to bring his family. He made his way to Boston and started a clothing factory. After he made enough money, he went back to visit his family in the small town of Korets in Ukraine. Even today Korets only has about seven thousand people. At the time, the small population was mostly Jewish, and many of the residents were killed or executed during the German occupation in World War II.

My grandfather, Bernard Israel Nirenberg—Papa Bernie to us—was conceived on one of my great-grandfather's visits to Korets. Charles finally made enough money to bring the rest of the family many years after he arrived in the United States. The whole family went through Ellis Island in New York and settled in the Jewish ghettos around Boston. My grandfather did not know English when he arrived and enrolled in a school program to learn the language. Charles died when Papa Bernie was thirteen years old, so he only knew his dad for about five years.

Bernie made his way through Dorchester High School and enrolled in Bentley College (what is now Bentley University), class of 1936. Bentley, founded in 1917, was primarily an accounting and finance school at the time, located in the Back Bay neighborhood of Boston. In 1968 the college moved to Waltham, a town about twelve miles west of Boston.

Bernie took up accounting at Bentley but only attended night school because he could not afford the normal university program during the day. He eventually obtained his bachelor's degree and became a public accountant, although because of a hearing problem, of which he was self-conscious, he did not pursue a CPA certification.

Bernie married Ida Kalish, whose family came from Poland—or Russia, as the border often shifted between the two countries. My grandmother—who we called "Nana Idie"—was never quite sure which one to claim as the country of her birth. Her father was an Orthodox Jew, in contrast to Bernie's father, whose family was not openly devout. But the traditions became part of Bernie and Ida's life together as a result of the typical family arrangement at the time—multiple generations sharing the same apartment. Ken Nirenberg, my dad, grew up in that Orthodox Jewish home, as Bernie had moved in with Ida's family. Every day Ida's father put on the tefillin, special boxes with leather straps that can be worn on the head and around the arm, containing parchment with passages from the Torah written on them.

Ken was not very religious—in fact, he rebelled against organized religion from an early age—but he had to go to synagogue every Saturday with his maternal grandfather. The latter, however, refused to learn English, even though he was in America and had carved out a career as a bricklayer. He spoke Yiddish. My father and he coexisted in the same bedroom without ever being able to really communicate because my dad never learned Yiddish. It was a rather strange situation for someone who has always proudly claimed to be "Jewish by heritage, not by religion." In fact, my father says he never really cared about any religious affiliation and argued quite a bit about Judaism with his parents. Today he claims to be more agnostic, though he is "leaning" toward atheism. That kind of attitude would come as no surprise to anyone who knew him as a younger man.

Kenneth Charles (named after his grandfather) was born in 1946 and raised in Boston. He grew up in Dorchester on the T's Mattapan line, in a house located behind a Hebrew school that he was not allowed to attend because it was Conservative. Like most Jewish boys, he had his bar mitzvah at age thirteen at his Orthodox synagogue—which was probably the last time he attended temple, except for when a relative had a bar mitzvah or other special occasions. He tried to go to the local synagogue after we moved to Austin, but it was during Yom Kippur and the synagogue informed him that he would have to pay to enter (which was typical during Jewish high holidays). He said, "I don't pay to pray," and that was that; he never went in again.

My father went to Boston Latin—the nation's oldest public school, which was actually conceived as a prep school for Harvard University. He attended for what is the equivalent of middle school and high school, where he naturally studied the classics, including five years of Latin and four years of French. From there he went to Brandeis University, west of Boston. He says he could have gone to Harvard because he finished ninth in his class (all of the students ranked one to seventeen at Boston Latin, except him, went there). But in typical fashion, Ken says he was not a fan of the tradition at Harvard, having had enough of it at Boston Latin. The irony, of course, is that Brandeis was founded as a Jewish university and named after the first Jewish U.S. Supreme Court justice, Louis Brandeis. My father graduated four years later with a bachelor's degree in economics.

But this was in one of the most tumultuous years in post–World War II American history: 1968. The Vietnam War was raging, with domestic protests escalating after the Tet Offensive in January 1968 revealed that the war was not going nearly as well as the U.S. government had been telling the public. It was also the year that

Martin Luther King Jr. was assassinated, followed by heightened race riots in cities across the country. Robert F. Kennedy, who was running for Democratic nomination for president, was also assassinated—all followed by the chaotic Democratic National Convention in Chicago. If you look at old pictures of Ken in these years and listen to his stories, it's clear that he was a hippie who regretted not going to Woodstock with his friends. One of his favorite memories was being in the audience when Bob Dylan went electric at the Newport Folk Festival on July 25, 1965. And he's always been vocally against war.

But I think my dad just wanted to explore the world on his own terms. He joined the Peace Corps right after graduating college. He was originally assigned to go to Turkey, but a devastating earthquake occurred there in summer 1968, so he was reassigned to Malaysia. After three months of training in Hawaii, including learning some Malay, he wound up in a small fishing village, Kuala Dungun, on the east coast of Malaysia. He taught secondary school there, primarily math and the sciences.

After his two-year commitment in the Peace Corps, my dad decided to re-up for an extra year in Malaysia's capital, Kuala Lumpur. He worked in the federal government's accountant general office helping to computerize the federal government payroll. While there, one of his Peace Corps friends who was engaged to a girl from India, set up a double date with his fiancée's best friend, Charlotte Castillo. I don't know too much about their dating life, other than that a short while later Ken and Charlotte were married in a small wedding in Kuala Lumpur. It was 1971. The newlyweds lived there for a short time, but because of a lack of job opportunities moved to Arlington, living with my dad's parents for a few months until he got a job as a computer programmer at Commercial Information Corp.

Growing up, I always thought I looked like my mother, and so did everyone else. I had jet black hair and the darkest complexion of the three kids, and in photos I was the spitting image of her father,

Andy Castillo. Charlotte (Castillo) Nirenberg has a complicated cultural background because Malaysia itself is mixed ethnically. She and her family were Catholics, primarily because her father was a devout Roman Catholic. In Malaysia, Andy—Granpappy to all of us grandchildren—married a well-to-do Eurasian woman. He had moved to Malaysia as a young man, having served in the army in the Philippines in the southern Mindanao region, and met Doris Blanche Hodges—Granny, my maternal grandmother. Doris's family was against their courtship and eventual marriage because Andy was working class, hustling to make money as a jazz musician, in stark contrast to their well-to-do family. He wasn't a pauper, but being married to a jazz organist wasn't quite what the Hodges had in mind for Doris.

The Hodges had social status. George, Doris's father, was commissioned in Glasgow, Scotland, as a game warden to help clear out the jungles in Malaysia, which, like India, was under British control. It was there that he met his Indian bride, Doris's mother. One of the earliest memories of my ancestry was learning that my Scots-English side of the family is descended from Sir Francis Light (1740–1794), an explorer of some notoriety after a career in the Royal Navy. Light founded the island of Penang and its capital city, George Town, in Malaysia in 1786. At Fort Cornwallis there you can find a statue of him. George Town is situated along the northwest coast of Peninsular Malaysia by the Strait of Malacca, considered to be one of the world's most strategic shipping lanes and choke points, effectively connecting the Indian Ocean with the South China Sea. Ironically, after several requests were initially denied, Light received official support for establishing a British colony in Penang as a sort of trade way station, after the need for it arose following the defeat of the British in the American Revolutionary War. Penang, often referred to as the "Pearl of the Orient," grew accordingly and today has a population of 1.7 million.

My mother's full maiden name was Charlotte Adelina Blanche

Castillo, after Sir Francis Light's daughter Charlotte Adelina Blanche Light. My mother was the light of her parents' lives, emulating them in every respect. As the eldest of three daughters and one son, she was a "proper" young lady who attended Catholic school and helped with tending to the siblings and cousins. In her teens, like most of the girls she knew, Charlotte grew into a dreamer—fantasizing about life in America and even joining a pop band as a bass guitarist. That never went very far, but she also fell in love with pop music of all kinds, particularly that of Brit megastar Cliff Richard. She started his fan club in Malaysia and would meet him several times during his international tours. To this day I still enjoy his music, having grown up hearing it in my house on my mom's record player nearly every day.

My mom became a naturalized American citizen during America's bicentennial in 1976. While she dropped "Blanche" from her full name, her Scots-English heritage has always been evident, as she spoke with a soft British accent. "What is your accent?" people often asked. She took that as a compliment.

A few years ago, after I described my family background to a friend, he bought me a subscription to 23andMe so he could see the results for himself. Sure enough, the entire Eastern Hemisphere was lit up, from Southeast Asia to Great Britain. It makes me proud to be an American, where all of those lines intersected, like they have for so many other families. And it makes me feel quite at home with nearly any ethnic group celebrating their traditions like family. I grew up a little frustrated not knowing which box to check on the "What is your ethnicity?" question during standardized tests. Now I feel blessed by it.

Our family lived a typical middle-class life in Massachusetts. Ken and Charlotte Nirenberg's first child was born in 1974: my older brother, Marc. I arrived three years later. Heather, the only native Texan, was born in 1985, five years after my dad's company, Commercial Information Corp., moved their headquarters to Austin. It was the beginning of the personal computer revolution, and his company focused on early accounting software and building multiprocessor, multiuser microcomputers for the business community. They were a niche company that built and rented out those machines, which came loaded with all the financial software for payroll and budget management a business might need. It was, as far as was known, the only company doing this at the time. Back then, computers didn't use graphic interfaces like Windows; it was all text prompts. My dad's company used a superior product that supported multiple processors, called Turbo-DOS, which was one of two disk operating system (DOS) products competing for market share at the time. The other one was MS-DOS (called PC-DOS if it was on a personal computer sold by IBM), from a little outfit called Microsoft. You know the rest of that story.

We moved to the far north side of Austin in 1980, to a modest single-family home on the edge of the city. It was the middle of the summer, and my mom told me that the triple-digit Texas heat gave me a fever she feared would take my life. I got over that, but as the seasons changed to winter, a blizzard brought a week of freezing temperatures and blanketed the city with nearly a foot of snow. It was a great introduction to Texas weather.

When I was old enough to attend preschool, my parents sent me to the Ponderosa school to socialize with other children my age. It wasn't easy at first. I was debilitatingly shy, afraid to speak even when the teacher called on me. But that year, 1980, my family went to see the Popeye movie starring Robin Williams, and besides being enthralled by the hero, who constantly got beat up and always came back to save the day, I somehow became compelled to dress like him: a sailor's cap from a theme park, some shin pads my brother used in his youth soccer league (my dad drew tattoos on them for me, and they worked perfectly as Popeye forearms), and one of Granpappy's old pipes that had found its way to our house. The teachers at Ponderosa figured that if they addressed me as Popeye instead of Ronny—since I was dressed like him—I would engage. They were right. I came out of my shell and made a few

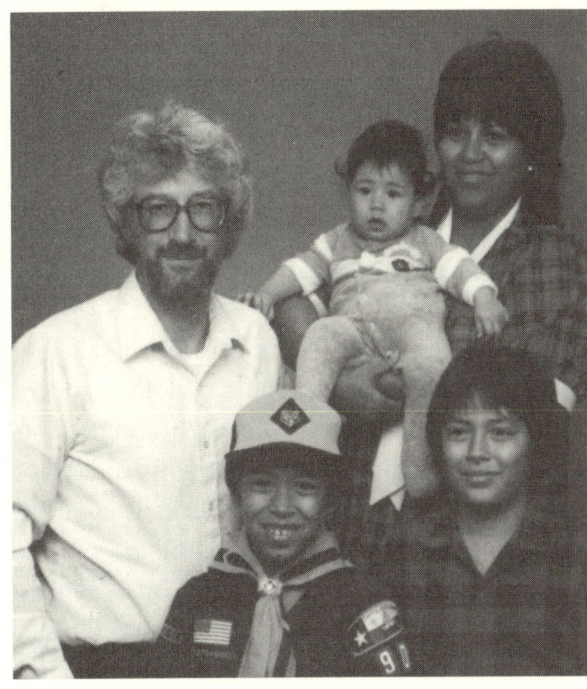

The Nirenberg family in 1985: (*clockwise from left*) Ken, Heather, Charlotte, Marc, and Ron.

friends, including Justin, who became my best friend for the next decade until his family moved to another city. By the way, I got that spinach tattoo on my left forearm when I was in my twenties, in part as an homage to Popeye, the first hero of my youth.

If you've seen the film *Dazed and Confused*, that is the kind of life I remember from those days. The families in my neighborhood had kids who were the same ages as Marc and me. We'd play in the streets, ride our bicycles to the edges of construction sites where the city was growing, and explore the undeveloped lots that seemed like forests to us. The boys hung out together, and the girls had their own separate groups. Bussing had been instituted in Austin's public schools by then, and besides lunchtime at the school cafeteria, siblings' birthday parties, and recess, the bus was one of the few places where all of the kids mixed together. The boys like me were obsessed with collecting G.I. Joe and Star Wars action figures, and in my neighborhood some of us found common ground by catching the early wave of freestyle BMX and skateboarding. We wore out a VHS tape of the movie *Rad*, and my brother and I got spike haircuts (we definitely weren't the only ones). Most of our free time was spent tooling around on our bicycles, taking them apart, putting them back together, and customizing them with parts from a Schwinn dealer or Cauthron's bike shop. I loved those times in our neighborhood, despite how fleeting they turned out to be.

Marc and I fought like cats and dogs, and it became a challenge for my parents to keep the peace. I never understood it—we were oil and water. I imagine I was just the pip-squeak brother trying to hang out with the older kids, which was not cool. And Marc did have the cool friends, while my friends and I were the younger, awkward dorks. He probably hated that and hated me for it.

Even in high school, I remember as a freshman intentionally bumping into Marc in the hallway (he was a senior at the time) and asking to borrow lunch money. I already had money, but I wanted the upperclassmen to see me talking to a senior. To Marc's credit, he gave me a few bucks. I never thanked him for that. As adults, later in life, we have become close friends—he was the best man at my wedding—and we've grown to respect each other. And I've grown to accept that he was—and still is—the cooler, laid-back brother. Erika reminds me about this all the time.

What I lacked in the social department I made up for with a wild imagination that kept me company during the lonelier times. I loved going to the movies, even by myself. My best friend, Justin, and I played with our G.I. Joe action figures and watched Arnold Schwarzenegger movies nearly every weekend. When my father—who, in hindsight, turned out to be a technology early adopter—purchased one of the first home video cameras on the market, we made crude stop motion animation movies with those action figures. Record, pause, move the figures, record, pause. They were not bad once we learned how to dub audio tracks over the finished product. My favorite movie to this day is *The Termina-*

tor. Justin and I re-created it scene-for-scene with our G.I. Joes, sound effects, and our own voices for dialogue. I've searched high and low for those home movies for years, but I still can't find our *Terminator* remake.

I did find the commercial I shot for my fifth-grade Webb Elementary class contest though. We were tasked with designing a new product and creating a marketing campaign for it. Right up my alley. I came up with the idea for what our team called Pasta Plus, a little fork with a handle to turn and wrap up spaghetti. The best (and only) Italian restaurant I remember in Austin in those days—Olive Garden—let me and my fifth-grade teammates dress up as waiters and film a commercial for Pasta Plus there. Our team won the contest, and the local news station ran a story about our product. By the way, many years later I saw that someone had invented that same product; it was even called Pasta Plus. We need to teach our kids how to patent good ideas!

I was also into drawing and writing back then, and I absolutely loved sports, especially baseball. Unfortunately I was never great at playing any of the sports I tried—my youth soccer stint ended after about two months of running aimlessly on the pitch and kicking the ball at the wrong goal. But around the time I turned ten, my love of sports, particularly baseball, came together in a self-published magazine I named *Baseball Monthly*. It eventually became *Sports Monthly* and contained articles, commentary, trivia, and drawings of all the major goings-on from a ten-year-old's perspective. I used the typewriter at home along with lots of Wite-Out and made copies on the Xerox machine at my dad's office. I assembled each issue one at a time with masking tape. After that, around the neighborhood I went, trying to sell it. Some willing neighbors kindly obliged me and purchased a copy (twenty-five cents each), but I'm sure it was more for moral support than for the sports insights.

While I was still dreaming of becoming the beat writer for the Boston Red Sox, I looked for every opportunity to hone my love

Sharing a love of the Red Sox with cousin Brian and Papa Bernie at Fenway Park, Boston, July 1994.

of journalism and sports. I kick-started a newspaper for our fifth-grade class and earned a writing spot at our middle school. A few years later, even though I hadn't taken any of the classes required to write for the high school newspaper, I begged them to give me a special assignment. I was relentless. One of my high school advisers told my dad, "I don't know what Ron is going to do when he grows up, but I think you're going to hear from him. And it might be in *Sports Illustrated.*" Perhaps the pinnacle of my baseball writing days came in 1995, when I saw a student essay-writing contest ("Why I Like Baseball") in the *Sporting News.* I immediately thought, "Now this is a contest I can win." After submitting my entry, I forgot about it amid the whirlwind of high school graduation and starting college at Trinity University in San Antonio. But during the first week of classes, the first issue of my new subscription to the *Sporting News* arrived. As I flipped through it, I was floored when I noticed my essay reprinted with "Grand Prize" in all caps on top:

The Sporting News "Why I Like Baseball" Essay Contest

Ron Nirenberg
Austin, TX
17 years old

Ever since my grandfather put his old five-fingered, web-less glove on my tiny hand, I was in love. For me, baseball means passion, innocence, and family. America's pastime will always be a sentimental part of my life.

The bright lights of Fenway shone down on us that Saturday night. The Red Sox were facing the Baltimore Orioles. I hadn't been to a baseball park before and didn't know many of the players' names, but I watched them excitedly. The vendors tossed bags of peanuts as my grandfather explained each pitch, swing, and toss of the ball. In his hand was his old five-finger mitt, worn and discolored from many games. I brought mine, too, in hope of taking home a souvenir. We didn't ever use our gloves, but by the end of the night, our hometown heroes had won.

At home, I decided to become a famous baseball player for the Red Sox. However, practicing my fastball up against the side of the house and playing homerun derby with my best friend, I realized that I would never become a great player. The hunger of the game wouldn't go away, though. I became a card collector, buying every Red Sox player I could find. My dad endured question after question about baseball rules each night. I borrowed baseball books from the school library and rummaged through old newspaper clippings that my grandfather kept. I even started my own newspaper, *Baseball Monthly*, detailing my predictions and opinions about the current Major League season. Though there would be no pitching future, I could be a fan.

Echoing life, baseball has been a source of disappointment and happiness; it is a common bond between grandfather, father, and son. Growing up with this game, it will always be part of me.

All that is still true. There have been few constants in the almost five decades of my life, but the Boston Red Sox are one. Every night before Jonah could read by himself, I read him the latest report on the team, whether it was the free agency rumors in the offseason or the gameday wrap-up. When he was a little older we read the origin story for most of us Sox fans, "The Curse of the Bambino." To this day, with few exceptions, Jonah and I still play hooky from school and work on opening day and watch the Red Sox season opener.

While the sports side of me was expressed mostly through being a fan—and fledgling baseball writer—I developed a great love of music. Like most kids at the time, when you went to middle school you had to take music class and choose an instrument in sixth grade. It was almost like choosing a dog from the shelter—you got to play around for a few minutes and then tried to make a decision you'd live with for years to come. For what it's worth, my brother had chosen the trumpet and loved it, and I wanted to be like him, but not completely, so I went to low brass and chose the trombone.

The trombone would be a focus of my life for the next six years as I played in the marching band, jazz band, and symphonic band and earned competitive spots in local and regional ensembles. Without an outlet for playing in college (unless I chose to major in music, and I didn't), my trombone days ended there. But music is in my family's blood, and it has remained a big part of my life.

On the edge of suburbia, everything seemed well and stable. My dad worked and my mom was a homemaker, taking care of the house and cooking dinner every night. It all seemed like a normal happy nuclear family of the 1980s. But like so many others, it wasn't.

Our parents tried to keep it behind the scenes, but Marc and I (and later Heather) occasionally overheard arguing. Mom and Dad could not as easily hide a growing iciness between them. Marc and I were still fighting a lot, and they assured us that they weren't fighting about us. But most of those increasingly rare times when we were all together were spent with our parents scolding me and Marc for fighting and ignoring each other.

One Saturday morning I walked downstairs, and my mom told me that Dad wasn't there anymore. He was gone. I must have been about six years old. Marc was much more aware of the world at the time than I was, but even if he was affected by it, he seemed to just go about his day. I remember the moment differently—the seconds went by like eternity. I lost it, didn't know what to do or how to react. I cried and crumpled to the ground. I still see the brown speckled carpet fibers that felt at once like a soft blanket and tiny little needles against my cheeks. The earth under my feet seemed to slip away. I didn't know what it really meant: "Daddy left."

Eventually I found out that my father had rented an apartment nearby, and I learned that this kind of rupture of our suburban family—and my childhood—was growing quite common among the kids my age. My dad would eventually move back in and then out again, and from then on I remember a distance between me and my parents, perhaps out of an instinct to find the earth under my feet again. Although I loved my parents and depended on them, I deeply resented their choice to break up what I had thought was an idyllic family.

Later in life, with a family of my own, I appreciate each of my parents as individuals who had their own pressures, hopes, and pains. I understand that life doesn't always turn out the way you think it will. People make mistakes. People deserve the grace of forgiveness. That goes for my parents too. I imagine it was their two different personalities that drove them apart. And although they loved each other, for a variety of reasons what they wanted out of life and what they could give to each other were just not compatible. I know it was hard for my mom to leave her homeland first and then leave her entire family in Boston. For my dad, it was the exact opposite—by the time he finished high school, he was anxious to leave home and explore the world.

When I was twelve my parents got a divorce. It was 1989. Heather was too young to fully comprehend what was going on. Marc and I dealt with the divorce in completely different ways. For my brother—by high school, a long-haired rebel with his own car—the lack of parenting gave him the opportunity to do whatever he wanted, and he did, sometimes getting into trouble. I had a much different reaction. I grew up fast. People say I became reserved, but I think I skipped the rest of my childhood and went straight to adulthood. We both experienced the common reality of Gen X latchkey kids, but Marc's angst was reflected outwardly while I bottled mine up. I started to have problems at school, and at times I got bullied. I only had a couple of good friends. Living through the separation of my family at the time, to survive I learned to block it out, stay occupied, and keep moving forward. Sometimes I cried myself to sleep, but that's all I would allow myself.

When my parents divorced, what I remember is being given a choice of where to live—with my mom or my dad. In hindsight, that was a lot to put on a twelve-year-old kid. Although both of my parents continued to live near each other in Austin and were very much in our lives with split custody, I chose to live with my dad while Marc and Heather initially lived with my mom. Marc later moved in with my dad and me before getting an apartment with his best friend, Larry, after high school.

Before the divorce, my dad was working a lot, so at home my mom was everything, including the primary disciplinarian. She taught us to let our imaginations run wild, to dream and believe that we could do anything and be anything we wanted. But, no surprise, Marc and I earned a lot of spankings. I dreaded the wooden spoon, but the worst was the belt. One time, at the age of eight or nine, I knew that fate was coming and ran to my room. I stuffed extra clothes for padding down my pants before my mom could get there. When she arrived, she could barely hold back her laughs as I received justice. I think that was the last time I ever got spanked. It didn't stop me from needing discipline; it just got more verbal, turning into real arguments from time to time. Maybe that is why I chose to live with my dad. I recall that he yelled at me only a few times, and on those occasions even a child's logic would say it was earned. He kind of left me to my own devices.

But being left alone meant I needed to figure out stuff that my mom used to take care of. As a result, I remember my dad being the one who gave me the organized, logical approach to my life, which I related to—along with a strong and focused work ethic. We also shared a love of sports. My mom, through thick and thin, gave me my emotional maturity and showed me how to empathize and imagine. Because I was raised Catholic and my dad was definitely not, my mother also gave me tradition and a deep sense of faith that I could turn to amid all of the familial chaos.

Interestingly, my mom never remarried and kept the Nirenberg name. For many years she had a great deal of resentment for my dad, not just for the divorce but for bringing her to this country and taking her from her family, twice. Indeed, much later she tried to establish her own life, independent of the man who in her mind had brought her away, and she had a falling out with her own family. I think she blamed my dad in large measure for all of that, especially when he got remarried a few years later to my stepmother, Carol Noble. Carol had two kids—Will and Anna—from a previous marriage, and she is the most nonjudgmental person I have ever met. Of all of the different personalities who have become part of the family over the years, she has accepted each one the same. She became the perfect balance to my dad, laughing at his jokes whether they were funny or not, and they've been together for more than thirty years now.

My mom's grief became an illness that she couldn't shake, although she would try to pretend nothing was wrong when we were around. In a way, I had to learn how to negotiate between my parents and between them and us. Conflict resolution on the fly. Still longing for the comfort of family I had experienced with everyone under the same roof, until the time I started my own family I tried to make peace amid any internal family fights and to soothe any sorrows. There were plenty. As my dad says, "Ron was the family peacemaker."

I envied Marc because, at least on the surface, it seemed like nothing bothered him. He kind of checked out to live his own life. Much later, I learned that his devil-may-care attitude was really self-preservation, an inner resilience. Because whether it is for our family, his family, his friends, or somebody who needs help on the side of the road, Marc has become the most reliable person I've ever known. I've never seen him fail to lend a hand when someone needed assistance—a stranger, a friend, or his once bratty younger brother. After graduating, he started college but soon found it wasn't for him. His skills working on our bikes (and then cars) ultimately translated into a career working on computer equipment and, eventually, cellular technology. He married and became a young father in his early twenties. His wife had some serious health problems, and along with trying to feed three kids and pay the mortgage on a single blue-collar income, his marriage faced serious strain from its early days. Just like our parents, after seventeen years it succumbed to the pressure.

But Marc was never daunted, and with a steady career of thirty years at AT&T fixing cell tower equipment, he has never ceased to be a devoted father of three daughters. Somehow he's continued to be the laid-back, fun one (again, at least, according to Erika).

Since she is so much younger than Marc and me, our sister, Heather, has always been the baby. She always got a little extra room to run, and boy, did she use it. I've always called her a gypsy because from the earliest moments until the time she became a married mom—not that long ago—she went wherever the wind took her, from sketch artist to flight attendant to chef to musician to licensed counselor. I have always admired that freedom. Heather is easily the most gifted and creative of the three of us, but rules didn't really work for her. She settled on a counseling career once she found her professional passion, after multiple starts and stops at college. She is growing her career and her family with her husband, Nick, a heavy metal guitarist and builder of custom motorcycles. Naturally.

For me, life immediately after my parents' divorce was a lonely and confused time. I kept to myself and learned to entertain myself, staying home quite a bit, which was the opposite of how I had been before then. My brother was doing his own thing as the age difference became more pronounced. By that time my best friend, Justin, had moved away to another city and a couple of other friends had moved to different neighborhoods, out of range for even our farthest bicycle rides. It was kind of a double whammy to a kid's spirit. Schoolwork slid, unsurprisingly, as my feet still didn't feel like they had found the ground. The first summer I lived in my dad's apartment, I got hold of a Sega console and spent the entire summer playing video games and walking to the local movie theater to watch the same two movies—*Indiana Jones and the Last Crusade* and *Batman*—over and over. In retrospect, I was avoiding the new reality. But it wasn't for naught; I forced myself to get up every day. I walked, I got lost in those fantasy worlds, and I learned to become self-reliant. My dad would give me cash to walk to the grocery store to get stuff for home. Life was more serious. I became self-disciplined.

That discipline was grounded in two things: faith, which through religious tradition reminded me of life when my family was intact, and weightlifting, which promised to take me once and for all away from being a kid, which I certainly didn't feel like anymore.

Two key moments helped to accelerate my life in a more positive direction. The first occurred one day when I was a sophomore at L. C. Anderson High School. Following a very mediocre freshman year, my English teacher, Ann Cowen, sat me down after class and said something to the effect of, "You have really got to figure out if you want to be here because you have a lot of talent, but right now you are going nowhere." For some reason, at that moment it clicked: I could use that same self-discipline I had learned and start applying it to my classes. After all, the books we were learning about sounded interesting—and they'd probably be even more interesting if I actually read them. I started to take notes obsessively, poring over every word of every textbook and novel until they were basically memorized. Reading everything and taking good, organized notes became an academic obsession, almost like a training regimen.

What became a real training regimen, though, was weightlifting. I got hooked on it by watching the show *American Gladiators*, which came on after *Saturday Night Live*. By then, my dad had moved into a house, and after watching these superhero-looking athletes compete against average joes I begged him to get a weight set for our empty house. I wanted to look like those gladiators. But at age fourteen, looking like a gladiator wasn't going to happen, and without any instruction—only images on TV—I knew just enough to be dangerous to myself. I went it alone, through trial and error, with no trainer or training on how to use weights properly. I lifted and lifted, injuring myself plenty in the process and eventually doing more harm than good.

You see, novice fourteen-year-old weightlifting boys normally don't have the genetics to look like a shredded adult American Gladiator. But that didn't stop me from trying everything. I found that by controlling what I ate, I got leaner and more muscular. In reality, though, I was losing a lot of weight and not necessarily building muscle, mostly because I was overtraining while slowly starving myself. In graduate school I would write part of my thesis on what sociologists now call "body dysmorphia"—a preoccupation with one's body that leads to a warped physical self-perception. Dysmorphia, I found, is quite common among male bodybuilders, and something I am now, thankfully, aware of. But I wasn't when I was fourteen. While it felt like the walls were caving in on me, I was still in control. The weightlifting and obsessing over what I ate continued through high school, and by the time I enrolled at Trinity University, I was a five-foot-ten 106-pound freshman.

Male eating disorders weren't something people talked about or even believed existed when I was growing up, and if not for that second key moment in my life, I might not have believed it either. The summer after I graduated high school, we took a road trip to visit our family in Boston. I was excited to go back to Fenway. The night before the game I was in Papa Bernie's TV room watching the Red Sox when Uncle Eddie, my dad's brother-in-law, came in. Like Mrs. Cowen, he told me that he was concerned about me, but this time it was about my weight. I had never heard that before; in fact, I had not considered it to be a problem. I was always in control, I thought, and men didn't have these kinds of issues. But I couldn't deny it—I was a beanpole. I was even embarrassed to raise my hand in class because my arm was so skinny.

As soon as I got home I signed up to meet with Craig, the trainer at my neighborhood gym. He taught me the basics of how to eat and train to reach my goals. I started counting calories so that I could avoid getting too few. From then to this day, I have never stopped training, continuously learning from books, experts, and friends about how to do it right. Later in life I competed in "heavy athletics"—bodybuilding, powerlifting, even traditional Scottish Highland Games and "strongman" events—but as those days passed, weightlifting became the force for keeping me physically, mentally, and emotionally balanced. It is critical to my well-being, so I make time for it, as necessary as sleep or getting to work on time. The gym—usually my garage these days—is a sanctuary, a place of peace no matter how intense the workouts.

Passed down through my mom, faith is another touchstone for me. We went to Saint Louis Catholic Church in Austin, and I remember many Sundays from my earliest ages passing time in the balcony pews with my brother. Sometimes my dad joined us. Growing up Catholic instilled in me a strong sense of tradition and comfort in the church, and when my family started breaking

VOICES OF SAN ANTONIO

The Reverend Raymond Judd Jr.

An extraordinary young man and I first met in a hallway of the Margarite B. Parker Chapel at Trinity University. That young man, Ronald Nirenberg, spent four years at Trinity pursuing his bachelor's degree. He was endowed with a strong voice and an inquisitive mind and spirit, and he wanted to know what truly was happening all over the university campus. He shared his scholarly ambitions and his pursuit of a fine education. He realized that I was the longtime university chaplain, and his curiosity persuaded him to get the details "of a beautiful chapel on a beautiful campus." A good question followed: "What's taking place in the chapel on Trinity Hill?"

As a result of our happy introduction, we became friends, and subsequently Ron became related to some of the chapel's activities. His comments and faithful participation created an environment where he built relationships and connections. One of my proudest memories is when he substituted as assistant minister in our chapel services.

I was then and am now grateful for Ron and students, faculty, and staff who valued him in many of the university's pursuits. He was held in the highest esteem for his daily involvement and energy both as a student and a graduate, especially on behalf of KRTU, Trinity's radio

apart that dogma was one of the few consistencies I could count on. Faith was a way to deal with my parents' troubles and their ultimate divorce, reminding me of when we were together but also that I still was not alone. I took to prayer to deal with my anger and disappointment, sometimes praying that Mom and Dad would get back together.

In my first year at Trinity University, I joined the Catholic student group, which held mass every Sunday evening. On Sunday mornings I attended the nondenominational service, devotedly station known throughout the city. Everyone seemed to be listening to the station, and KRTU owes a significant debt to Ron's leadership.

During the period following Ron's graduation, in 1999, our paths rarely crossed. We were busy and fulfilling our commitments. Several years later my wife, Mary Jane, and I were invited to a large party, and suddenly there appeared our friend Ron. His strong voice and sincerity instantly brought back fond memories of his time on the Trinity campus. We were delighted by the opportunity to learn about his pursuits. As we talked, Mary Jane and I both had the same thought: "Ron is headed for the political world where he is desperately needed."

We were so pleased, though not surprised, when we learned that he was running for San Antonio mayor. He has now admirably served four terms. We have always supported Ron through his terms in office, and we have never been disappointed.

We are brought to the present book. How pleased we are that Ron's name will be remembered in a memoir. We may not know what the future holds for Ron at this time, but we are assured that he will be a valued leader wherever he is.

The Reverend **RAYMOND JUDD JR.**, Trinity University chaplain emeritus, was the school's longest-serving chaplain, ministering to the campus community for more than thirty years.

listening as Trinity's revered chaplain Raymond Judd Jr. gave his sermons. Reverend Judd spoke to students in a way we could relate to and inspired us to think beyond ourselves. We became friends, and I soon became one of the student deacons. He encouraged us to pursue our faith but not in a dogmatic way—rather, to ask questions and consider how religions across the world are expressed differently but are based on some universal values. These values included the Golden Rule (treating others the way we wanted to be treated); a belief in the inherent dignity of people; a respect for all of God's creations, including nature; service before self, especially in serving the poor and vulnerable; and the importance of personal integrity (or doing the right thing, especially when no one is watching).

When I arrived in San Antonio, I felt like I had been thrown into the middle of the ocean, this big city that I did not know, away from family and friends. As the world seemed to expand in all directions from my new vantage point at Trinity, these universal values appeared as buoys in each of Judd's sermons, helping me to know exactly where I was and where I needed to go.

At Sunday morning services, I saw classmates I knew weren't Christians. But they were as attentive to Reverend Judd's words as I was. In hindsight, this is where my faith and spirituality became a passion I still hold for interfaith dialogue. Trinity is a small campus, too small to become tribal, and everyone welcomed each other to learn from each other's customs and traditions. Ironically, despite my Jewish roots, at Trinity I learned about Judaic traditions for the first time and attended my first seder. And I gained a curiosity about all of the major religions. My best friend was raised in the Hindu tradition. I dated a girl who taught me about Buddhism. Muslim classmates shared their customs around Ramadan. For someone like me, with an active and inquisitive spiritual life, there was no better place to be.

Even though San Antonio is only eighty miles south of Austin, it wasn't easy leaving home in 1995. My family had already fallen apart, but at times it felt like I was still trying to hold it together. Still, it wasn't long after I arrived on campus that I felt like my feet had found solid earth beneath them again. Trinity's Margarite B. Parker Chapel is iconic and sits in the heart of the campus. By the end of college, it had become a second home to me, central to my growing love of my new hometown.

THE WORLD IS A BIGGER PLACE

Although I looked forward to going back to Austin and seeing family on breaks, it took about one semester at Trinity University for it to feel like home. There was comfort in the new routines, and I believed in my gut that whatever adversity I encountered there would be of my own making. I would get out of my college experience what I put into it. It took me a little while to understand that the real growth (and fun) would come from forcing myself out of my comfort zones. College is supposed to nurture and expand one's worldview and intellectually challenge many of one's assumptions. It certainly did all of these things for me.

But there was a practical side to college as well. While I knew I'd need loans and scholarships to pay for it, my parents made us believe that our education wouldn't end at high school. That was a privilege I didn't understand at the time but certainly do now. An undeniable truth about today's economy is that to be financially independent, you need a college degree or some other postsecondary credential, like a skilled trade or technical certification, that qualifies you for a well-paying job. Without either of these, making ends meet is virtually impossible; you'll have to string together several lower-paying jobs just to pay the bills. That's the situation for so many families that get trapped in the cycle of poverty: children whose parents are struggling are more likely to struggle themselves, eventually raising their own families in similar circumstances.

All this is exacerbated by the fact that higher education has gotten so expensive that it's out of reach for an increasing number of students. During college and in the years that followed, I was often reminded of that as I began to meet more people who became the exception—the first to pursue a postsecondary program—within their family. They described overcoming so many obstacles and talked about how college was their ticket out of poverty, sometimes mentioning family members who didn't "escape." Those stories still stick with me today, including Erika's story (more on that later).

In retrospect, even having the option to attend college was powerful. Before I ended up at Trinity, my mind had been set on Rice University in Houston. I longed for the kind of classical college experience that was romanticized in the movies *The Dead Poets Society* and *Rudy*, which had transfixed me just as I was beginning to think about college. Rice certainly had that reputation—"the Harvard of the South," they called it. I definitely did not want to go to a school where I'd be one of several hundred students in the same lecture room. That meant no University of Texas at Austin, even though when I was in high school, everyone in the top 10 percent of their graduating class was granted automatic admission.

Apart from the idea of gigantic classes, my reluctance toward UT may have been the result of the impression I got of the university when I attended Texas Boys State, held at the campus in summer 1994. The competitive program, sponsored by the American Legion, aims to provide qualified high school students an opportunity to learn more about how government works, particularly at the local, county, and state levels. It was my first immersion into the inner workings of the political system in Texas. The other participants and I stayed in Jester dormitory—one of the designated dorms for UT freshmen—which itself was the subject of an intractable urban legend. The story goes that Jester was designed by a team of architects who specialized in prison facilities. It turned out to be an Austin myth, but I still remember the pull-out vinyl beds—about the size of a surfboard—and the tiny Folsom County sinks. Although UT is widely recognized for its academic and athletic standing, I was not going to be a Longhorn.

With acceptance letters from a couple of old East Coast schools (Tufts University and Brandeis University, which held the reputation as two of the nation's most expensive colleges) and no real financial assistance, I decided, at my father's suggestion, to check out Trinity. He said the school offered as good or better an education at half the price. It also used the Common Application, which meant that I simply needed to check a box, and essays, test scores, and application materials would be sent to the school along with any other schools I selected on the form.

Trinity wasn't even on my radar; the only thing I knew about it was from vague memories of the red brick buildings and the inside of Laurie Auditorium, where I attended an event for Texas seventh graders taking practice SATs. But my dad was keen on the school, and he convinced me to take the short hour-and-a-half drive down to San Antonio, which my family and I had visited a handful of times as tourists. I toured the school as a prospective student, and it was appealing, mainly because the people at Trinity seemed like they wanted me there. The campus itself was a bubble—reminding me of that classical college life I wanted, yet nestled in the heart of a sprawling metropolis. The lower campus, where the students' dorms and athletic and dining facilities are located, was situated in an abandoned quarry. The upper campus, composed of the academic buildings, library, student union, and Laurie Auditorium, hovered above. My dad said the school reminded him of his alma mater, Brandeis, even down to the red brick buildings. And with a student population of about 2,500, the class sizes would be relatively small; I knew I wouldn't be lost in a crowd. To top it off, the school offered me a partial scholarship, and the total costs to attend would be a fraction of what I would pay in the Northeast. I wouldn't owe nearly as much in student loans. It turns out that going to Trinity became one of the best—and most important—decisions of my life.

Trinity is primarily an undergraduate school, rooted in the liberal arts and sciences, with preprofessional programs offering a few master's degrees. It was founded in 1869 by Cumberland Presbyterians in Tehuacana, about forty miles east of Waco. Its first class consisted of a hundred students. In 1902 it relocated to Waxahachie, about thirty miles south of Dallas, where it remained until 1942. The mascot for Trinity, the Tiger, was drawn from the fact that in 1916 the Detroit Tigers major league baseball team held its spring training in Waxahachie; the name stuck, replacing the Trinitonian. In 1942 Trinity moved to San Antonio, where it eventually purchased an abandoned limestone quarry encompassing more than a hundred acres in an area just north of downtown. Famed architect O'Neil Ford was commissioned to design and develop the master plan of the campus, which still bears his imprint. The so-called Skyline campus, located "on the hill" with its beautiful, unique views of downtown, was completed in 1952. The Murchison Tower in the campus center, at only 166 feet tall, remains one of the city's highest points. The same year as its centennial celebration, in 1969, the school and the Presbyterian Church ended their legal ties, signing a covenant that memorialized their shared history.

I buried myself in my work as soon as I got to campus. Were there enough hours in a day for eating, sleeping, and the three-to-one ratio of reading to class time my high school counselor told me about? I had every waking hour written down, blocked out, and accounted for. That lasted about a month, when things started to loosen up as I got the hang of it. Still, it was all work and no play. That included a walk down to the "dungeon" before the first semester officially began. This was how students referred to the campus newspaper's basement office—a nickname the *Trinitonian*'s headquarters deserved, with no windows, awful lighting, and a persistent smell of mildew. I was hoping to get on as a staff writer at the paper.

After the upperclassmen there explained that they didn't give jobs to first-year students during their first semester, they offered me an unpaid internship as a fill-in reporter. I snapped it up. It wasn't the first time in life and it wouldn't be the last time that I followed a calling to do work despite the lack of a paycheck.

The *Trinitonian* was a legitimate business operation, though the student staffers didn't look like people you'd trust with your money. The office had recently been outfitted with new Mac computers running QuarkXPress and Netscape, but the newspaper itself was laid out by hand. Every Thursday night the editors finalized all the copy, printed the articles, and pasted them onto the pages in designated spaces that wrapped around advertisements the marketing team had sold.

During the next several months I became a reporter, mostly covering random campus events. My first break came when I got an assignment to cover a school football game after the beat reporter called in sick. The editors liked my work, and they gave me my own beats—including the San Antonio Iguanas (minor league hockey), the San Antonio Missions (minor league baseball), and the Trinity women's basketball team, which was on its way to building what eventually became an NCAA Division III champion. My writing and work ethic were impressive enough that I became the sports editor my sophomore year.

The Missions played on the far southwest side of town in the new Wolff Stadium, and the Iguanas played on the East Side at the old Freeman Coliseum, so my San Antonio world was opening up beyond my dorm room. I was meeting people I had never encountered in the small world of Austin. In my first six months of college I must have encountered more diversity—ethnic, socioeconomic, political, you name it—than in my first eighteen years in Austin. A lot of it was right there at Trinity, including within our publication's ranks.

I became friends with Hunter, a gay student who worked at the yearbook, which shared our offices. We helped each other with the coursework for our communication industry class. The only gay student I had known at my schools in Austin was a woman who was the subject of incessant bullying. I'm sure there were others, but they didn't tell anyone and no one asked. This was a time when the most frequent insult you heard among boys was "fag," and no one took note of how its use would affect other students. But the fact that Hunter was gay was no secret to anyone, and he was given the same respect as everyone else among his peers. That was a clear moment where the world opened up more for me, and I began to connect with the principles of acceptance and inclusion that Reverend Judd preached about.

If life in San Antonio was changing how I viewed the world, I was also determined to change the way I viewed myself, including physically. I was still a beanpole when I reported to campus, and Uncle Eddie's words were seared in my mind. I became intensely focused on getting to a normal, healthy weight, so I followed Craig the trainer's prescribed routine and advice in minute detail. No deviations—every set, every rep, every calorie was counted. The regimen was another block to add to my daily schedule, along with class, reading, sleeping, and eating. Slowly but unmistakably, my body started to transform. I felt better, more confident. From those moments forward, weightlifting became significant part of my life; it is still an essential part of my mental and spiritual balance. That's also why I put that can of spinach on my forearm.

In my ensuing years at Trinity, I explored more of San Antonio. I discovered that it was a city of incredible diversity and many apparent contradictions: at once old and historic, embracing its Mexican roots, even as it was sprawling, the seventh largest city in the country, with huge areas of poverty hiding in plain sight. Everyone, even strangers, seemed to treat everyone else like a cousin. Aside from the drab downtown buildings, it was the most colorful place I'd ever seen, especially during the annual spring Fiesta activities. And the new mayor, Howard Peak, an adjunct professor at Trinity, talked nonstop about the importance of the environment and creating more parks. As I had fallen in love with Trinity my first year in college, now I began to fall in love with the city. By the time I graduated, I knew this was my new home.

Because I enrolled at Trinity as an aspiring journalist, I recognized pretty early that I wanted to major in communication. Robert (Rob) Huesca taught the intro course—Media and Industries—during my first semester, and he suggested I sign up for the first-year seminar he was teaching on sports and American culture. Normally the seminars are assigned randomly, but since it was so suited to what I wanted to do, he got me in the class. Rob became my major adviser, a friend, and an important mentor, helping me to sharpen my critical thinking abilities and develop the skills of academic inquiry. His classes were fascinating and he was a terrific teacher; he challenged us to examine our perspectives and biases even on the most mundane things while always questioning "the authorities" and how and why institutions are formed. I took all of his classes, a great mix of the practical and theoretical.

As I delved deeper into the academic world of communications, writing papers nearly every month on human communication theory and persuasion, I soon grew out of wanting to be a sports journalist. Being a sports beat writer and interviewing the same coaches and players week in and week out started to become monotonous. I kept up with the practical side at the *Trinitonian* and later gained more experiential learning with Trinity's radio and television stations, but the school had turned me from a journalist into a scholar.

Trinity strongly encourages students to study abroad for a semester, usually during junior year. It is yet another way to broaden one's worldview, to immerse oneself in other cultures, and to challenge assumptions about life outside one's comfort zone. I had visited Mexico with my family when I was eight or nine years old, but it was just across the border in Nuevo Laredo. As far as international travel goes, for a Texan that's like barely dipping a toe in the water. So, I thought, when would I ever get this opportunity again? The tuition normally paid to Trinity would go toward a college overseas for a few months. I'd see a new part of the world, and I'd get course credit so my college career didn't miss a beat. It's one of the best things anyone can do, particularly at that formative age. It certainly was for me. To have a four-month visit to a foreign country, to engage with the local people and customs, and to really learn about the town, province, and country—this quickly reveals the things you've taken for granted. While you gain a new appreciation for the place you've left, you also begin to feel a uniquely human compassion for others by living with people on the other side of the world.

While I was thinking about where to study abroad, I saw the movie *Braveheart*, and there was a lot of talk about Scotland in media circles at the time that caught my eye. I explored the country on paper and found that the University of Glasgow offered courses in film, one area of practical college media experience I did not yet have. In addition, by studying abroad there I could discover and connect with my Scottish-English heritage. So I chose to attend the University of Glasgow, the fourth-oldest university in the English-speaking world, founded in the fifteenth century. From the beginning, the institution was a hotbed for political, moral, and economic philosophy, along with the natural sciences. Among its famed alumni are Lord Kelvin and Adam Smith, the "father of economics." The university's namesake, Glasgow, is the largest city and economy in Scotland. It has been and remains an active port city, located on the River Clyde in the Western Lowlands. Legend has it that the city was founded in the sixth century, although settlements were located there for centuries prior. These included Roman communities from when the empire ruled over most of Britain. Glasgow is still known for its architecture and museums, and for its serious football (soccer) fan clubs—better known as gangs—which were notorious and often violent, partic-

On a peak in the Highlands. Stirling, Scotland, October 1997.

ularly at matches between the two old Scottish Premier League rivals, Celtic (green and white) and Rangers (blue, red, and white).

I enrolled for the fall 1997 semester. As it turned out, the film class I came for required a number of prerequisite courses I hadn't taken. So I decided to immerse myself in the history of the place instead and signed up for Celtic Civilization and Scottish History. (There was a time when I could tell you all of the details the movie *Braveheart* got wrong about the Wars of Scottish Independence.) Basically I was a cultural tourist for several months, listening to history lectures during the week and traversing the beautiful old country on weekends. My flatmates at Cairncross House were students from all over the world who also chose Scotland as a temporary home, and we enjoyed learning each other's stories and customs as we were learning about this new country. We took turns cooking—Guinness stew was my contribution—and traded travel tips, like where to get the best deals on a rail pass, how to sneak into first class, and how to hitchhike safely. Stirling, Inverness, the Highlands, Edinburgh, the Isle of Skye—we explored them all. To this day, I still believe I found paradise in a little dot on the map at the northern tip of the Isle of Skye: Flodigarry, which at the time was the home to a hostel, a pub, and a limitless view of the night sky and the ocean at the northern end of the world.

I became good friends with a student from Singapore named Raj, who taught me a bit of Malay, my mother's native language. I kept all of the new words and phrases in a journal, ready to impress my mom when I got home. Raj was a little older than the rest of us and more worldly. He knew multiple languages, so by the time we left Cairncross House many of us could swear in Cantonese.

Our flat was a bit like a little United Nations, a few Americans mixed in with a bunch of students from all over Asia, Europe, and the United Kingdom. We stayed in touch for many years, before time eroded those connections. But while we were in Scotland, we were every bit a new family, showing each other that the world is a bigger place, creating opportunities to connect with other cultures. These experiences no doubt further shaped my life and, I'm sure, theirs.

Before I got to Scotland, my college experience—even when I was with my classmates—was all work and no letting up. Every hour was prescribed for advancement of some aspect of my life. But in Glasgow my job, literally, was to explore and to get good at it. With my new Cairncross family, I also started to explore the city at night. In the UK, with a legal drinking age of eighteen, alcohol was not taboo, and beer was everywhere. So my flatmates and I did as the natives do and headed into town to visit pubs and music clubs. We went to rock concerts and poetry slams. I grew facial hair and a mustache and let my hair grow out. I looked like the 1990s version of a hippie. Without realizing it, during those months in Scotland I transformed yet again. It almost felt like I had grown out of my old skin, accelerating a spiritual, intellectual, and physical transformation that was underway in San Antonio.

I really did come back a different person, and in many ways a better person, certainly more aware of the world and more comfortable in it. I enjoyed almost every moment of my time in Glasgow, except for getting deathly ill with tonsillitis on three occasions, usually for a week at a time, with a fever of 104 degrees. The third time I went to see the priest at the cathedral to get anointed with oil, because nothing else seemed to work. Doctors told me that after several severe bouts of tonsillitis, my tonsils were becoming progressively more prone to serious infection, and the damp cool weather of Scotland only made it worse. I got them taken out a few years later.

Now and then, I dream about returning to Scotland, and I know I will one day. Back home, I got rid of the mustache but let my hair keep growing to shoulder length. By the time I would graduate a year and half later, I would be unrecognizable from the freshman who had walked onto campus. Fresh back from Scotland, a young man fully about town, I wore cowboy boots, bell-bottoms, polyester shirts, and what amounted to a mop haircut. I was finally fully enjoying the college life.

When I got back to Trinity in the spring of my junior year, I found the *Trinitonian*, which had been trending downward, in what I thought was embarrassing shape. Bad writing, bad layouts, and too boring to bother with. It was really an awful college newspaper. I had declined a staff position to go overseas, but I continued to write a column every now and then. I wanted nothing to do with it, but finally, in spring 1998, several of my colleagues at the paper urged me to apply to the campus publications board to become the paper's editor-in-chief for the upcoming academic year. I had always thought that if I came back to the paper I would run the whole thing and turn it around. And I did. I started from scratch, hiring all of the staff, reporters, photographers, and more. And boy did we turn it around.

Nothing really newsworthy happens regularly on a small campus like Trinity, and for the most part, by the time a weekly newspaper has covered it, it's old news anyway. So we made a strategic decision to shift to a tabloid-style presentation, similar to the *New York Daily News*: big full-page photo with headlines splashed on the cover that begged you to open the paper. The *Trinitonian* was not a tabloid per se, but we'd liven up a mundane story by approaching it from an unusual angle. After the historic flood of 1998, we ran the headline "Water World" with a front-page photo showing students in the freshman quad splashing around in stagnant, knee-deep rainwater. The inside cover had an alert from the campus health department: "After flood, tetanus shot might be good." A special photography series featured interesting automobiles parked on campus. We took on controversial current events by inviting guest columnists, often Trinity professors, to write side-by-side point and counterpoint opinion pieces on the same subject in the weekly "Face-Off." And I always signed the weekly staff editorial so people would know that it was my take on a hot topic, not that of some anonymous publisher.

We aimed to be open and transparent about the news-making process while inviting people, especially students, to engage with the paper's content—not just read it—and to feel like their engagement mattered to the rest of the community. I certainly felt like it did. And I suppose this work was the first spark of what would later become a passion for increasing civic participation that has been a common thread in my life ever since.

We spiced the paper up. And we had fun with it, like filling all of the random empty spaces that didn't get sold by the advertising team with in-house ads for the paper itself. (My favorite was an AP picture of a triumphant Pope John Paul II tagged with "*Trinitonian:* Wholly Trinity.") Most of all, we just made it a better, maybe even a great, student newspaper. And we ended up taking it from a downward spiral in 1998 to winning "best college newspaper" in the country by the American Scholastic Press Association in 1999. I believe we laid a successful foundation for the *Trinitonian* that has lasted to this day.

With that culminating experience my senior year, I continued to balance coursework, the newspaper, a new social life, and my weightlifting regimen like so many spinning plates. I busted my tail from start to finish and graduated summa cum laude in May

At Miller Fountain, Trinity University, on graduation day, May 1999.

1999. My time at Trinity was life-altering, and for the first time I felt what it was like to not waste any effort. I had done my best. But I also realized that there were no guarantees and no roadmaps for life after college. I knew what I didn't want to do—become a sports beat writer, at least for now. And after applying for jobs to teach journalism in high school, I figured out that there weren't many jobs in journalism unless I wanted to work in the media.

I took the advice of my dad and my adviser Rob Huesca and decided to take my newfound enjoyment of communication studies to the next level and apply to graduate school. I sent applications to at least a dozen schools with programs in culture and human communication and was rejected from all but two: the

University of New Mexico, which offered a partial scholarship, and the Annenberg School for Communication at the University of Pennsylvania. I had never heard of Annenberg, but Rob told me to apply because he wanted to see how far I would get in the process (thinking I had no shot, since I wasn't good enough for state schools like UT and Indiana University). What he didn't tell me was that Annenberg was regarded by many as the best communication graduate program in the country, if not the world.

I had already booked my flight to Albuquerque to check out the University of New Mexico when I received a letter informing me I had been accepted to Annenberg and inviting me to visit Philadelphia on the same weekend. Included in the letter was the financial aid statement, which was the same for all students: total tuition remission and an apprenticeship (a research or teaching assistant gig with Annenberg faculty) that paid about nineteen thousand a year, enough for an apartment. I canceled my flight to New Mexico and told the woman I was dating at the time, "I'm moving to Philadelphia."

Just like that, one part of my life ended and another began. Again, an inflection point, but this time it wasn't just education and experience I gained at a top institution. It is also where I met my wife.

Erika Prosper was born in Weslaco, Texas, on September 3, 1974. She is about three years older than me. Weslaco gets its name from the W. E. Stewart Land Company, which founded the town a little more than a hundred years ago. The community is located in the Rio Grande Valley in the southern tip of Texas, between Harlingen and McAllen, about seven miles north of the Rio Grande. Erika grew up in the colonias, which were (and still are) unincorporated, low-income, substandard housing developments that emerged in the 1950s along the U.S.-Mexico border. The residents were mostly Mexican migrant workers, and their communities usually lacked basic infrastructure or services such as sewage treatment, water, and paved roads, as the colonias were on unregulated properties outside of city limits (even in 1999 when I first visited Erika's family, her grandmother's neighborhood was still unpaved, had no sidewalks, and only a few years prior had been hooked up to running water). Erika grew up in two colonias, one near the city and one about ten miles outside of Weslaco, which she and her family moved to when she was six years old.

She lived in an environment that consisted of a collection of families within a family, which was typical of the migrant worker life. Her parents, sisters, grandmother, and uncles and aunts lived and worked together. To Erika, in some ways it seemed like a happy childhood compared to what many people have because she was always around family. But even as a young child she worked long days, sometimes in onion fields, other times in cotton fields. In the summer she and her extended family migrated north to cooler climes in a caravan of sorts, sometimes to New Mexico and up to Michigan or Wisconsin, where they picked apples. She essentially worked this migrant cycle every year up until high school.

Erika's family was poor. And as she recalls, along with that poverty often came domestic violence and substance abuse. She remembers the adult males, especially her uncles, frequently beating their spouses, her aunts. It became par for the course to her, and it wasn't until she grew up that she realized how wrong this was. The women took the beatings, saying nothing. Erika told me, "This is how we lived; this is just the way it worked." Her grandmother had lived in a horribly abusive marriage; indeed, Erika's grandmother says her husband was "an evil SOB." But he was the one who had brought the family to the Texas-Mexico border in the 1960s, eventually settling in a colonia. By the time Erika was born they all lived under one roof, and it was loud, very loud. She could hardly find a quiet place or any privacy. She thinks she ended up being such a great student primarily because there were all of these after-school programs for students, and they were just as valuable to her educationally as they were in terms of providing a retreat of quiet and calm away from the chaotic environment at home.

Erika's grandmother, Abundia, came from an Indigenous tribe in the Mexican state of Michoacán, located west of Mexico City along the Pacific coast. Her birth father, Constantine Prosper, was from Laredo, Mexico. But he and her birth mother divorced when Erika was barely a year old, so she doesn't know anything about him. She considers her adoptive father, Jonah French Gray, to be her real father. Jonah and Pat Gray, her adoptive mother, were teachers who devoted themselves completely to improving the lives of their students in the Rio Grande Valley public school system. In the process they became foster parents, taking in several troubled students who had difficult home lives that interfered with their education. After an episode of abuse in which Erika was taken out of her own home, Pat and Jonah became her foster parents when she was sixteen years old and adopted her when she was twenty-three. The adoption was a significant and emotional moment in all of their lives. I remember it because Erika and I were already together. Pat and Jonah have always been in-laws to me, although Erika's birth family is also a part of our lives.

If you know Erika, she is one of the most focused individuals you've ever met. Her ability to block out noise, process information, and focus it into strategic action is unmatched. This was present—quietly—at her youngest ages, when she would figure out shortcuts to make the days in the fields as a migrant worker a little less backbreaking. And it was ever visible as a student. She excelled in every grade, earning honors wherever she went, including Weslaco High School, where she finished fifth out of five hundred students. She was accepted at a number of colleges, but she was destined to become a Longhorn (Pat and Jonah took their students on field trips to see the University of Texas at Austin to give them something to aspire to). Erika still takes pride in putting the "Horns Up" whenever it's appropriate, sometimes even when it's not.

She continued to excel at UT, completing two majors, one in a liberal arts honors program "designed to provide a broad, liberal, and challenging education for a limited number of students whose high school class standing and admission test scores indicated strong academic potential and motivation," and the other in advertising. As a child, one place where Erika could get lost amid all of the noise at home was watching television shows, even the commercials. She fell in love with the storytelling she saw and, over time, got very good at understanding the formulas. (Incidentally, this is a skill that drives me nuts. We love watching movies together, but Erika usually knows what's going to happen—even in movies she's never seen—and tells me before it does.)

In her first year at UT she heard Lionel Sosa give a talk on campus. Sosa, a San Antonio native, had become a prominent business and political adviser on a national scale, pioneering Hispanic advertising and representing some of the world's largest companies at a time when the advertising giants of Madison Avenue did not remotely understand or appreciate the Hispanic market. His mission to improve the Latino experience in his community and beyond naturally pulled him into politics, where he helped Texas senator John Tower and Presidents Ronald Reagan and George W. Bush, among others. Lionel's career spans multiple generations and countless successful businesses and elections. He was named to the Texas Business Hall of Fame, and in 2005 *Time* listed him as one of the twenty-five most influential Hispanics in America.

In typical Erika fashion, on that day in 1993 she confidently approached Lionel after his talk, shook his hand, and said, "I'm going to work for you one day." This would come to pass, and it is the reason we ended up back in San Antonio.

The story of how Erika and I met has become a little legend within our circle of family and friends. In spring 1999 the Annenberg School made their application decisions exceptionally late, so by the time I was notified in April and invited to visit later that month, I had to scramble schedules. I'm sure I wasn't the only one. Usually, "prospective day" was actually a weekend for college seniors who were accepted to Annenberg to visit and get to know Penn. It was meant to be a Philadelphia version of what I had encountered during my visit to San Antonio and Trinity University. But since our acceptance letters were so late, this year's Annenberg "prospective day" was not very well attended—only Dannagal Goldthwaite, a student from Delaware, and I were able to change plans quickly enough to attend. So, rather than create a big program for the two of us, Annenberg organized a tour and a few meetings with faculty and turned us loose with the rest of the graduate students.

As soon as I arrived, I was told several times that I had "to meet the other Texan in the school, Erika." I guess the folks at Annenberg thought I'd be more comfortable if I knew they had experience with foreigners like me. Erika, they said, was super nice, whip-smart, and very cute. And she was a Texan. I remember thinking at that point, "I'm going to like this place."

Annenberg's graduate program at the time was a two-year terminal master's degree with an option to apply to continue on for a doctorate. The summer between the first and second years was an apprenticeship where students gained practical experience toward an area of study by working in a business or organization while being paid by Annenberg. For students who didn't pursue a PhD, the apprenticeship often parlayed into a full-time job. Erika was admitted in 1998, a year ahead of me, so she was looking toward her second and final year while planning her apprenticeship. The evening I arrived in Philadelphia, the dean of the school, Kathleen Hall Jamieson, took all of the graduate students to dinner in the Old City district—the most historic area of Philadelphia—to celebrate the end of the academic year. The dinner also provided an opportunity for the Annenberg School to show off its students, as well as the interaction between those students and faculty, to potential new recruits.

The dinner was held in a private room at City Tavern, a building designed to recreate the historic tavern that served as a meeting place for the Founding Fathers attending the Continental

Congress in 1774. The wine and conversation flowed nonstop, and I could barely keep up. I was amazed at the intellectual sparring, not just between students but between faculty and students, and between faculty themselves. And every time Kathleen—as everyone called her—spoke, all debate ended. I could tell how much everyone in the room revered her. About a dozen Annenberg faculty members, a handful of staff members, and thirty students were present. This was the first time I met Erika, but as I found out during our conversation, it was not the first time I had laid eyes on her. Erika told me that she had played women's club lacrosse at UT. During her time on the team they played—and destroyed—their Trinity counterparts at a game in San Antonio in 1997. I remembered that game because I covered it for the *Trinitonian*. If I recall, many of my classmates were furious with me the next day because I gave a pretty accurate account of our drubbing.

After dinner several of us went to Chaucer's, a local bar popular with graduate students and some faculty, and continued the conversations—some heavy and some you'd expect from a bunch of twenty-somethings with only time on their hands. It was already past midnight when Erika said she had to get home. I offered to walk her home, which was about five blocks away near Rittenhouse Square in Center City. Maybe it was a little show of our shared Southern hospitality, but at least in my book, a young woman wasn't supposed to walk home alone late at night, certainly not in the middle of a big city like Philadelphia. When we got to her door I hailed a cab and gave her a "nice to meet you; see you next year" hug.

I'll never forget what happened next, though, because in my heart I still believe the cab driver was my guardian angel. It was one of those moments when you get an unexpected push in a direction by something divine.

"Cute girl. You going to marry her?" he said.

Without thinking, I replied, "Yeah, I think I will."

After that Erika and I went our separate ways for the summer—Erika to San Antonio for her apprenticeship with an advertising agency led by Lionel Sosa and me back to Austin to get ready for the move to Philadelphia.

It wasn't until the fall semester that I started thinking about that interaction in the cab. It was strange that I had responded that way out of instinct, and I was interested in getting to know the girl who made me do it. There wasn't any interest beyond that initially; Erika was already dating someone, and my new classmates and I were having the time of our lives exploring the Philadelphia scene. Going out on dates here and there was more trouble than it was worth, frankly. But whenever we were in the same place, I was drawn into Erika's orbit. She was beautiful and brilliant, and she fascinated me.

Finally, as the semester wore on, our friends started to whisper that even though we were casually dating different people, we should be dating each other. I had never asked Erika out directly, but eventually, over the course of our conversations, I guess she figured out that I was working my way up to it. Before I got the nerve to ask, she basically told me there was no way she'd ever go out with me, so I shouldn't bother asking. I wasn't a serious prospect.

Then she smiled and said, "But you didn't ask." *What an enigma*, I thought.

Later, one night at a house party on campus, Erika and I found ourselves in conversation over a pitcher of mango margaritas she had made. We were joking about how all of our classmates said we should be dating each other, and by that time even the guy she was dating—another classmate—had said the same thing. So, finally, I asked. And this time I got it all out, uninterrupted.

She stared at me for what seemed like an eternity, then laughed and said the only way she would ever go out with me was if I cut my hair (which was shoulder length and beginning to grow in all directions) and stopped wearing all my vintage clothes. She was setting a bar she thought a nonserious guy wouldn't want to reach.

Sitting behind Erika in class at the University of Pennsylvania's Annenberg School for Communication, January 2001.

She proceeded to put it into a written contract, which we both signed, with Erika probably thinking it would end my awkward interest in her. It did not.

To her great surprise, at our next stats class I showed up clean cut, wearing a pair of slacks and polo shirt. I went from hippie to preppie in a day.

Erika tells me that at that moment she thought, "Now I *have* to go out with him!"

It was December 1999, and on our first date we went to the movie *Notting Hill*, a great rom-com starring Julia Roberts and Hugh Grant. After the movie we returned to my place, where I made Erika a late dinner of chicken and rice. She was impressed by my cooking and manners, but apparently what sealed the deal for a second date was my spotless bathroom. She thought that if I cared enough about her to clean the bathroom, I must have

VOICES OF SAN ANTONIO

Carolyn Marvin

In 2018 the faculty and students of the Annenberg School for Communication at the University of Pennsylvania invited Ron back to Philadelphia to share his thoughts about his journey to public office. A triumphant homecoming was organized for a special graduate we were extremely proud of. When he took the stage, however, there was a surprise.

This two-term councilman and newly minted mayor of one of America's largest cities, a preternaturally talented (as we knew from following his career) engager of audiences, was suddenly tongue-tied. He fumbled his words. He was halting and uncertain. This brief display of nerves before he settled into a compelling story of his path to public service and his vision of democratic culture astonished us.

Later he confessed to having been overcome by the accomplished gathering of scholars before him, a community he held in awe and cared very much about being worthy of.

Those seconds revealed something central about Ron—not only his gratitude to those who have helped form him but also a fundamental humility in recognizing what other people in the world have to offer. Not just faculty and students at the university but citizens he regularly encountered, former mayors he interviewed on YouTube as a candidate, the city he was deeply honored to serve, and countless others. Here was a member of the political class who was not only the opposite of full of himself but also a person who radically valued the gifts of all he met.

There is a connection between this and Ron's time as a student. His master's thesis, which I supervised, examined the culture and experiences of bodybuilders training to compete in a local contest.

In pursuit of a noble ideal, bodybuilders transform themselves through ordeals of body and mind. A study of such folks might seem like an odd project for the academy. Not everyone "got" the investigation. But from the beginning Ron zeroed in on the dedication and striving for excellence that made this supportive and caring community special; he wanted the world to see it, too. It was a great thesis, sensitive and informative about its topic.

Can bodybuilding camaraderie and competition be preparation for political office? I doubt it occurred to Ron. But the links are there.

Ethnography, the framework for Ron's project, makes overlooked communities legible through the methods of deep engagement. Its best tool is observing with patience and curiosity what people do and what it means to them. It prizes empathy and the cultivation of human connection by a researcher who learns how to be part of the cultural context. This is also how good leaders bring citizens from all conditions into conversation with one another to fashion a resilient, decent, and resourceful civic community capable of identifying and implementing its dreams for the common good.

The tireless commitment of bodybuilders to the heroic perfection of classical myth also bears a family resemblance to the leadership ability to inspire citizens with an aspirational vision of democratic possibility, and the staying power to overcome any obstacle that stands in its way. Nor can we forget that bodybuilding, like politics, is fiercely competitive!

When the contest he was investigating was finished, Ron had proudly captured a coveted runner-up prize. He finished his thesis. He moved on to become program director of the Annenberg Public Policy Center, a laboratory of best practices for building democracy. Here there were new lessons to learn ahead of San Antonio.

But those who taught him had no doubt that his perceptive and searching study of bodybuilding, achieved through active participation in a supportive community of fellow bodybuilders, ingrained priceless truths. Truths about how worthy goals undertaken by passionate, serious people create empathy, inspire and sustain nurturing communities, and give rise unabashedly and uncynically to a better world.

CAROLYN MARVIN is the Frances Yates Professor Emeritus of Communication at the Annenberg School for Communication at the University of Pennsylvania.

something going for me. What she did not know at the time is that I always kept my bathroom that clean. In any event, I think she finally realized I was a serious guy. We really fell for each other that December. And we have been together ever since. Within a couple of weeks of our first date, I informally asked her to marry me, and Erika gave a qualified yes, saying perhaps someday soon.

During the winter break I went down to the Rio Grande Valley so I could meet her parents, Jonah and Pat, her grandmother, Abundia—the matriarch—and all of her aunts, uncles, nephews, and nieces. Her uncles thought they'd embarrass me by asking me to try some chile pequins—tiny, super spicy peppers—off the bushes. They didn't realize that I'd been enjoying chilis hotter than that in my mother's cooking since I was a child. I earned their respect immediately. Over spring break Erika and I returned and drove to the Gulf Coast at Port Aransas. I formally proposed to her, although I didn't have a ring—and of course I had already asked a month before, almost immediately when we started dating. It already felt like it was meant to be.

We were walking along the beach in the darkness, holding hands as the waves rolled up across our feet. Erika was kicking some of the water at me, and I stopped and said, "We should get married." She said, "Yes, it's time."

Whoa! It's happening, I thought. Although we had talked about getting married many times, it didn't seem real until that moment. You know that line from *Jerry Maguire*—"you complete me"? Life inserted it here. It wouldn't all be smooth sailing, though. Erika had already landed a permanent job with Lionel Sosa's firm starting after her graduation in 2000 and would be moving to San Antonio. I was one year behind and wouldn't finish in Philadelphia until the following summer. We decided to plan a wedding for summer 2001, which would allow plenty of time for me to graduate and find a job in San Antonio, and for us to start the rest of our lives together.

THE MAYOR OF JAZZ

In summer 2001 I found myself a twenty-four-year-old married man. Our San Antonio wedding in July was mostly a reunion of friends from graduate school and a strange—but super fun, I'm told—montage of traditions that represented our multicultural heritage: a lasso adorned with *milagros* around Erika and me as we exchanged vows under the chuppah, after which I broke a glass under my heel and the mariachis began to play. My father-in-law, Jonah, performed the ceremony as an elder in the Reformed Church of Christ, and after a quick stage change, Erika and I danced to our wedding song, "Crimson and Clover" by Tommy James and the Shondells, still my favorite song of all time. It was definitely a ceremony planned entirely by two kids in their twenties, right down to the PowerBars and Hot Tamales—party favors meant to represent the two of us—on each table in the banquet hall.

We honeymooned on the cheap. We had to. After we chose New Orleans for a long weekend, Erika's parents, who knew and loved the city, gave us three one-hundred-dollar bills for the purpose of getting three fancy meals in different restaurants they selected. I was a long way from having a foodie's taste at that point, but those three dinners remain some of the best I have had in my life: Brennan's, the Court of Two Sisters, and Tujague's. We spent the nights drinking, dancing, and listening to music on Bourbon

Street and the mornings falling in love to chicory coffee at Café Du Monde. It was two months after my graduation from the Annenberg School and three months before 9/11; the air hadn't become as heavy and still as it would become in the wake of that tragedy. From our tiny hotel room in downtown New Orleans it seemed as if everything—life itself—was accompanied by jazz music.

Erika and I returned home to our apartment in San Antonio, where she was beginning to take on more responsibilities in strategic planning for Lionel Sosa's ad firm, Garcia LKS, and I had just begun full-time as the national web editor for the Annenberg Public Policy Center's Student Voices Project. It was a position I had accepted first as a graduate student apprentice while the pilot was being conducted in San Antonio in fall 2000. I chose that over an offer from NFL Films in summer 2000 because it allowed me to be with Erika, whom I had just fallen madly in love with, in San Antonio. Even though working for Steve Sabol would have been pretty close to a dream gig en route to my dream job (writing for the Red Sox), given the choice between love and career, I did what most hot-blooded boys in their twenties would do, and it turned out to be one of the best and most important decisions of my life.

Student Voices was a determinedly nonpartisan civic engagement initiative funded by the Pew Charitable Trusts, the Carnegie Corporation of New York, the Annenberg Foundation, and others that aimed to study how young people can best learn about and participate in local government. We developed curricula for middle and high schools that taught about how local government worked by engaging students directly with government officials, media, and each other on issues they cared about in their communities. Some of those officials in the nine years I worked for Annenberg included an upstart mayoral hopeful named Cory Booker taking on the Newark political machine; a young state senator named Barack Obama making the unlikely leap to a U.S. Senate campaign; Rudy Giuliani, who was staying on as mayor to lead New York City through the darkest days of 9/11; his successor, Michael Bloomberg, who, after successfully rebuilding New York, would go on to become the country's leading philanthropic voice (and funder) in support of mayors and cities; and brewmaster-turned-mayor/governor/senator John Hickenlooper. Back in San Antonio, I recall how Julián Castro's voice seemed to penetrate even as a somewhat unpredictable new member of the San Antonio city council.

While I had no real interest in the government business I was being exposed to in the twenty-two cities where we worked, I absolutely loved getting the students interested in their communities and showing them how to use their voices. My job involved a lot of travel across the country to get more school districts to adopt the project and curriculum, and in each of our project cities I curated local news articles each morning from daily newspapers and stations so that students could keep up with current affairs. In each city, from Seattle to Tulsa to Philadelphia, students also engaged in Speak Outs—online forums in which students talked with each other in civil debate about pertinent issues in the news—that I moderated for accuracy and civility. They organized civic fairs in their schools and came up with Youth Issues Agendas that represented their collective voice. And they pushed local leaders to make change on things that would improve the lives of their communities. I remember one group of students in Pittsburgh who studied their city budget and argued how one hundred thousand of their tax dollars could be better spent to repair and paint a bridge that many of them commuted across every day. The city council ultimately agreed, and the project was completed quickly.

The issues were all relevant to the general public: police presence in neighborhoods, publicly financed stadiums, public transportation, smoking bans. You'd be surprised how intelligently these teenagers, not yet old enough to vote, engaged in the issues, often more so than the adults they were reading about. Simply because they were given the information and told that their opinions mattered, the students behaved as model citizens. My time with Student Voices planted a deep belief about our democracy that I still return to when optimism seems hard to come by: young people are the foundation of a healthy democracy. Perhaps it was easier to see this in an era that predates smart phones and social media apps, but when young people have access to accurate information, the skills to interpret that information, and the understanding that their voices are important, our democracy is strong and resilient.

I turned a study nook adjacent to our bedroom into my home office, where I would log in before dawn to scour the news in all of these cities and prepare them for students' morning classes. These were the days before Zoom, WebEx, and gigabit internet speeds (DSL was about as good as it got), so while much of my work was online, I managed my small staff and the project sites through conference calls and frequent flights to cities across the country, including Philadelphia, where the Annenberg Public Policy Center headquarters was located. Student Voices was my main responsibility, but the head of policy center, Kathleen Hall Jamieson, brought me into an increasing number of projects. Justice Learning and Justice Talking were initiatives that brought lessons from landmark Supreme Court cases into classrooms and National Public Radio stations, respectively. FactCheck.org, the pioneering website that provided in-depth analysis of the accuracy of claims made by public officials, led to a classroom spin-off called FactCheckED, and all of these initiatives got rolled up under an umbrella we called AnnenbergClassroom.org. Before I knew it, my professional life had become consumed by a nonpartisan mission to create active, informed citizens. And while the projects proved effective for their aims (Annenberg studies showed that students who were engaged by these initiatives for more than one semester exhibited long-term civic participation, including voting when they reached the age of eighteen), I wouldn't realize the salutary effects they had on me until a few years later.

The Student Voices program seemed like a natural fit since

I had always had an interest in education. At my high school I founded a chapter of Future Teachers of America, and at Trinity I started taking education courses, thinking that teaching high school would be an option after college. I even applied to Trinity's master of arts in teaching program before I received the letter to attend the Annenberg School. Through Student Voices, I was scratching a professional itch to become a teacher, inspired by the role that Mrs. Cowen and Trinity professors Rob Huesca and Donald Van Eynde—and so many other important teachers—had played in my life. We were empowering an entire generation of students with the knowledge to participate in the world, and I loved it. In hindsight, if I hadn't entered a life of public service in politics, I might have become a teacher. Erika still thinks I should.

I loved the job with Annenberg, but by 2007, when Erika and I were starting our family, there was a huge downside: it was grant funded. Mind you, a major study had proven the efficacy of Student Voices by that time and our funds from Pew, Carnegie, and the Annenberg Foundation Trust at Sunnylands were not in jeopardy. But having to apply for renewal every year was not a whole lot of job security, especially when by 2008 Erika had decided to change careers and start consulting on her own and the subprime mortgage crisis had sent the U.S. economy into the worst tailspin in our lifetime. I had experience with start-ups, having established a fitness and nutrition consulting company—Nirenberg Fitness Training—a few years prior in 2003, so when Erika left the ad firm after eight years, I helped her set up ColectivaMente Consulting, a market research company. She ran the company and conducted all of the research and strategy for business clients who wanted to understand their markets better, while I handled the administration. Effectively, by 2008, I found myself with three jobs—managing operations for ColectivaMente, managing a client roster of fifteen in my weightlifting and fitness training studio, and serving as program director at the Annenberg Public Policy Center—and not a single one could guarantee a paycheck from one year to the next.

When Jonah was born in June that year, we began to look at life—and our careers—through the lens of his future. As they say, becoming a parent changes everything. But just as our prayers were answered for good health for our son, they were answered again for health in our careers. One of our ColectivaMente clients—H-E-B Grocery, among the country's largest and best run private companies, according to *Forbes*—offered Erika a job only months after she started consulting. She accepted the offer and became director of customer insights for H-E-B, where she has worked ever since. Headquartered in San Antonio, H-E-B is an incredible company, beloved by their customers and employees (called partners) all over Texas. Erika's team handles qualitative research of all kinds. If there is a challenging question that needs to be answered about nearly any aspect of the business, from markets and products to customers and partners, Erika's team designs and directs a research strategy to find an answer. It's an intensely creative and rigorous process, and I've come to understand why her previous bosses used to say she is one of the most brilliant strategists they've ever known. Too bad she really dislikes politics.

While Erika was growing into her new roles as an H-E-B executive and young mother, and when I wasn't traveling to visit project sites for Student Voices, my day consisted of bouncing between conference calls, training clients at the studio, and changing diapers. Erika had returned to work, and without any good childcare options nearby and no family in San Antonio, I became a stay-at-home and work-from-home dad for the first year of Jonah's life. I could write a whole book about how this altered my life in profound ways, and maybe one day I will. But long story short, that year gave me an intense respect for the role of caregivers, and it sharpened a growing desire to find ways to spend my life in service of a better world for the younger people who will inherit it from us.

I'd often finish those days sitting on my back porch when Jonah and Erika were asleep, looking up at the stars and meditating or praying silently, asking for guidance. I found myself pleading to God to understand how I should live so that I served what I was beginning to see as my purpose: to leave the world a better place, especially for Jonah and his generation.

When Jonah turned one and a slot opened up at a nationally accredited early childhood center, Erika and I agreed that it was time to enroll him for his own development. The next step was for me to find a job with more financial security. While this meant that I would have to give up some flexibility, including no longer training my clients in the weight studio I had built in our home, we were parents now and that stability was more important. The first place on my list to look for work was my beloved alma mater, Trinity University. The school had introduced me to San Antonio, Jonah's birthplace and the city where Erika and I had firmly planted our roots, and I still had many friends on campus.

I had already let Rob Huesca know I was on the job hunt, and in early 2009 he called me with an opportunity. The communication department—where I already knew most of the faculty—might have a staff opening to manage the university's noncommercial radio station, KRTU 91.7 FM. The position had two functions: first, teach classes in management and marketing by having students learn about the broadcast industry, and second, manage a professional staff and volunteers, including those same students, who kept the FCC-licensed jazz and indie rock station operating. I was already familiar with KRTU. During my last semester at Trinity a decade prior, I had convinced the faculty to allow me to host a classic rock show that explored how classical music had evolved into rock and roll. It was all bullshit. I really just wanted to spin my growing collection of classic rock albums on the air, and KRTU was a classical/jazz format station. But they agreed to it, and until I graduated I spent every Wednesday night from midnight to 2 a.m. hosting *The Revolution* for the San Antonio listening audience.

The KRTU job would require a big pay cut, putting me back

at my starting salary when I was first hired full-time by the Annenberg Public Policy Center in 2001, but it was 2009 and the economic crisis was in full effect. It was a tough time in our lives. We had just bought a home near the daycare center, were trying to establish steady-paying careers, and had lived through the death of our daughter, Sophia. Now we had a one-year-old son. Erika and I were seeking stability wherever we could find it, even if it meant we had to live like we had something to lose for the first time in our lives.

We were also having to adjust to each other as a couple nearing our tenth year of marriage. We each had volatile upbringings in dramatically different ways, with hers being marked by violence, noise, and feelings of abandonment. As she says, it was disconcerting being married to this nice, relatively quiet guy. She was always waiting for the other shoe to drop, feeling that there must be something else going on with me. In the early years of our relationship I was every bit as hot-headed as she was and only added fuel to the smallest of fires. The most minor arguments often ended up with her threatening to leave me, mostly just to provoke another reaction. I can understand why a lot of couples don't make it much further than this in marriages. It took a lot of learning and commitment to each other and our future together, and a lot of swallowing of pride by both of us. We sought some counseling, and eventually we learned to navigate through our differences.

That's why I always say that being married to Erika has kept my feet firmly planted on the ground. I had to learn how to pick my battles, humble myself—which, it turns out, is an important skill in public life—and de-escalate rather than withdraw, a habit I had gotten into after witnessing so many of my parents' arguments. Both of us had to learn each other's insecurities and practice not taking every minor quibble to DEFCON 1. Erika began to understand that my workouts were not time away from her but essential for my mental and emotional health. Together we had to agree that no argument is worth exposing Jonah to the kind of familial volatility we experienced growing up. We celebrated our twentieth anniversary in 2021. It's a wonderful place to be when your partner knows when you're bothered or hurting and how to address it, especially when the wounds are not visible. I love it because we both have an instinct to make each other laugh unexpectedly with just a look, not a word, when things escalate.

In search of stability at a place I knew and loved, I took the job at Trinity to run KRTU. But that wasn't before one of the station's donors, a marketing executive from a local auto dealer, decided to apply for it as well, as a "gig to enjoy in retirement." Money talks, and the station needed to build its brand, so the faculty board hired both of us and split the general manager job in two. I was in charge of programming, personnel, and compliance, and he was in charge of development (fundraising). We soon clashed, and while we had plenty of disagreements about how to perform each other's jobs, to be quite honest, the faculty board broke a cardinal rule in business: make sure people know who is in charge. Our age difference was certainly another factor. But in noncommercial broadcasting the program drives development, so my work and the station's direction undoubtedly drove my colleague out, which was a good thing for both of us and for KRTU.

I developed a strategic plan for KRTU to expand the audience and build financial capacity. Those who didn't like the direction or couldn't keep up soon left. I had to find a new music director—one of the most critical positions—to curate the programming. I was referred to Kory Cook, an enigmatic musician with an encyclopedic knowledge of jazz and eclectic taste. When I called him, he was driving a van aimlessly through Oregon after breaking up with his girlfriend. He agreed to check out the station, and within a couple of weeks he was on board. I also hired JJ Lopez, a dedicated KRTU community volunteer who had taken part-time fill-in positions at the station before but had never shaken the "interim" title because he was still in school. JJ was one of the most dependable people I had ever met at the station, and I hired him immediately as our operations director. Finally, I hired one-time volunteer Monica Reina, who had left an uninspiring job and was looking for a career that would get her excited to come to work every day. She became my management assistant. By the way, two decades later the three of them were still running KRTU (as I write this, Monica is station manager and JJ is the general manager), which is the best jazz radio station in the country.

Two key objectives of the strategic plan were to launch a marketing campaign we could execute for no cash and to begin the process of building a new tower to boost the station's signal reach beyond the 8,900 watt capacity that barely played over the tops of buildings in downtown San Antonio. For the latter, to expand the broadcast signal, I began the long bureaucratic process of filing for a new FCC permit. Spoiler alert (and an early taste of how the federal government operates): the license was granted but not until several years later. For the former, I enlisted J. C. Pagan, an experienced advertising creative and volunteer host of our *Blue Note Hour* to come up with images and taglines for a campaign to build awareness. The "I AM JAZZ" ads featured photos of a range of people enjoying music: young, old, blue-collar workers, suits, hipsters, and so forth. The idea was to show how America's original art form—jazz music—united everyone.

We didn't have money to put into marketing, so everyone volunteered for the effort—in front of and behind the camera (even a barely two-year-old Jonah posed with headphones), and I traded underwriting spots on KRTU for ad space in newspapers, magazines, other radio and TV stations, and billboards along the major interstates. Within a year we had ads running all over town, and all it cost us was a few twenty-second "thanks to our sponsors" spots during each broadcast hour. Our underwriting revenue doubled, and we began to build capacity to develop more programming and plan for the future.

One of the programs we had to develop was a proper celebration of KRTU's tenth anniversary since adopting a full-time jazz format, which made the station among the country's few remaining "real" jazz radio stations. (At the risk of offending some readers, KRTU is real jazz, not smooth jazz. Coltrane, not Kenny G.) Although KRTU was launched in 1976, it wasn't until 2001 that it converted to jazz full-time to fill an underserved market. So the big question was how to properly celebrate the station's format anniversary in a way that uplifted the station, the music, and our listeners and donors and also helped KRTU grow its audience.

The answer was inspired by a familiar place. As I was taking command of my role at KRTU, I felt an itch left from my experiences at Annenberg. Julián Castro, a young San Antonio city council member during our Student Voices project, had just become mayor (as expected), and he started a community visioning initiative called SA2020. The goal of SA2020 was to bring the city's diverse people together to create a community-driven vision and strategic plan. I had seen a few of these exercises before (in particular, I remembered Tulsa mayor Bill LaFortune's Vision 2025), but this time it was happening in my hometown and I wanted to get involved. Castro had also brought together an impressive group of people, from business leaders to college students, and he was committed to a community-led process and vision, not something that would be buried in government bureaucracy like so many other projects. My interest was piqued.

So I attended the first SA2020 meeting in 2010. Hundreds of people gathered at a local school, and facilitators separated everyone into smaller groups focused on a number of topics ranging from arts and culture to transportation. I decided to take a seat at the economic development table, as I figured businesspeople would be there who might be helpful to KRTU as sponsors or donors. It was 2010, and I didn't know many people in the business community or in politics, both of which were well represented at SA2020. I sat across from a woman who introduced herself as Carri Baker. It turns out that she worked at a local law firm and had just become chair of the Greater San Antonio Chamber of

Commerce. She was joined by several other businesspeople, all representing different businesses and chambers of commerce—the Chinese Chamber, the Taiwanese Chamber, and so on. I had never realized there were so many chambers. That was interesting enough, but the conversation that ensued took me by surprise. For nearly the entire twenty minutes we were given to discuss a vision of economic development in San Antonio, our conversation revolved around how the city's economic potential hinged on the arts and culture scene, where the city derives its unique identity. It's true: San Antonio has a unique culture, drawn from its history as a binational community at the crossroads of the Americas, a place where people had to fight for everything they had, from land to rights to respect. Its heritage as a military fort—and now a military city home to nearly 250,000 veterans—is also infused into everything, giving San Antonians an unrelenting sense of duty to one another and a feeling of honor in service. All of that mixed into what is known now as "puro San Antonio"—a certain swagger and devil-may-care attitude about what other people might think. It dawned on me during our conversations at the economic development table with Carri that our arts, cultural, and historic heritage is indeed San Antonio's economic competitive advantage. By the time the meeting ended, I felt I needed to come to the next SA2020 gathering, not just for KRTU's sake but also my own.

The idea that the arts and culture community was San Antonio's unique economic advantage convinced me that KRTU—a media platform for that very community—could be a force for advancing the city's arts scene, including the art of jazz. That became the idea behind the tenth anniversary celebration. KRTU would celebrate a "Year of Jazz" in a way that could lift up key members of the arts community and their inherent cultural value to the city. For the next six months I visited with arts organizations all over San Antonio to develop collaborations that would allow us to host a concert at their facilities in exchange for us highlighting their organization on the air. Jazz is as diverse as America itself,

Announcing the Year of Jazz lineup with Bill Christ (*left*), general manager of Trinity University's KRTU-FM radio station, at a reception with community leaders, August 2011.

and for every organization that agreed to participate, the station would feature a band that played jazz music reflecting their mission. In the Guadalupe Cultural Arts Center on the West Side, it was Chicano-inspired West Side soul. At the Carver Community Cultural Center on the East Side, it was a tribute to Miles Davis. The Southwest School of Art celebrated its French roots with a concert of Parisian jazz. A member of any organization participating in the Year of Jazz could attend all of the concerts for free, so it was a great way for arts patrons of all kinds to be exposed to cultural opportunities they might not have experienced before. For KRTU, it was about introducing all of these dedicated members to our station and our music. And for the city, it was about showing off the diversity of our cultural heritage—our identity and economic advantage—at a time when we were thinking big about the future. Talk about collective impact.

That was the picture I painted for Mayor Castro when I took a page out of the Student Voices playbook and approached him with an ask: declare the twelve months starting with October 2011

Mayor Julián Castro reads *Charlie Parker Played Be Bop* with accompaniment by saxophonist Jim Waller during KRTU's Year of Jazz kickoff, October 2011. Photo by Jennifer Whitney, special to the *San Antonio Express-News.*

as "A Year of Jazz in San Antonio." I was elated when he agreed. But he couldn't say no because of the second part of the pitch: Erika had given me an idea to have a song created for the city as part of the yearlong celebration. Rather than just a song, I suggested to Aaron Prado—a KRTU volunteer and former music director who happened to be a gifted pianist and composer—that he compose a suite of original jazz that would tell the city's story through the language of jazz. We could even have it narrated so that listeners were escorted through our complicated history. The last movement of the suite should be about where we are today—aspiring for a bright future, SA2020 and beyond. Aaron loved the idea, and the *San Antonio Jazz Suite* was born. I told Mayor Castro about it, and he loved it too, especially when he learned that the last movement would be titled "SA2020."

The *San Antonio Jazz Suite* was debuted in October 2011 by the

King William Jazz Collective and the San Antonio Symphony in front of a live audience at Brackenridge Park. Aaron played the piano, and the whole thing was narrated by Spurs legend Sean Elliott, who was incredibly easy to approach about such an outlandish idea. His dad was a big jazz fan too, so he was excited about the project. Mayor Castro kicked off the event by reading Chris Raschka's *Charlie Parker Played Be Bop* to the many kids who were in attendance. After all of the performances, the jazz suite finale was played as the sun set, and the Year of Jazz followed with twelve months of concerts all over town. A reprise of the *San Antonio Jazz Suite* closed out the year at Trinity's Laurie Auditorium in October 2012. This time it was narrated by San Antonio's first poet laureate, Carmen Tafolla. It was a resounding success, with KRTU's stock continuing to rise within the arts community, and the only check I needed to make it all happen came from Graham Weston, founder of Rackspace and an SA2020 tri-chair, who donated seventy-five thousand dollars—not because he loved jazz but because he saw that the kickoff would be a helluva way to showcase Brackenridge Park, a place he was increasingly interested in preserving and activating. Collective impact.

Carri and I kept in touch, and she was also impressed by our work at KRTU. We started sponsoring the music at chamber events, which provided additional revenue and visibility for the station in front of potential donors and sponsors. She was so impressed by how I was creating value and running the station as a successful start-up that she encouraged me to sign up for the Leadership San Antonio (LSA) program. LSA was created in 1975 by the Greater San Antonio Chamber of Commerce to help identify and develop community leaders. Having graduated some two thousand participants over the years, it is now considered the premier program of its kind for existing and emerging leaders in Bexar County and surrounding areas. The program goes beyond personal and professional development; rather its overarching goal is to educate and inform leaders in the vital areas affecting San

VOICES OF SAN ANTONIO

Doc Watkins

It's uncommon to move from a career in the arts to one in politics. Behind closed doors, musicians and artists love to tear their politicians apart; one would almost think they were natural born enemies. Yet at their core, art and politics are after the same thing: the greater good for the benefit of the community.

Both fields also share the common trap: an orchestra conductor can be given to vain glory as easily as a senator. But the basic aim is the same. Not unlike a city council member, one enters a profession in the arts to serve the community. It's a difficult, often thankless, job that requires constant sacrifice for the good of the village.

So it was not entirely surprising when Ron Nirenberg, my friend and station manager at KRTU 91.7, threw his hat into the ring of local politics. Back in those days Ron was a "jazz cat," the face of the greatest local radio station exclusively featuring jazz. I loved it—and still do. In our earliest conversations, Ron often mentioned areas of the community that he felt needed improvement. I realize now that he was hinting at something.

My own experience with KRTU was transformative. In 2008 I received my doctorate in classical music studies from the University of

Antonio and to increase participants' involvement in the life of the city. In 1992 the San Antonio Hispanic Chamber of Commerce joined LSA as a cohost, increasing and diversifying the participant pool. To be eligible, participants must have demonstrated leadership and held responsible positions in their profession and must show a sincere commitment to serving the community.

I was accepted into LSA Class 37 around the time KRTU's yearlong celebration kicked off. Given my past experience with Annenberg, and now SA2020, my interest in the city's civic affairs

Texas at Austin, only to realize I wanted to play jazz instead. One day I declared to my wife and friends that I was now a jazz musician; my sanity was questioned shortly thereafter. Pursuing a career in jazz in San Antonio seemed about the worst idea one could think of, but somehow it felt right to me.

As a recovering classical musician in my late twenties, I found a simple strategy for learning jazz: I took any gig that would have me and listened exclusively to KRTU while I was driving. (I often took the scenic route to the grocery store for maximum effect.) I fell in love with KRTU and marveled at the sincerity of its programming. I learned more about jazz from listening to the radio than any university could have taught me.

Fifteen years later I'm blessed to own multiple jazz clubs and to have played a small part in the city becoming a cultural hub for jazz worldwide. I often chuckle to think that a small radio station in San Antonio (wait, not Austin?) has had such an effect on a global scale for one of the greatest art forms the world has ever known.

Thank you, Mayor Nirenberg, for your decades of service to the San Antonio community. We need more jazz cats in politics.

DOC WATKINS is a jazz pianist and band leader and the owner of Jazz, TX, a restaurant and jazz club in San Antonio.

went into overdrive. Every month we spent a full day doing a deep dive into different aspects of how the city functions—the water and electrical systems, the military, the health care sector, environmental protection, government, and more. To say I enjoyed it would be a massive understatement. Almost immediately it became far more interesting to me than the day-to-day grind of running the radio station. I learned about how the city operates, and I connected with a number of people from across the city who were making things happen. I was constantly fed a wealth of information on the challenges facing the city as well as all of the opportunities for it to grow, expand, and prosper. I remember telling Erika that the experience with LSA created a spark that I hadn't felt in a long time; I felt like public service was calling me.

I had been at KRTU for a couple of years by then and had built a solid team. My work had evolved into business development, creating connections within the community, and bringing in revenue while building the brand of jazz as far and wide as I could. And I was a devotee, especially after auditing a jazz history class during the first year I took the helm. Jazz is the original American art form and one of America's three greatest exports, along with baseball and democracy. I quoted the jazz greats with ease: "If you have to ask what it is, then you'll never know" (Louis Armstrong) and "Jazz washes away the dust of everyday life" (Art Blakey). Jazz is the quintessential American art form because it's multicultural, it's free-form, and it's first and foremost improvisational. No performance can ever be replicated. You will never hear the same song twice, unless there is sheet music. As Miles Davis said, "I'll play it first then tell you what it is later." The station's mission gave me a passion for the music and our role in preserving it. Learning and appreciating improvisation in jazz would even later serve me well in politics, but in 2011 there was something missing.

Some of my favorite jazz musicians are John Coltrane, Miles Davis, Stan Getz, and Thelonious Monk, artists from the golden era of jazz. Although rock and roll was my first love, I learned to love our programming and our mission, which was largely done to advance the arts in general and the music specifically being created in our city. That put KRTU (and me) in the center of the city's music scene, and I got to know Jim Cullum, Ron Wilkins, Spot Barnett, Bill King, George and Aaron Prado, Doc Watkins, and so many other wonderful local artists. In fact, I recommended Doc for the LSA program, and I think that kickstarted his interest in the business side of his music, which eventually turned into one of the premier live music venues in Texas: Jazz, TX, located in the

Pearl district just north of downtown. I suppose I was so much into the jazz scene—and giving off civic leader vibes by showing up all over town—that *San Antonio Express-News* music writer Jim Beal started calling me the "Mayor of Jazz."

With all of this community involvement, however, I still couldn't shake the feeling that I was missing something. I began to listen more to that calling. One evening after spending the day with LSA, I said to Erika, "Maybe I should run for city council. What do you think?"

"Sounds like you've already made up your mind," she said. "Do it."

That's when our lives changed again. And eventually led to me becoming a very different type of mayor.

MEET YOUR NEIGHBORS

It was an intersection of faith, fortune, and opportunity that paved the way for my entry into San Antonio politics. When I was hired at Trinity, my days as a stay-at-home dad were over, which meant that we needed to find a day care for Jonah, who had just turned one. Erika and I looked for a quality early childhood program, and we found it at the Block and Dreeben School for Young Children, a National Association for the Education of Young Children–accredited center at the Barshop Jewish Community Center (JCC). We decided to sell our house to be closer to the JCC, which was quite a distance away (San Antonio is a city of nearly five hundred square miles), and found the perfect place practically across the street. It was late 2009, and I had not yet started to think about San Antonio politics, but the location of our new school and home would turn out to be a stroke of political luck.

San Antonio operates under a council-manager system of government, and there are ten single-member city council districts of roughly equal population. At the time, each district elected one representative to the council in May of odd-number years, for a maximum of four two-year terms. The eleventh council member is the mayor, who presides over the city council and is the only member elected by the entire city.

The city council essentially functions as the city's legislative body, with a city manager appointed to act as its chief executive, responsible for the day-to-day management of city operations and the execution of council legislation. San Antonio's council-manager form of government has been in place largely unchanged since the adoption of the city charter in 1951. The first major change occurred in 1977, when the city faced pressure from the U.S. Department of Justice over lack of Hispanic representation on the city council; a charter amendment was passed in a citywide referendum that created district-specific elections for the council. Prior to that, council members were elected at-large, which led to virtually all representatives being elected from the affluent Anglo-majority parts of town on the city's North Side. The seminal change was intended to democratize local politics, and it did exactly that, resulting almost immediately in a more racially diverse council. Four years later, in 1981, District 1 (the center city) elected María Antonietta Berriozábal, San Antonio's first Latina councilwoman, and Henry Cisneros, its first Latino mayor in almost 150 years.

Erika, Jonah, and I found ourselves right next to the JCC, just inside the border of District 8, a place we would later learn is one of the most diverse areas in an already diverse city. The district is on the city's northwest side, straddling Interstate 10, one of the fastest growing parts of a fast-growing city and home to the South Texas Medical Center, the University of Texas at San Antonio, some of the most affluent neighborhoods along with one of the highest concentrations of subsidized housing, and the entire religious and ethnic diaspora of San Antonio. Politically, it is divided right down the middle. Coincidentally—or perhaps not, given the skills required to govern—it is also a district that has gotten a reputation for producing effective public servants, such as former state senator, Bexar County judge, and mayor Nelson Wolff.

Councilman Reed Williams was one of those highly regarded public servants when we moved in, and after one productive term in which he guided the city's electric utility out of a financially catastrophic nuclear energy deal, he announced early into his second term that he would not seek reelection. This was right before Christmas in 2011, and I had just had that conversation with Erika.

There was, however, a practical side to the matter at the time. Another feature of the city charter that had not been changed since 1951 was the council members' salary (or lack thereof). In 1951, San Antonio was a growing southern city of just over four hundred thousand people, but it was hardly the bustling metropolis it is today. Council members (including the mayor) got paid a stipend of twenty dollars per weekly session for what amounted to part-time work. That's what the pay was when Lila Cockrell became the first female mayor of a major American city in 1975. That's what it was when Henry Cisneros stepped out of city hall after fourteen years (eight as mayor) in 1989, and when Julián Castro left the mayor's office for President Barack Obama's Department of Housing and Urban Development in 2014.

The twenty dollar stipend became a bit of a running joke in San Antonio, and despite the fact that everyone knew it limited council members to those who either had other sources of income (legal or otherwise) or who, in the case of then–council member Rey Saldaña, still lived with their parents, voters rejected an amendment to institute a salary for council in 2004. For the most part it ensured that the council was not at all reflective of the working-class community; many of the tenured council members were retired or independently wealthy. This finally changed in 2015, when voters elected to amend the city charter and institute a salary for council members equal to the median family income in 2014 ($42,722), with an additional 35 percent for the mayor ($61,725).

But that wasn't the case in 2011. Erika and I really had to think about the financial ramifications of me entering politics. We decided that if I won, I would continue working at KRTU.

Erika also recalls "activating our friendship group," because we knew we'd need a village if this was going to work. Martha and

Mike Flores, our trusted friends for more than a decade, organized a brunch at their home one Sunday morning in January 2012 for our closest circle of friends in San Antonio. "Dr. Mike" was then vice president of Palo Alto College in the Alamo Community College District and would later become chancellor in 2018, winning several national awards along the way. Martha is a creative marketing executive who worked with Erika before she started her own boutique firm. They were some of our closest family friends; we had known each other for more than a decade and were all going through the same life stages in the same town, at the same time.

Between Martha's creativity and Erika's strategy, the brunch table was a diverse collection of expertise, ideation, and encouragement. And other than Mike and me, they were all Latinas—I knew I had better come prepared. I stayed up all night before our meeting, writing about the San Antonio (and District 8) that I knew and the priorities I thought needed work: transportation, development, public safety, water quality, and so on. I typed up nine policy white papers, each describing the issue from a high level and laying out actions I would support to solve them. I knew that even a year and half away from the next municipal election, for this group—which included a friend of a friend, Theresa Canales (the only person with campaign operations experience), I would need to have good answers to the questions "Why?," "Why now?," and "Why you?"

I finished the policy papers with a new resume and a one-pager on my values that included three questions I thought were essential for every public decision, questions that have continued to guide my thinking ever since:

1. Is it fiscally responsible?
2. Is it fair and ethical?
3. Have we done our homework?

With our friends group activated and my statement of purpose composed, the next several months were learn-as-you-go—the education of a candidate—starting completely from scratch. While I knew how local government worked and had spent a decade in public policy research in a range of cities, I hadn't a clue about local politics or how a campaign worked. In many ways, that naivete was a godsend. If I had known what I was getting into—how all-consuming it would be and how it would knock me and everyone close to me out of our comfort zones—I probably never would have begun. (I came close to quitting once soon after we began and I realized I'd have to put in nonstop work that took me away from Jonah, walking every accessible neighborhood for the next year and half and raising money to pay for a campaign since there was no way we could afford it on our own.) Theresa became my first "campaign manager," which meant teaching me campaign 101, starting with how to block walk: going door-to-door to listen to residents' concerns and sell ideas instead of magazines and candy bars (or jazz radio). Lionel Sosa—who at that point, despite his local, state, and presidential campaign experience, was simply, to us, Erika's former boss and my former personal training client—was thrilled, along with his wife, Kathy, to help me with communications strategy. Martha agreed to handle all of the creative.

I called Reed Williams, then the current council member in my district, to pick his brain on what serving on the council was like and what he thought the most pressing issues were for our area and the city. Williams was a retired oilman turned politician with an academic's brain. I had never spoken to him before, but I knew that he was sharp and detail oriented. He had a reputation as a policy wonk and often surprised people with hyper-technical words they'd never before heard in a Southern drawl. I told him about my background with the Annenberg School and my budding interest in running for office. He graciously took the meeting. It was the first of many meetings with people all over the community.

I met with everyone I could (starting with those Theresa, Lionel, and the rest of the team suggested), with each meeting leading to several more. I was introduced to Betty Sutherland, a former assistant to several consequential San Antonio mayors. "Miss Betty" was known as the great connector and a whisperer among the titans of the business community, and she became one of my fiercest champions and advisers for the next decade. She led me to Red McCombs, Ed Whitacre, Bartell Zachry, Tom Frost, Lowry Mays, Gen. Joe Robles, and Bill Greehey, all of whom eventually became supporters. She connected me with Janelle McArthur, one of the only experienced political fundraisers in town, who came out of retirement "one last time" to help me get started. Betty then introduced me to retired real estate pro Charlie Conner and his wife, beloved former city councilwoman Bonnie Conner, who became my campaign treasurer. Bonnie was still adored by the neighborhoods she served in District 8, so that was an immediate boost to our grassroots campaign. Betty also encouraged me to meet former mayor Howard Peak, who had started the linear parks system and become one of the staunchest proponents of protecting greenspaces in the city. Howard and I immediately struck up a friendship, and I committed to continuing his work.

Finally, Betty set up an appointment with Phil Hardberger, mayor of San Antonio from 2005 to 2009, who left office as one of the most popular politicians ever to serve in the city, having guided the city through the aftermath (and neighboring evacuations) of Hurricane Katrina, the restoration of the San Antonio River, and a great expansion of public spaces, including parks, Main Plaza, and the famed River Walk. He was so popular, in fact, that on the way out of office he led an effort to extend term limits from four years to eight, greatly transforming the landscape for future city leaders to implement a long-term vision for the future.

I got to the Starbucks at Houston Street early, so I could find a table and make sure I got my nerves under control before Phil arrived. From the window, I saw him saunter across the street, walking along the sidewalk like an average guy. It all seemed surprisingly normal for someone who basically walked on water in terms of local politics. He was stopped a few times before getting to the door, as people seemed to greet him like an old friend. He finally walked in.

I waved awkwardly to get his attention and then extended my hand. "Hi, Mayor Hardberger," I said. "It's an honor to meet you. I'm Ron Nirenberg. Thanks for taking the time to visit with me."

Phil Hardberger was a rarity in politics. A retired B-47 bomber pilot, he became a renowned civil rights attorney who later ascended to chief justice of the state Fourth Court of Appeals. Then, coming out of retirement in 2005, he became the first mayor in modern history not to have served previously on the city council. In nearly every meeting I had, from neighborhood leaders to business icons to current and former elected officials, Hardberger was regarded as the epitome of leadership and one of the most effective mayors in city history. After taking office in the wake of scandal, in which three sitting council members were indicted for bribery, he restored city hall's credibility and ably navigated natural disasters, record infrastructure investments, and an expansion of the community's parks system.

Phil and I got right down to it. He asked me basic questions about myself, my education, why I wanted to serve on the council, and what my plan was to get there. I asked him about the things he did as mayor, the things he thought were left undone, and any advice he had for someone who wanted to serve. His interest was heightened when I mentioned that I was the son of a Peace Corps parent. During the time my dad served, Phil was executive secretary of the Peace Corps, appointed by the director, Sargent Shriver. He seemed excited by the idea of a council member with an appreciation of international relations and offered one of the many memorable quotes he would give me over the years, this one paraphrasing a young Mahatma Gandhi. As mayor, Phil said he wanted the windows and doors of San Antonio to be open

With former San Antonio mayor Phil Hardberger at his law office, in the final months before the city council elections, March 2013. Photo by Jonathan Alonzo.

to the world, so that "the culture of all lands [would] be blown about [our] house as freely as possible." He put his time where his mouth was, restarting the city's sister city program, which had laid dormant for nearly two decades. He connected San Antonio with Chennai, India, and started efforts to establish a relationship with Germany that I was able to finalize in my first year as mayor.

Our conversation continued for another thirty minutes, meandering between global affairs, water policy, city council politics, and the challenges of balancing family life with being a public servant (you can try, and you should try, he said, but you really can't). As the meeting wound down, I gave Phil my white papers and asked for feedback. He was taken aback. He said he'd never met a candidate who wrote white papers about policy and what he'd do if elected. We ended with Phil promising to read the papers

VOICES OF SAN ANTONIO

Phil Hardberger

I first met Ron Nirenberg at a downtown coffee shop next to my law office. He said he was interested in running for city council. As I had been mayor, a meeting like this was not an unusual request. What was unusual was what he brought with him: a book-length white paper dealing with the several needs of our city and his ideas for addressing these issues. He gave me a copy of the manuscript so I could read it at my own pace. I did read it—and learned from it.

The study was comprehensive in its scope. All of our major issues were there: low wages, poor education, potholed streets, income inequality, and bad housing. The paper showed many hours of research and thought. It was a good summary for an incoming mayor, even though his race was for a council member position. Ron recognized the problems but also had solutions for dealing with them. This sense of preparation permeates everything he does. He is ready. He stays ahead of the problem.

Most candidates concentrate on the politics of getting elected. They spend little time thinking what they will do, if anything, if they are successful in becoming an officeholder.

Ron is also spiritually prepared for leadership. He is, more than anything, a good man. He is a family man and good citizen. He incorporates his family challenges into community challenges.

and offer his thoughts. And while he reminded me that he had a rule not to endorse anyone for city office after he finished his tenure as mayor, we left the door open for future conversations. Phil would eventually become one of my primary mentors and a dear friend. He still says that his first meeting with me was one of the most impressive he had ever had with someone running for office—again, thanks to all those white papers. He says I was the

Ron made a powerful impression on me from the first meeting. I knew he would be a good public servant because he rules from the heart, and his heart is pure. He has his priorities in order. Like all of us, some of his ideas are better than others, but you never have to worry about his motivation. His ideals do not change. The ideas may change, but not the ideals. They are locked in place.

I always supported Ron because of those ideals. He is willing to take on the big issues—workforce training, better housing, income inequality, keeping a healthy environment. These are long, complex issues with few clear, complete victories. But the fight for a better life is the soul of the American Dream. There is glory in the struggle in and of itself. As Gandhi said, "You must be the change you wish to see in the world."

This is what I saw in Ron that first day he came to my office. I see it today. He is guided by the goal of making a better America. In Nature's inexorable cycle of life, we run against the clock. There is much to do and little time to do it in.

Ron is strong, knows the pathway, and has the energy to do much. Of our leaders, we can ask for no more.

PHIL HARDBERGER, a lawyer and former chief justice of the Fourth Court of Appeals, served as San Antonio's mayor from 2005 to 2009 and is currently a board member of the Phil Hardberger Park Conservancy.

first one to come in with such detailed and realistic plans on issues affecting the city.

And so it went for the next several months, working deeper into the neighborhoods and constituencies of District 8 and the rest of the city. I soaked it all up like a sponge—I couldn't wait to get off of work each day to get back to discovering more about this amazing city. Every person, every question, every answer poured right into me and informed the next steps in my growing "campaign" (a word I finally had to get used to saying).

Eventually we built a web page, Martha designed a logo, and Lionel put together a push card. My friend Jonathan (Jon) Alonzo, a Pulitzer-worthy photographer, took photos along the "trail." And Kazim Fahim, a former coworker of Martha's who had just opened his own creative shop, compiled Jon's photos with my white papers into a glossy twenty-eight-page booklet, "Vision for District 8." It was essentially my treatise about the district I wanted to serve. I gave a copy to anyone and everyone I could. I left them at the doorstep when no one was home. We were rolling.

When I hired a professional campaign consultant several months later, he told me that he was glad I had written the white papers before I hired him because he would have strongly advised against a client putting their positions and promises in writing. People would remember all those promises, he said, and many would form an opinion about me based off of that alone.

"Isn't that the point?" I said. It was important to me that if I was going to run for city council I needed to stand for something and be crystal clear about what it was. I knew from then on that I would have a strained relationship with politics as usual if I were to strive to be a statesman, as opposed to a typical politician, like my father preached. It's cold comfort, but when the political noise gets too much to bear, I still remind myself of that.

I tried to be everywhere that people were. Exactly one year before the council election, the city had called a $596 million capital improvement bond election to improve streets, facilities, parks, and more. It was May 2012, and I went to poll sites in District 8, greeting voters as candidates do, except of course I was not on any ballot since the District 8 election wouldn't be held for another year. I handed out the push cards that Lionel designed like a sneak preview for a movie that would be coming to theaters soon: "In spring 2013 ..."

Then I walked. And I walked, and I walked, and I walked. Indeed, I wore several pairs of shoes until the soles were hanging off (Erika saved a pair as a memento). You quickly learn how to be efficient, such as walking up one side of the street and down the other, returning to the car, and driving it to the next street, all the way through the neighborhood.

I learned some of it the hard way. For instance, in one of my first solo walks I parked in the middle of the Hunter's Creek neighborhood, which was the district's heaviest voting precinct, just down the street from where we lived. I had gotten a list of voters in the area, and I started walking around, visiting every home on the list. Some eight hours later I was only about one-tenth of the way through because I was using a presidential election cycle list, which is much longer than a city council voting list. In San Antonio, unfortunately, it is typical to have only 10 to 15 percent of registered voters turn out for the May city council and mayoral elections (as opposed to 50 to 60 percent in November presidential elections). My time at Annenberg showed me that voter apathy is a vicious, dangerous cycle that ultimately erodes the essence of a democracy. Elected officials tend to focus on the voices of those who engage, and the voices of those who don't are drowned out or ignored, leading to more distrust and disengagement. Unless there are intentional efforts to bring those silent or ignored voices to the table—a focus on equitable representation—the result is policymaking that poorly reflects the needs of the entire community, especially the underserved. And the apathy cycle continues. Block walking is one way to break that cycle.

Eventually I knocked on the doors of thousands of homes in my district, some several times, in dozens of neighborhoods across forty-nine local precincts. On weekends I'd start at 8 a.m. with a backpack loaded up with my walk lists, door hangers (including a stack hand-signed with "Sorry I missed you!—Ron" in case no one was home), water, and snacks, and I'd walk until the sun went down. On weekdays I walked after work until sunset.

Block walking District 8 while running for city council, March 2013. Photo by Jonathan Alonzo.

What I found during all those months was that diversity is not a statistic or an abstraction. It is the strength of a community. Our city was made up of many different kinds of families, all with their unique challenges and aspirations. Their own cultural backgrounds and beliefs. But we all share the same city, and if we are going to thrive together, we need to appreciate that our personal perspectives and experiences are not the same as everyone else's. I immediately recognized that my job as a public servant is not about having all the answers; rather it is about bringing people together to understand who they share the community with—to see and meet their neighbors—so that we can find common ground to tackle those many challenges together. I still believe this to be the key to good public policy. If only we could better know and appreciate who our neighbors are, whether they are across the street, across the city, across the country, or even across the globe.

I created an online Facebook album called "Meet Your Neighbors" that featured the stories of dozens of different families in District 8, their hopes for our community, and photos at their homes. Veterans like ninety-three-year-old Maurice, who was getting accustomed to living alone; the three-generation home of Olga, Anna, and Fernanda, who told me how their family's lives revolved around the parks; and Lydia and Joe, who were retired and on fixed income and needed their elected officials to remember that. One of my favorite editions of "Meet Your Neighbors" was at the home of Fabian, who was outside doing yardwork with his son, Fabian Jr. Fabian Sr. said he loved San Antonio because "it feels like a family-oriented city. Everyone says hello to their neighbors," while Junior told me, "I love that everybody watches out for each other in San Antonio." Eventually "Meet Your Neighbors" became our unofficial campaign slogan and a mantra I would carry throughout my time in office. It also reinforced how much I had fallen in love with my city.

My main opponent in the 2013 election was Rolando Briones, who was a politically connected engineer in town. He was a prolific donor to dozens of local political candidates and officeholders from San Antonio to the Rio Grande Valley, and not surprisingly his boutique engineering firm did quite well securing contracts from public entities. As a result, when he announced his campaign around the same time I did, which was extremely early for a city council race, he was immediately deemed the front-runner. He turned a Hummer into a campaign vehicle, adorned with his image and logo, and hired every local political consultant and fundraiser, just to make sure they were occupied and could not be hired by anyone else running for District 8. Briones had all kinds of money, all of the business establishment, with whom he frequently rubbed elbows, and all of the insider political establishment, who he had consistently supported with donations over the years. His campaign ended up spending the most money in the history of San Antonio city council races (approximately $450,000, although it has been speculated that he spent much more in his own money). A typical open seat city council campaign at that time would run $75,000 to $100,000. Early on, I figured he was trying to intimidate me into dropping out, but that only motivated me more, as did my distaste for the kind of quid pro quo politics he seemed to be playing. That much was still burning in me from my days at Annenberg, teaching communities about the way good government should work.

There was one consultant named Kelton Morgan who hadn't engaged in local campaigns in a while. I was introduced to him through another Leadership San Antonio classmate, Magaly Chocano, who happened to have a tech firm located near his office. Kelton and I agreed to meet for margaritas at La Gloria in the Pearl complex. We talked about the city a bit but mostly about our political views. He said he was a Republican growing disenchanted by the brinksmanship in both parties and that our politics lacked smart, committed, practical professionals who wanted to serve the public. I told him I didn't want to run a partisan race and that, as the son of a Peace Corps volunteer who had already had a career in civic engagement initiatives (which some would say makes me a natural Democrat), I valued getting things done and bringing people together. So while I was definitely not a Republican, I wanted to let my values and actions speak for themselves and avoid feeding into the polarization of our city. I was turned off by the growing political polarity, even at the local level. I just wanted our elected officials to represent the community's best interests, focus on the important things, and spend their money wisely. Kelton and I hit it off over that discussion, and although we eventually parted ways many years later, we established a relationship that would change my life and lead to many tough but successful campaigns.

For fundraising, Betty introduced me to Janelle McArthur, Phil Hardberger's fundraiser who had retired when he did. She still maintained a rolodex as vast as Betty's and was just as respected by the pillars of the San Antonio business community. Well into her eighties at that point, Janelle agreed to come out of retirement to help me after we had a conversation similar to the one with Kelton. Phil also helped by giving her a friendly nudge.

Briones ran an aggressive, and in many ways, ugly campaign, eventually pushing disinformation directly and through surrogates about me that bordered on the absurd. I certainly got my first taste of what some politicians—or would-be politicians—are willing to do in order to win. Letters arrived at the houses of some of the wealthier areas in the district warning against my "inexperience," alluding to a "liberal agenda," and ridiculing my professional background by equating it with being a "college dee-jay." Later, during the runoff, a pink flier circulated with a photo of me during a bodybuilding competition with the image blurred from the waist-down, making it appear like a lewd photo. The accompanying text proclaimed, "ron is pro abortion & pro homosexual agenda,""ron is anti 2nd amendment,""ron supports castro's liberal agenda," and "ron voted twice for obama!" among other things. My logo was also copied at the bottom, except with the "O" in my name replaced with the Obama reelection campaign logo.

Kelton kept me and the team disciplined and reminded me that those kinds of desperate, negative tactics meant the Briones camp was concerned about us, even if it would have been an understatement to refer to me as a dark horse when we started. So I just stayed busy, continuing to meet with people and walk everywhere I could. In those one-on-one meetings, most of the insiders told me they had to support Briones because of what he'd done for them, but they were impressed by my vision, work ethic, and background. I asked them to keep an open mind and know that I looked forward to visiting with them and earning their support after I won.

Talking to people at their front door was different. If I could keep the conversation about city issues, I usually won them over.

But if they just wanted to know my view on abortion (I support a woman's right to make her own health decisions) or guns (I believe in commonsense gun regulations that keep dangerous weapons out of the hands of people who are a danger to themselves or others), it was a toss-up.

Over the following months I continued walking every day. I would go up to homes, and if people answered the door and gave me a chance to talk to them, I would immediately tell them who I was, what I was running for, and a little bit about my background. I told them I was president of the Summerfield Homeowners Association, an HOA I joined a couple of years after we moved into District 8. The association meetings were usually not well attended, and typically retirees were the only ones who came. They had asked me to join and soon asked me to run for president because I was an anomaly—a young homeowner who was interested and actively participated. Erika thinks I joined just to find out why our neighborhood association bills were so high; I wanted to know exactly what we were paying for. That was probably part of it, but I was truly interested in neighborhood affairs. And although small scale in relative terms, it gave me valuable civic experience.

I also told voters that I worked at the Annenberg Public Policy Center, which brought me to twenty-two cities and helped me learn about what worked and what didn't in communities across the country and gave me the opportunity to teach people how to get involved with the life of their city. Finally, I mentioned that I was currently teaching and running the radio station at Trinity University. All of these things often opened up broad areas of discussion, most of it having to do not with politics but with life in general. I usually closed the conversations by asking people if they had any questions, if they had any concerns for the neighborhood, district, and city, and finally, if they would consider voting for me for city council.

Although District 8 was very diverse politically, the municipal turnout at that time typically skewed conservative, so many of the questions I received had to do with whether I voted for President Obama or my position on abortion. I was straightforward and honest in my response, as opposed to my opponent, who although he was a Democrat and donated prolifically to local candidates, told everyone the opposite and branded himself a Republican to appeal to the conservative electorate in the district. He told people he did not vote for Obama, but we found out that he had donated to the Obama campaign. While someone's vote is their own personal business, it becomes a legitimate issue when they make it part of their campaign and then you find out they are lying. When people asked me why they should vote for me and not one of the other candidates, my response was essentially the following: "I'm going to level with you. I'm going to be honest with you. You might not agree with everything I say or do, but frankly I would want someone in office with integrity over somebody who you might agree with more on certain issues but who is not going to tell you the truth."

Then I'd tell them about the three questions I always asked myself before making a decision, beginning with, is it fair and ethical? Because even if you like all of my answers on the issues, we can't possibly predict every issue we'll face in the years to come. Of the thousands of doors I knocked on, only a few were slammed in my face, almost all over the issue of abortion. But the encouragement from neighbors, who often expressed pleasant surprise over a candidate coming to their home to personally ask for support, provided the fuel to start back up the next day.

Bonnie's neighborhood of Hunter's Creek was ground zero—the District 8 battleground—in that first campaign. It had an exceptionally large voting population, and I went back three or four times as we noticed that some houses with my sign on the front lawn changed it to Briones. I wanted to know why, and being competitive, I thought I could win these homeowners over if I could find out what mattered to them. Primarily I wanted to correct the disinformation that was streaming out of the Briones campaign.

After talking with me and hearing the facts, most would put my sign back up.

No one was going to outwork me. But the Briones campaign had dozens of paid staff and seemingly no limit to their resources or money. Some of those resources included insider connections that helped boost Briones's profile. One puff piece in a local magazine featured his moral stand against the CEO of the San Antonio Water System (SAWS) ten years earlier, when Briones had refused to eat a raw egg during a strange morale-building exercise and lost his job there because of it. Another cover story in the *San Antonio Business Journal* featured Briones, alongside former mayor Ed Garza, as a visionary engineer who was changing the landscape through the groundbreaking public projects his firm was involved in.

Of course, all that glitters is not gold, and we knew Briones was a prolific donor to local elected officials' campaigns. It wasn't hard to conclude that my campaign had to take a stand against pay-for-play politics and cronyism. Still, we needed a break.

It finally came in January 2013, when the *San Antonio Express-News* reported on the front page that Briones had completely fabricated the story about his firing from SAWS. In fact, a year prior to the supposed egg incident, he had been fired for accepting gifts from vendors before and after they were awarded publicly funded contracts he was working on at SAWS. This led to more fact-checking of his claims, and even though he outspent me nearly five to one, the playing field became much more level. Phil Hardberger, who had resisted getting directly involved in municipal campaigns after leaving the mayor's office in 2009, arrived at my next fundraiser and made a speech about integrity while holding up a raw egg. He endorsed me that evening and encouraged the shocked—but amused—audience to do the same. Mayor Peak agreed to record a video conversation with me about parks and the environment, which we posted on social media. Former mayor

Henry Cisneros recorded a get-out-the-vote script for a robocall to District 8 voters. The tide had turned.

On election night in May 2013, I received the largest number of votes in my district but not a majority. Because of a late-entry third candidate, my 49.53 percent was close but still thirty-four votes shy of an outright win. There would be a runoff election.

I remember telling my dad before the vote count was in that after eighteen months of nonstop campaigning, the negative attacks, and the odds we had to overcome, I hoped I either won or lost. I didn't know if I could start from scratch in the runoff and endure another month of all-out campaigning.

"You've come this far," he said. "If you're in the runoff, run to win."

We drove to the election watch party at Naples pizzeria after the early results came in and it was clear I was in the lead. I kept hoping over the next several hours that election day would boost us over the 50 percent threshold to avoid a runoff, but it didn't happen. I kept thinking, "What am I going to tell these supporters and volunteers to convince them to do this all over again?" It was one of the most challenging speeches I had given. I was scared to death trying to motivate them again and hit the campaign trail for another month—and raise more money, especially against someone who had insiders in his pocket and for whom money was not an issue. Much to my surprise, however, the energy in the restaurant was pure elation. To our team, we had done the impossible. Our upstart, underdog campaign had just defeated the entire political establishment in the city's highest profile race. Now we just had to go get thirty-four more votes. Lionel Sosa suggested "34 Votes" as a campaign rally cry, and it seemed to catch on.

Election day in San Antonio is held on a Saturday in May, and the next day was Mother's Day. It drove home the point that the sacrifices I would accept as part of my political life would also extend to my family. We called a strategy session with my campaign team bright and early that Sunday morning, and the team included Erika. Instead of spending the day relaxing and being celebrated, she was hard at work helping me prepare for the runoff.

I had a wonderful campaign team and eager volunteers. Two young people who had shown up to one of my first campaign events really stood out in our grassroots efforts. Chris Stewart was a right-leaning undergraduate at the University of Texas at San Antonio (UTSA) and student government president with a deep knowledge and passion for politics, while his friend Noah Howe had just graduated from Churchill High School and considered himself a standard-bearer for the next generation of Democrats. I appointed them as my field directors for the runoff effort. Chris set up a war room in his parents' house, and they quickly organized a Saturday morning recruitment meeting for more student block walkers. The two of them, along with other student government leaders at UTSA, created UTSA Students for Ron, a group encouraging more students to get involved and vote, especially since the university's main campus was located in the heart of District 8. (After the election, Chris, Noah, Hannah Beck, and other UTSA students kept the organization going and focused on issues we were championing in the District 8 office, like transportation reform. The organization was formalized into the nonprofit Move San Antonio, which many years later spread to other campuses and cities as Move Texas.)

Chris and Noah would continue to work in formal staff positions in my office, and Chris would eventually become my chief of staff while he was still an undergrad, maybe the youngest in San Antonio city council history. A lot of college-age people were involved in this campaign, and that would continue as I moved forward, even after I became mayor. This has been one of the most fulfilling aspects of my public service career, something that continued from my days at Annenberg; young people believe they can bring about positive change, and when they are given opportunities, they do.

In those days I didn't have a campaign office or headquarters. It would have been a waste of resources; we needed to be walking the neighborhoods. My unofficial campaign headquarters was the Starbucks at the Alon Market shopping center near my house. We never let up, and the momentum and positive energy seemed to build from one day to the next. On election night we won the runoff convincingly, with nearly 54 percent of the vote (53.84 to 46.16 percent for Briones). I was elated, and at the second Naples pizzeria party that night, I gave Jonah a big hug and planted a kiss on Erika. That photo appeared on the front page of the paper the next morning.

The work began immediately, and it was unrelenting. From council sessions twice a week to committee meetings, constituent hearings, and neighborhood association gatherings, my new job as a council member went from before dawn to well after dusk every day. When I came home, it was increasingly challenging to take my mind off of work. I was routinely out the door before Erika and Jonah awoke and back on my laptop answering messages and emails well into the night after they fell asleep. At first I tried to keep my position at KRTU going (it was the one with the paycheck, and the council was still a twenty-dollar-a-week "volunteer" job). But three months in, the hours at city hall crowded out any possibility of that, and Erika and I decided it would be best for me to focus solely on being a good council member. I left KRTU, and we buckled our financial belts, thankfully having retired our student loans and car notes a few years earlier. We essentially became a one-income household, with Erika as the primary breadwinner; otherwise, my public service story likely would have ended right here.

Between the pace of life as new parents and relatively new careers for both Erika and me, my council tenure went by in a flash. At home, Jonah was a precocious preschooler, headstrong and curious about the world around him, particularly the things he could observe directly like the parks and natural areas we often tried to escape to on weekends. One evening we took him to the Bracken Bat Cave to watch millions of bats emerge—a breathtaking tornado of them spiraled up and out of the mouth of the hundred-foot-wide cave, floating away over the horizon as the sun set. I described to four-year-old Jonah how Bracken was the world's largest colony of migratory Mexican free-tailed bats—housing approximately twenty million of them—and that the cave helped replenish the water we drink whenever it rains. I also told him that I was working to protect the cave from being overrun by a new development that planned thousands of homes in the area. From that moment on, every day when I got home Jonah asked me, "Have you saved the bats yet?" Eventually that question and many subsequent conversations with Jonah turned into a priority list he developed for me: Save the water, save the land, save the bats, and save the air.

I picked up the mantle of water and environmental policy on the council and became a staunch advocate for managed growth. Using the lessons from the Year of Jazz of a broad, albeit loosely affiliated, coalition aligned toward a collective goal, I assembled a public-private coalition that raised twenty-one million dollars to purchase the land surrounding the Bracken Bat Cave and place it in a public trust, allowing us to preserve its natural state forever. I traveled up and down the I-35 corridor across multiple jurisdictions: commissioners courts, city councils, neighborhoods, philanthropy, businesses, Republicans, Democrats, even the U.S. Army (because of their nearby training areas), and the U.S. Department of the Interior.

No one took ownership, but everyone took an interest. I recognized that in order to get it done, the cause just needed someone to lead it. So I did. In the end it took more than a year, but together the Texas Nature Conservancy, along with Bat Conservation International, the City of San Antonio, the U.S. Army, and several others, were able to do as a team what none of them would consider individually. The Edwards Aquifer, the bats, the Hill Country landscape, and the trees that provide habitat to native endangered species were spared from the march of urban sprawl, at least for now.

One year into my tenure as a city council member, I was reminded of why I had fallen in love so quickly with San Antonio—it was a confluence of people and organizations with their own unique purposes uniting for common cause when they were called to it.

Later during my first term, I led an effort to gain voter approval for continuing the Edwards Aquifer protection program along with the Howard W. Peak Greenway Trail System, named after former mayor Peak who had started it fifteen years prior. Both of these sales tax initiatives had proven wildly popular over the previous decade, acquiring easements to conserve land over the aquifer and to build out the hike-and-bike trail system that was approaching a hundred miles long. We fended off repeated attempts by Republican-dominated state legislatures to gut our environmental protections, including tree protections and regulations that restricted the amount of impervious cover over the aquifer. These efforts culminated in the development of the city's first comprehensive plan, called SA Tomorrow, that took the SA2020 vision and developed a policy roadmap to achieve it, from environmental sustainability to multimodal transportation to land development. I was a cochair of SA Tomorrow, along with Darryl Byrd, a highly respected entrepreneur and consultant who had led SA2020, and Afamia Elnakat, a UTSA scientist who had an uncanny grasp of the science, regulatory, and community implications of our work.

During that first term, I recall being yelled at a lot. Every Wednesday evening we had a public comment period in which citizens could sign up to speak on any topic they wished. Sometimes those sessions lasted for twenty minutes, and other times they went until the wee hours of the morning. Each citizen had three minutes to speak, though Mayor Castro occasionally reduced the time allotted if more than 150 people had signed up.

For a freshman council member, those sessions were fascinating, scary, enlightening, infuriating, hilarious, inspiring—it depended on what the person had to say. I really honed my poker face during those months. There were pleas for fairness and complaints about service. Petitions to strike down laws and demands to create new ones. And many, many demands for things that we had no control over. We even got hexed and cursed a few times (I made sure to get a *limpia* from Erika or a blessing from a *curandera* whenever that happened). All kinds of people came to the public comment session, from average neighbors to business types to folks who scheduled their lives around the Wednesday evening opportunity (those were the regulars).

On one occasion an older woman named Theresa, who lambasted us every week at the public comment session for something she claimed the city did, turned to me after she finished yelling at all of us, and said into the microphone, "You should listen to Mother Teresa, who said, 'Do good anyway.'" I wrote that down and taped it to my desk on the dais, and it got me through some tough times on the council over the next four years. I later found out that the quote was from a longer text by Kent M. Keith and later attributed to Mother Teresa of Calcutta; a revised version was found on the wall of Shishu Bhavan, the children's home she founded in 1955. It goes like this:

> People are often unreasonable, illogical and self centered;
> Forgive them anyway.
> If you are kind, people may accuse you of selfish, ulterior motives;
> Be kind anyway.
> If you are successful, you will win some false friends and some true enemies;
> Succeed anyway.
> If you are honest and frank, people may cheat you;
> Be honest and frank anyway.
> What you spend years building, someone could destroy overnight;

Build anyway.
If you find serenity and happiness, they may be jealous;
Be happy anyway.
The good you do today, people will often forget tomorrow;
Do good anyway.
Give the world the best you have, and it may never be enough;
Give the world the best you've got anyway.
You see, in the final analysis, it is between you and your God;
It was never between you and them anyway.

Perhaps the most formative experience of my council tenure came a couple of months into it. Mayor Castro and District 1 (downtown) council member Diego Bernal launched an effort to update an ordinance protecting people in San Antonio from discrimination based on race, sex, creed, color, and so forth. With increasing concerns about discrimination against members of the LGBTQ community, we were being asked to consider a change to the nondiscrimination ordinance (NDO) that added sexual orientation and gender identity to the protected classes. Kind of a no-brainer, I thought, although I found out quickly after I declared my support publicly that not everyone agreed. In fact, over the course of two months of public testimony and debate, often going well into the morning hours from the 5 p.m. start, council chambers became a raucous and divided place, filled to the rafters, with one side in vocal opposition, suggesting that adopting the ordinance would lead to damnation of ourselves and the city, and the other side enduring those attacks and asking for the basic dignity of not being denied services or accommodations at public places because of who they loved.

As the representative of a conservative-leaning district, I got many angry letters and phone calls warning me to vote against it or suffer the consequences. All of the council members who declared support soon had recall elections launched against us. It was quite an introduction to council. After winning a bruising runoff election a few months prior, I was being told that I'd be terminated if I voted with my conscience. I made a decision in the heat of the moment that I still hold firm to: if doing the right thing costs me my job, so be it. At least I could look back and be proud of what I did. The updated NDO passed 8–3. As it turned out, none of us were forced into a recall election, and of those who ran for reelection, all were elected.

That formative experience cemented my belief in the power of mutual understanding—the whole idea behind those "Meet Your Neighbors" posts during my campaign. Countless times, courageous parents, siblings, coworkers, and others testified to the dignity of all people, pleading with the city council and the audience of public speakers—including those in opposition—to get to know the people the nondiscrimination ordinance would protect. On more than one occasion I saw the raucous chambers disarmed by appeals to mutual respect. One speaker who brought that message was clergyman Tom Heger, who blended a unique literary humor with perfect recall of biblical scripture. The late Reverend Heger, pastor of Beacon Hill Presbyterian Church, would soon become a good friend, always offering sage advice (or jokes, whether or not the occasion required it) until his passing in 2024. His words called for understanding, not necessarily agreement, and people listened.

I was at the beginning of my tenure, and it remained a time of great promise and progress. Then in spring 2014 the San Antonio political scene turned upside down when Castro officially announced that he had accepted an offer to become the secretary of Housing and Urban Development (HUD) in President Obama's administration. He told me he was going to do this earlier, in February, when we were both flying to El Paso to attend a tour of the Kay Bailey Hutchison Desalination Plant, but the official announcement had to await the administration's vetting process. In San Antonio city government at that time, when a mayor left before finishing his or her term, the city council chose an interim mayor to complete the term. The council then selected the replacement for the council member who became interim mayor from a slate of candidates in his or her district. On the flight, Julián suggested that I had better start thinking about who I would throw my support behind on the council. Immediately, I had two thoughts. First, I was not happy that he was leaving because I thought he was a good mayor. And second, I wondered why I shouldn't put my name forward. That's exactly what I did.

Once it became known I was putting my name in the hat, my phone started blowing up. Kelton Morgan, who had become my chief political adviser and consultant by then, and Christian Archer, Hardberger and Castro's former political strategist, both told me I had to act fast to try to garner council support. There was a lot of jockeying around in the council that July among those who wanted to become interim mayor and those who were being courted to support one person over another.

In retrospect, putting my name forward ultimately created tensions and expectations that rippled through the next few years. But it also helped fortify a resolve to keep our city moving forward. I was understandably considered (and called) brash for being a first-term council member and thinking I could leap into the mayor's office. To be honest, though, and no disrespect to my colleagues at the time, I believed Castro had our city on the right path forward, and I believed I could keep it on track and build on that momentum. It wasn't to be, as the pundits predicted, as my fellow freshman Shirley Gonzales and I were both unable to secure support from our colleagues. The votes were divvied among two three-term council veterans, Ivy Taylor from District 2 on the East Side and Ray Lopez from District 6 on the West Side. In the final round of voting I threw my support behind Ivy Taylor, who I thought would hold a fair line in the ongoing and tough contract negotiations with the local police and fire unions. She also agreed to move forward on developing a comprehensive plan for the city, which we eventually dubbed SA Tomorrow.

In part because of a promise not to run for a full term as mayor if selected, and despite a vote against the NDO, Taylor succeeded Castro as mayor in July 2014, becoming only the second woman and the first Black mayor elected in San Antonio. For a brief period that measure of political and social progress was universally celebrated in the city. The council was united, and Mayor Taylor commanded an easy supermajority for every action. But that harmony began to erode as she began to see me in a different light: an ambitious young politician and a possible threat.

In my first council term I was able to move the needle on some of the initiatives that were important to my constituents. Along with environmental and water policy, the comprehensive plan, and efforts to improve citizen access to council deliberations and records, I took a lead on technology policy. This included an initiative to pull together all of the city's major public agencies to collaborate on broadband access and cybersecurity, with the latter eventually becoming the Alamo Regional Security Operations Center, where today cyberthreats are monitored and defended around the clock. Voters took notice of District 8 office's work ethic and responsiveness, whether to the smallest neighborhood issues or our efforts to shape citywide policy on development regulations, so I had a relatively smooth reelection in 2015, winning with just over 72 percent of the vote.

The council term was equally successful in many ways, but it was also more difficult. Despite her pledge not to run for reelection, Mayor Taylor ran against two highly experienced politicians from our local legislative delegation, state senator Leticia Van de Putte and state representative Mike Villarreal, and pulled off an upset victory in the runoff. As the term began, it was clear that she had turned her sights to me, assuming that I would run for mayor against her eventually. Truth be told, I had no such intent, at least if she was doing a good job. In fact, we were aligned on important issues—water security, development and housing, the comprehensive plan.

But I heard explicitly from city hall insiders at the time that

Mayor Taylor and her advisers felt they needed to separate themselves from me, because I had previously shown that I wanted to become mayor. One of them told me that my North Side colleague Joe Krier in District 9 was given one job, and that was "to bury Ron Nirenberg." She and her team began to put up roadblocks to my initiatives in hopes of limiting my impact. Whether or not this was her personal intent, we started to diverge on key issues and over which direction the city should go. The city's momentum stagnated, and she began to court support among conservatives as a way of shoring up a base she thought she would need against me. In reality, I supported her reelection in 2015, her first electoral victory for mayor, but our relationship consistently deteriorated after that.

My vision for what the city could be and what I could accomplish never changed despite the increased complexities of being on the council and the hostility from the mayor's office. But I clearly felt I was being isolated, and I was no longer enjoying the job. I figured I had three options: be satisfied with having little influence as a dissenting voice on an island, finish my term and walk away, or run for mayor and try to change the conversation. Well, I don't quit. And I also wouldn't be happy just talking about change, so I chose to run for mayor in order to move our city forward. Mayor Taylor's paranoia of me running against her became a self-fulfilling prophecy. After months of discussion—and another crucial conversation with Erika—I decided to run for mayor as the only way to do my job.

THE CITY YOU DESERVE

San Antonio is a city that celebrates hard work, and it rallies behind the underdog. While the slogan "Keep San Antonio Lame" emerged in the 1990s as a way to mock a laid-back, old-fashioned atmosphere (in contrast to "Keep Austin Weird" just up the road), residents eventually began to wear it with a sense of pride. It became a source of strength: forever going against the grain, the city is undefeatable because it just doesn't care what other people think. Some call it authenticity, or IYKYK (If you know, you know). It's no wonder that the San Antonio Spurs, unceasingly bemoaned by sports commentators as "boring" and "overrated" on their way to dominating the NBA for twenty years, are interwoven in the fabric of the city. How satisfying it has been to watch Tim Duncan—the "Big Fundamental"—known for his casualness on and off the court, quietly win five NBA championships and become one of the best players in league history.

And it's also no surprise that San Antonio was the birthplace and incubator for so many movements and organizations at the bedrock of human rights in our country, the Mexican American Legal Defense and Educational Fund, La Raza Unida Party, and the Southwest Voter Registration Education Project among them. Throughout history the city has been the place where the underrepresented and marginalized have found a champion. Emma Tenayuca led workers strikes against the pecan industry in the

1930s. In March 1960 religious leaders and Black residents paved the way for San Antonio to become the first southern city to voluntarily integrate lunch counters. In 1968, not long after Dolores Huerta and Cesar Chavez began organizing labor, Our Lady of the Lake University in San Antonio hosted the U.S. Commission on Civil Rights to hear testimony about civil rights violations experienced by Mexican Americans in the Southwest. Fifty years later the city government provided seed funding to launch the Mexican American Civil Rights Institute, the first of its kind in the United States. San Antonians are proud to fight the powers that be, if those powers trample the dignity of others. It was in this community that I was finding myself increasingly isolated on a city council led by a new mayor whose deputies identified me as a political threat.

As I started preparing to run for mayor, I first asked Erika for advice, as I always do. She is keen to say, though, that when I ask for her advice it almost always means I have already landed on a course of action and am simply seeking support. She knows she has a veto, but she's never used it. As for my dad, whose counsel I always sought on serious matters, after I described my vision and my predicament, his response was definitive: "I think you should do it."

I bided my time for the next few months, first and foremost to see if my situation at city hall might improve under Mayor Taylor. It did not. I sought out more advice on whether to run for mayor and whether there was a realistic path for success. My cabinet at that time, which consisted of Bonnie Conner, Betty Sutherland, Kelton Morgan, Lionel Sosa, Mike Flores, and attorney Jorge Herrera, encouraged me cautiously. Kelton said he didn't see an immediate path to win but would come up with one. In the meantime I began to raise money for either reelection to city council in 2017 or a run for mayor. Because I was still on council, my campaign donations could be no higher than five hundred dollars. (It is one thousand dollars for mayoral candidates.) By July 2016, a year ahead of the next election, I had raised more than a hundred and fifty thousand.

The *Express-News* reported that "Nirenberg won't say whether he's running for mayor, but the level of his fundraising says he is." The truth of the matter is I had already decided.

At about that time Kelton came back and said, "There's a path. It's a narrow one, and you have to run a perfect race, but there's a path." He urged me to delay a final decision and announcement until after the presidential election already heating up between Donald Trump and Hillary Clinton. It was very hard; I knew what I wanted to do, what I needed to do, but I hated the idea of playing coy about it. So we waited. And waited. In the meantime I kept reaching out to people across the city and raising funds, although most of the city's establishment political and donor class had already decided to back the incumbent. We also heard that Mayor Taylor's camp warned potential donors that if they contributed to me, they'd be iced out by her as mayor.

Meanwhile the situation was deteriorating on city council. Mayor Taylor dissolved a committee I was chairing on the SA Tomorrow comprehensive plan, which she had strongly supported. She also dropped Amy Hardberger, water rights attorney and daughter of Phil Hardberger, from an important committee that oversees the policies and fees to promote sustainable development and rein in urban sprawl. Sprawl is an urgent issue to me, which was underscored by SA Tomorrow, and besides being a close ally I considered Amy as one of the city's most knowledgeable people on water and environmental issues. There was definitely some political gamesmanship going on. It became evident to me that Taylor's decision to replace Amy, who served as a potential brake on overly rapid and careless growth in the city, was also aimed at satisfying some developers, who contributed significantly to the mayor's campaign finances.

After months of waiting, speculation, and eventual sniping between the mayor and me (after staying quiet for a year, I began to call out her bad decisions publicly), I officially announced my candidacy for mayor on December 10, 2016, becoming her first challenger. At that point, although the election was only five months away—in May 2017—the formal campaign season for local office in San Antonio followed a very compact timeline.

After candidates file for election in January and the real race begins in earnest, those who have already laid the groundwork for a successful campaign by raising money and building a support base and team are separated from everyone else. It became clear that unless there were any late entries who were already well known, the race would be mainly between Taylor and me. I immediately focused on widening my circle of supporters, introducing myself and my vision for the city to likely voters but also, harkening back to my lessons from Annenberg, to young people and those who had not been previously engaged in local elections. Among others, that led me to David Lesch, my coauthor for this book, through the kind auspices of our dear mutual friend Bill Clover, who had gone from being a strong supporter and donor during my jazz days to being the same during my political life. Bill and David were both professionals in international commerce and diplomacy, respectively, and formed the core of a small policy group advising me on San Antonio's role in the international community. I formed several other policy groups on other parts of my campaign platform, from energy policy to transportation, economic development, housing, and so on.

I made the official announcement at the old campaign headquarters for Phil Hardberger and Julián Castro at Broadway and Tenth Street, close to downtown. In San Antonio political lore, it was kind of famous as an undefeated campaign headquarters. It was somewhat of a coup that I was able to get a lease on the building several months prior to the kickoff. (If the chattering political class had been looking closely, that fact would have all but confirmed my intentions to run for mayor.) There was a small office and an outdoor parking lot that had been a used car deal-

Announcing bid to become mayor of San Antonio, with Jonah, December 2016. Photo by Scott Ball, *San Antonio Report*.

ership. It was the perfect place for events and volunteer efforts like phone banking and block walking launches, and it was right on the route for the two main Fiesta parades, Battle of Flowers and Fiesta Flambeau. Hundreds of people could fit there for an outdoor event.

I remember talking to María Antonietta Berriozábal, who for ten years served District 1, which encompasses central San Antonio, including downtown. After I had taken tough but correct stances on neighborhood and environmental issues during my council tenure, she became a key supporter and adviser, particularly on housing. María found herself in a similar position as me during her time on council, and she made the same decision to eventually run for mayor. In 1991 she barely lost in a runoff to Nelson Wolff in the mayoral race. During my many discussions with her in preparing to run, she shared her research and advocacy on water and housing. She gave me copious notes and research papers and told me that she had gotten the council (and then-mayor Henry Cisneros) to agree that the city needed a comprehensive housing plan to address the community's diverse needs. But it was never done. I promised her that if I was elected, I would get it done.

María also told me she had four hundred people at her mayoral campaign kickoff and that I should try to get that many people at mine if I wanted the city to take me seriously. That seemed impossible to me, so I was thrilled (and a little surprised) when, on that cold morning in December, I walked out to a crowd of more than five hundred. The lot was buzzing with a cross section of the community—young and old, businesspeople and neighborhood activists, liberals, conservatives, and just about everyone in between. It was like the diverse District 8 coalition that had propelled me onto the council, just so much larger.

The event began with Bonnie, Lionel, and Jorge warming up the audience. As the crowd swelled right at ten o'clock, Erika introduced me, and I started my speech with the words, "I'm Ron Nirenberg, and I'm running for mayor of San Antonio." Just as planned, Will Long, a friend and devoted campaign foot soldier, went onto the roof and unveiled a huge sign on the top of the building that read "Ron for Mayor." I finally put an end to all of the speculation, laying out a vision we called "The City You Deserve," a prosperous, equitable, and sustainable city where every family and business can thrive. After my short speech, Lionel introduced two campaign videos and urged the crowd to help us raise the funds necessary to put them on TV. In those spots, I pitched for a San Antonio "that listens to you, that treats you with respect, that spends your tax dollars responsibly and openly. You deserve a city whose leaders are ethical and accountable and a mayor who has a vision for a bright and successful future."

We also streamed the kickoff on Facebook Live, which hadn't really been used in local San Antonio campaigns before, and later learned that almost two hundred thousand people viewed it before the day ended. With that, we started using Facebook Live at most of our events. It was free to use and, combined with our growing grassroots support, we figured it would help us level the playing field against a much better funded incumbent. A friend and former war correspondent–turned–news anchor, Jeff Goldblatt, who had just left the local CBS affiliate, handled our social media efforts. Each week we hosted question-and-answer sessions with the community on Facebook Live, routinely drawing thousands of viewers.

The kickoff went well, and my announcement generated a lot of buzz around town. But it was right before winter break, and as soon as the crowd disbursed we were left in the quiet, empty office wondering how we could possibly sustain the momentum for another five months.

But Kelton had a good plan, and we worked methodically, starting with building the volunteer base and walking the neighborhoods, just as we had for city council, except citywide now. I walked every single day, and so did our ever-growing (and diversifying) team of volunteers. With my field director, Juany Torres, and backed by the data analysis of consultants Kelton and Bert Santibañez, we pounded the streets, visiting neighborhoods all across the city, and listening to residents' stories—their challenges, their fears, their hopes for their families and their city. It was such a wonderful experience to meet so many San Antonians from so many different backgrounds. We started up the "Meet Your Neighbors" program again, adding video interviews produced by Jeff. If you consider all of the block walking over the past twelve years, my team and I visited more than three hundred thousand individual homes in the city. In all of those conversations, I've seen a defining spirit of this community: resilience, compassion, and hometown pride emanate from every corner. Perhaps this is also what we mean by "puro San Antonio."

Lionel added his own marketing genius to the campaign, figuring out how a relatively low budget could make big impact. We already had social media going for us, but we needed signs, and to be effective we needed a lot of them. The typical roadside campaign sign is four by eight feet, and for a citywide election we needed hundreds, an expensive proposition. Lionel suggested that we spring for twenty special four-by-eights, in full color with a giant photo of me (a very expensive proposition) standing in what he called the "Superman pose." It had become a bit of a trademark look for me: white dress shirt, sleeves rolled up, with my tie loosened and my hands on my hips. That was basically my block walking uniform. Rather than setting the signs up horizontally, Lionel had them printed and installed vertically in random locations across town (even more expensive given the additional lumber and labor needed for this kind of installation). The effect was immediate. People noticed this big photo of me standing above all of the other political signs, promoting "Ron Nirenberg—For the City You Deserve." People were actually going around looking for them because they were so unusual. Many residents took photos of the signs and posted the images on Facebook and Twitter. We couldn't believe it. Lionel had done it again.

Along with the creative efforts and our block walking, the campaign organized about seventy-five house meetings all over town. Amir Samandi, a nonprofit leader and former foreign service officer I had met through KRTU, introduced me to Judy Hall. Judy was an old hand in the lonely world of Democratic campaigns in Texas and had most recently run "AlamObama," the local effort to support fledgling presidential candidate Barack Obama's campaign. She already had a network of progressive people who would host gatherings for me, on most occasions in their homes. We started with maybe a dozen or so people at these meetings, but toward the end of the campaign the attendees frequently exceeded a hundred people. The meetings were located all over the city, and at each one we recruited new volunteers, received small donations, and got commitments for new house meeting hosts. Each meeting was an opportunity for me to hone my stump speech, and I was getting pretty good at it, with a question-and-answer session

VOICES OF SAN ANTONIO

Lionel Sosa

Before I met Ron, I met his then fiancée, Erika Prosper. My wife, Kathy, and I owned a small ad agency, and Erika was about to graduate from the University of Pennsylvania. She called for an interview, but we had no openings. She kept calling. Once we met her, we had to hire her. She's that good.

Before long, we met Ron, a quiet and polite young man whose inner confidence escaped me at first. He was working at KRTU, the jazz radio station in town. He gave me one look and decided I needed a personal trainer. He volunteered to drive thirty miles to our home in Floresville to help me put a little muscle on. It didn't take.

A few weeks later Ron and Erika shared wedding vows in a beautiful downtown setting. It was clear then that this would be a strong marriage.

When Ron decided to run for city council, he asked if I would help with messaging. I agreed, and he got two for one. Kathy and I jumped right in. This would be a tough, close, exciting race. Ron began the campaign at a disadvantage: no name recognition and no political experience. Against all odds, he came from behind to beat an opponent with more money, better name awareness, and stronger political connections in a tight run-off that no one predicted.

A short three and a half years later, Ron decided to run for mayor. "It's too soon," I said, "You haven't finished your second term as councilman. The current mayor is doing okay. She's made no big mistakes, and she's very popular. Wait two more years. You'll be ready then." Most of his close advisers agreed.

But Ron had other ideas. Winning was the longest of long shots to everyone but him. In his mind, this was his moment. He didn't flinch. He didn't hesitate. "I'm doing it," he said. "Are you with me?" All we could say was "of course."

He got to work. First he outlined a detailed long-term plan for the city's future. Then he assembled a team of experienced and dedicated advisers. He picked up the phone to raise the hundreds of thousands of dollars needed to run a solid campaign. He made more calls to secure the big-name endorsements he needed. He put together a team of novice and veteran volunteers. He knocked on thousands of doors in every part of town to look voters in the eye and ask for the vote. He prepped for debates like a champ and used his "Superman" physique to project strength.

Erika and their eight-year-old son, Jonah, were by his side at every turn.

Ron wasn't supposed to beat Ivy Taylor. But he did. He *willed* himself into office.

And throughout his twelve years as a public servant and San Antonio's leader, he has remained the same man he's always been—smart, humble, caring, ethical, appreciative, consistent, devoted to his family and to his city.

Ron delivered on his promise as mayor to help build the city San Antonians deserve.

LIONEL SOSA founded Sosa, Bromley, Aguilar & Associates (now Bromley Communications), the largest Hispanic advertising agency in the United States, and served as the Hispanic media consultant for eight Republican presidential campaigns.

to follow. I felt energized by the interactions, and collectively we could feel the momentum building.

While I was getting more comfortable on the political stump, I was still a policy wonk. Using the input from my policy groups, I compiled policy papers, which we turned into a new version of the "Vision for District 8" booklet from my first campaign, this time titled "The City You Deserve," "La Ciudad Que Usted Merece" for Spanish-speaking households. We distributed thousands across the city. Jon Alonzo once again provided the photos, and Kazim Fahim put it all together.

The booklet was another effort—like four years earlier in my first campaign—to be transparent about who I was, why I was running, and what I planned to do if elected mayor. By now, Kelton had accepted this as my MO, despite the conventional political wisdom suggesting I should say as little as possible to give future policy positions as much flexibility as possible. The booklet also reminded voters about how I would make difficult decisions on their behalf (Is it fair and ethical? Is it fiscally responsible? Have I done my homework?). After outlining the main challenges I believed San Antonio was facing in the future—intense population growth, a rising cost of living (especially threatening vulnerable families), the loss of economic momentum over the past twenty years due to short-term thinking, and increasing threats to our natural resources and environment—the bulk of the thirty-two-page booklet detailed my platform.

First up was transportation reform to "get San Antonio moving." Growth and lack of adequate infrastructure investment were leading to increasingly congested—and more dangerous—roadways. My agenda centered on tackling what had become third rails in San Antonio politics over the past thirty years (no pun intended): building a modern multimodal transportation network and redeveloping the San Antonio International Airport. The latter, by the way, was starting to become the butt of local and national jokes. I argued that San Antonio leaders needed to muster the political will to put mass transit back on the ballot (where it had failed before) and to create a comprehensive transportation system that integrated all mobility options, from sidewalks to bicycles, cars, buses, and eventually, rail.

Next I described my plans for what city government could do to stimulate the local economy, starting with empowering the "workforce of tomorrow" through workforce development, partnering with the public school systems, and expanding access to high-speed internet. In addition, because so many San Antonio families find economic opportunity through small business and entrepreneurship, the plan called for more active engagement with that sector, particularly using the city's contracting power to provide opportunities to developing businesses. Finally, because I always considered a mayor's job to be "salesman-in-chief," we would aggressively recruit business investment and relocation in growth industries that leveraged San Antonio's core strengths and assets: cybersecurity, technology, renewable energy, manufacturing, and the biosciences.

I then laid out a plan for public safety that called for ensuring that our emergency response and prevention capacity matched the city's growth and complexity. In particular, I argued that our community could not afford for its leaders to play politics with public safety; properly supporting these critical functions and adding police, fire, and disaster response capabilities (which were desperately needed) meant we also needed to maintain fiscal discipline with all of our resources. My plan also called for completing what I had proposed as a council member two years before: a regional security operations center where all public agencies would collaborate on the cyber defense of public assets.

I summed up my agenda on improving the overall quality of life in San Antonio as "putting neighborhoods and families first." Walking as much as I did all over the city, I felt I had a pretty good handle on the struggles many San Antonians faced but few talked about openly. I argued that if we were truly to be a great city it was time to end "San Antonio's losing streak on domestic violence, child abuse and neglect, births without prenatal care, substance abuse, homelessness, and income disparity." This is also where I planted the flag that María Antonietta Berriozábal and I had talked about: if I became mayor, we would finally make equitable investments in our community and deliver the long-sought goal of a comprehensive housing policy. That meant working with businesses and community leaders to mobilize public and private sector resources to lift the city's most impoverished neighborhoods while streamlining development codes and policies to lower the cost of doing business. Quality of life in San Antonio also meant that as the city grew, we should consciously "celebrate our culture and heritage." Too many cities lose their identities when growth and investment accelerate. I knew San Antonio was poised to become a great American city, but I didn't want us to lose our soul in the process.

Finally I outlined my plan for bolstering ethics and accountability at city hall, which had hit another low point in recent years after multiple council members—including Mayor Taylor—were found to be violating conflict-of-interest standards related to doing business with the city as an elected official. In each case a council majority waived the provision to let their colleague off the hook. I wanted to simplify yet strengthen the ethics code and empower an independent ethics review board that wasn't beholden to the officials they were trying to police. (The ethics board and its rules and recommendations are all appointed and overseen by the city council itself—how dumb is that?) The plan called for various efforts to increase accessibility and participation in city government too.

The last page of "The City You Deserve" was a photo of Erika looking up at a tiny five-year-old Jonah clinging to me after one of my state of District 8 community town halls, with a quote from the video Lionel showed at our campaign kickoff: "I want our children to know that when we had choices to make, we acted boldly to build San Antonio into the great American city."

We handed out the booklet everywhere—events, block walks, through mail and email. The publication was a big hit at the house meetings. It showed that, despite the higher stakes and bigger platform, I was the same policy-focused, average neighbor who had taken the pundits by surprise a few years earlier. It showed that I was seriously listening to our community and I had specific ideas and plans for tackling the city's challenges. It may be one of the reasons Mayor Taylor's team made a significant strategic error in their campaign.

In a very short election season (essentially five months from January to May), and with the advantage of incumbency (more money, establishment support, and the platform of mayor to dominate media attention), Kelton said that Mayor Taylor should be favored to win if all she did was coast to the election. But she didn't. Our team had been working methodically for months, building our grassroots support, fundraising, developing a real policy agenda. Perhaps she couldn't coast. But it was a mistake for her to agree to debate me early—and often. The *Rivard Report* hosted a mayoral town hall for us in January, before the filing deadline had even closed, and I notched an early and convincing win. The crowd was made up of very engaged young professionals, political insiders, and neighborhood leaders, and they were all put on notice: it's going to be a real race. The debates, hosted by media outlets, neighborhoods, business associations, and more, continued all the way through early voting and then again in the runoff. While Taylor's team may have wished they could stop debating me after agreeing to the first event, she couldn't stop participating in the debates or it would risk looking like surrender. We participated in nearly fifty debates in all, with most ending the same as the first.

It was at one of those forums that Taylor made another error in judgment. This time it went viral. *San Antonio Express-News* col-

Challenging Ivy Taylor at a mayoral candidate debate at the Tobin Center, March 2, 2017. Photo by Tom Reel, *San Antonio Express-News*.

umnist Gilbert Garcia moderated a forum hosted by the Nonprofit Council of San Antonio, which wanted to probe our plans for dealing with issues related to poverty, community health, and domestic violence. In one of the questions Garcia asked us to identify the root cause of systemic poverty. It should have been a slam dunk for Taylor, who had worked at a nonprofit housing provider before spending five years on city council representing the East Side, a historically redlined area of San Antonio that now had a high rate of families living in poverty. Instead, perhaps trying to sound more memorable than right, she said plainly that poverty is a result of "broken people...not being in relationship with their creator... and not being productive members of society." Yikes. Taylor had frequently cited her faith in governing (it was one of the reasons she gave for voting against the nondiscrimination ordinance that extended protections for sexual orientation and gender identity), so I didn't think much of it. But for the audience—especially online—she was clearly blaming poverty on being godless. Within forty-eight hours the story was everywhere—from social media to the *Washington Post* to *Time.* Taylor tried to add more context in subsequent interviews, but the damage was done.

For what it's worth, my answer was as esoteric and unmemorable as hers was wrong. I described how we were losing a commitment to a social contract—I called it the public common—and said that families have different challenges for a variety of reasons, including a lack of opportunity, and that we have not made an effort to rectify those challenges through equitable investments. Subconsciously I was distilling all of the stories I had gleaned from walking from house to house over the past five years. I was thinking about how the first step to breaking cycles of poverty was to get people to know their neighbors in order to understand the challenges those who are struggling face. That was necessary before expecting people to care enough to want to help. I was determined to win the election so I could start that work.

Our team felt good going into the general election. Fiesta—the eleven-day citywide party that celebrates San Antonio's diverse cultural heritage and generates money for nonprofits—took place during early voting, and it provided plenty of proof that we had built serious grassroots momentum. My campaign office was along the main parade routes, and I walked up and down the street handing out stickers and our "City You Deserve" Fiesta medals. The energy was palpable. On election day, May 6, 2017, Kelton was cautiously optimistic. I went to his office to wait for the early returns, as was our tradition, and when I got there he was arguing with a couple of his pundit friends who said that I wasn't going to make the runoff. They said I ran a good campaign but Mayor Taylor was either winning outright or going to a runoff with Manuel Medina. Medina was an entrepreneur with a suspect history of political and business dealings in Mexico. He had recently wrested control of the Bexar County Democratic Party by becoming a self-styled populist chairman—like a left-wing, local

Donald Trump—and getting many of his loyalists to take over as precinct chairs. His campaign consisted of attacking city government (especially Taylor and me) and the media. At one point his team picketed at the *San Antonio Express-News* after they ran an article examining his political history in Mexico.

But all the bluster and bashing resulted in his receiving 15 percent of the vote. I melted into Erika's arms as the results came in, showing that I was easily headed to a runoff with Taylor. We had both shocked all of the observers—me with a surprisingly strong 37 percent, and Taylor with a lower-than-expected 42 percent. A crowd even larger than the kickoff greeted us at the campaign headquarters, and the mood was pure elation. Although we had to start back up again and campaign for another month before the runoff election, that night almost felt like a total victory because the momentum was clearly with our campaign. The writing was on the wall, and from then on there was an air of inevitability. The political establishment—as fickle as it is—immediately realized that I could, and probably would, be the next mayor, and as a result, started sending donations and endorsements. Medina, now out of the race, announced that he was supporting me.

As nice as all that was, I was reminded of what my dad meant about the difference between statesmanship and politics. Taylor's team went on full attack mode. Her communications team, which included political consultant Colin Strother and former journalist Greg Jefferson (who would later become the *Express-News* metro editor), turned up the negative messaging, launching the website LiberalRon.com and calling me out as inconsistent and too much of a lefty for San Antonio. Kelton reminded me that, just like with Briones's pink flier during my first campaign, it was just a sign that the end was near for our opponent.

Judy Hall, who in addition to her political chops was a psychologist by training, became my guru in those difficult days, helping keep my head in the game. She organized another twenty-five house meetings during the runoff (sometimes three a day), and I

Being sworn in as mayor of San Antonio inside the city council chambers alongside Jonah, June 21, 2017. Photo by Jonathan Alonzo.

kept walking the neighborhoods alongside our now massive team of volunteers. I reminded them (and myself) that as hard as they were working, no one would outwork me.

The month of May flew by. When we put a new version of a commercial up on the local networks, it felt like we were stretching a lead. On June 10 the crowd at our headquarters grew even larger. The tallies came in and I won the runoff election 55 to 45 percent. I hadn't written a victory speech (I figured that would be bad luck), so I took an index card and scribbled some notes. I went up on stage and thanked Mayor Taylor for her years of dedicated service, I thanked my family and my team, and I reminded people why we were working so hard and what we meant by "The City You Deserve." By the way, an artist and supporter—George Cisneros, brother of former mayor and HUD secretary Henry Cisneros—found that index card on the ground the night of my election. A few years later he brought it to me, framed. It stayed on the bookshelf in my office for the next five years as a humble reminder of where it all began.

I gave Erika a big kiss (which ended up on the front page the next morning), and an exuberant eight-year-old Jonah joined us onstage and leapt into the air. The crowd stayed late into the night, and passersby on foot, in cars, and on bicycles stopped to join us. A little later that month San Antonio would officially begin a new era with a new mayor. There was an enormous and collective sense of relief, satisfaction, and anticipation of the road ahead. In the community that rallies together, we were ready to start a new chapter.

There was also an enormous sense of gratitude to our family members, friends, supporters, and volunteers, all of whom were so critically important to the cause. What I wasn't prepared for, however, was the fact that this sense was also shared by the community. It felt like our family got larger, like it wasn't just Erika, Jonah, and me anymore. It felt like it was Erika, Jonah, San Antonio, and me. And that feeling was being reciprocated. I have tried to describe it to others; being mayor makes you feel as if your community, the people you are responsible for, are part of your own flesh and blood. You experience all of the joy, pain, anger, and triumph that they do.

In something that has become a tradition, the day after the election my entire family descended upon San Antonio and we gathered together to have a meal. That year it was barbecue. We ate at King's Hwy Brew & Q, off of North Flores Street. In between eating tons of barbecue, chatting, laughing, and reminiscing

VOICES OF SAN ANTONIO

Gordon Hartman

I had the opportunity to get to know Ron during his first mayoral campaign. I knew of him as councilman from District 8 but had not chatted with him until he ran for mayor. He was in a battle to unseat Ivy Taylor after she decided not to abide by her pledge not to run for election as mayor if she was appointed by the city council. This decision caused me to pause my support for the incumbent mayor, and I welcomed the opportunity to better understand Ron and his thoughts about San Antonio's future. Initially I had some reservations, but I felt that he would quickly grow into the job. He did.

Ron and I did not always agree, but he was always willing to listen and engage in productive dialogue to learn all sides of an issue. Working closely with him, I watched a man who had the focus and determination to review all of the options before he made a decision. He often knew his decisions would not be popular, but he was always true to his belief in what it would take to make San Antonio a better place for all.

Ron is shy, does not joke around much, and does not enjoy the limelight. I think that is what I like about him the most. He is in it to make his community a better place and not to advance himself. That is the type of leader we all want. San Antonio has been blessed to have a leader with those qualities for eight years, and because of that the city still has the charm of a small city even as it grows. We are a city on the rise, but we have not forgotten who we are or where we came from. Kind of like my friend Ron.

San Antonio native GORDON HARTMAN, a former homebuilder and land developer, sold his companies in 2005 and founded the Gordon Hartman Family Foundation and Morgan's Wonderland, the world's first theme park for people with special needs.

about the campaign, people stopped in to tell us how excited they were about what was next for San Antonio. There was a palpable optimism in the air that had been missing for a while. At the end, I stood to thank everyone. Erika noted that I was wearing my white-collared uniform and that after I ate all of that barbecue there was not one stain. She said I was off to a good start.

But I knew I wouldn't be able to keep my shirt clean for long.

BIG CITY, LONG VIEW

On June 21, 2017, I stood at the podium of San Antonio's municipal chamber, a stately three-story-high room that holds about five hundred people and once served as the lobby of the Frost National Bank headquarters. Alongside Jonah, who had just turned nine and was holding my left hand, I took the oath of office. I felt the gravity of that moment, made all the more urgent by the fact that Jonah was now pushing four feet tall, and the stakes of our work seemed to grow by the day as Donald Trump wasted no time in stoking anxiety and divisions in his first six months as president. Jon Alonzo took a photo of that swearing-in from behind us, and a few years later Erika gave me a painting of it by Cristina Sosa, Lionel's daughter, for my birthday. It has hung in my office ever since, one of my most treasured possessions. Since our faces are not visible (I'm facing forward and Jonah is looking up at me), the portrait is a constant reminder of why I chose public service: always looking forward, accountable to future generations for leaving the world a better place.

Usually when I tell people that San Antonio is the seventh largest city in the United States—or more accurately, the seventh most populous city—locals roll their eyes because throughout the modern area, we haven't seemed to operate like other big cities, and visitors are shocked. It's trite, but visitors and residents still say the city feels like a small town. As of 2020 the municipality's

1.5 million people are spread out over nearly five hundred square miles, with an additional million-plus residents in the metropolitan area. Annually one of the country's top three fastest growing areas (and often number one), we have plenty of room to grow. The downtown area is unique, with the legendary Alamo (which, in addition to the four other Spanish colonial missions in San Antonio, compose the only UNESCO World Heritage site in Texas) surrounded by a modern city and landmarks like the River Walk and the Tower of the Americas. Historic neighborhoods, a medical center, military bases, live/work/play economic development hubs, retail districts, and more form approximately thirteen developed and emerging "nodes" stretching out from the city center that are distinct centers of life. One of my priorities has been to connect them all with reliable mass transportation, something San Antonio has never had. After a decade of ideating, planning, and political haranguing, I'm proud that we are finally building mass transit.

The small town atmosphere people talk about, however, is less about the built environment than it is about the people. Spend a day here and you'll know that San Antonians have a strong sense of community. Hundreds of years of Indigenous community life confronted by colonial settlement, migration from every corner of the world, conflict, and political upheaval (San Antonio voted to stay in the Union, by the way, during the Civil War) will test the limits of social cohesion. In the case of the people of San Antonio, the result has been a common identity that bridges those cultural differences and has strengthened community bonds. There is plenty of conflict and strife, of course, and a good amount of it has been based on marginalized people's struggle to get a seat at the table. Yet in San Antonio, sooner or later, they eventually do.

And what you'll find notable here is a baseline level of respect and courtesy afforded to all people, and it's a lot deeper than what one might call Southern hospitality. It's an implicit recognition that if you're standing in San Antonio, you're standing on common ground, sharing common interests, celebrating shared heritage, history, and purpose. Like any big city (or small town), we have our challenges, but to put it simply we tend to get along. People from outside of San Antonio see and feel that, a vibe that is in stark contrast to the anonymity of life in some other big cities.

San Antonio was named on June 13, 1691, when Franciscan priest Damián Massanet, traveling with a small expedition led by Spanish Texas's first governor, Domingo Terán de los Ríos, arrived at a Payaya Indian settlement along the Yanaguana River. That day happened to be the feast day of Saint Anthony of Padua, or in Spanish, San Antonio de Padua, so Massanet held a mass and christened both the site and the river "San Antonio" in Saint Anthony's honor before continuing on to East Texas.

It took another twenty-seven years and a second Spanish expedition to the area before friars, soldiers, and Indigenous Payaya and Pastia peoples began work on a mission and presidio in 1718. The Mission de San Antonio de Valero was named after both Saint Anthony and the viceroy of New Spain, the Marqués de Valero, although it came to be known colloquially as the Alamo, perhaps due to a grove of nearby cottonwoods (*álamo* in Spanish). About a mile away, on the banks of the San Antonio River, Presidio San Antonio de Béxar was constructed as a fort to administer and protect the Spanish mission, along with an office and residence for the presidio captain, later used as the Spanish governor's palace. Dozens of soldiers and their families were stationed at the military complex, or Plaza de Armas (which became home to city hall in 1889).

To secure Spain's hold on the region against French ambitions, King Philip V authorized a group of families from the Canary Islands to settle near the mission. The year-long trip over land and sea was arduous, but in March 1731, sixteen families arrived at the presidio. By July, they had laid out a villa to the west of the presidio, which became San Fernando de Béxar, the first civil settlement in Texas. Today, some San Antonio families trace their

Presenting King Felipe VI and Queen Letizia of Spain with the keys to the historic arts village (and San Antonio's oldest neighborhood) La Villita at the Spanish Governor's Palace, San Antonio, June 17, 2018. Photo by Suzanne Cordeiro, AFP.

lineage back to those first Canary Islanders, and we celebrate that history with three Sister City relationships between San Antonio and the Canary Islands. During my final year as mayor in 2025, I established the most recent relationship with Lanzarote, the homeland of most of the original settlers. From its earliest establishment, San Antonio was the confluence of international cultures and commerce, a military community, and a community of faith. These three pillars of society continue to define it today.

San Antonio was part of the Spanish Empire and remained that way until 1821, when it became part of the Republic of Mexico from 1821 to 1836, following Spain's granting of independence to Mexico in 1821. The republic's Constitution of 1824 provided that each state in the republic should create its own constitution. The state of Coahuila (a province today in northern Mexico that borders Texas) and the former Spanish province of Tejas were combined as the state of Coahuila y Tejas. One of the main problems for the Mexican government in inheriting Texas was that it was sparsely populated, untamed land, so the government allowed the Tejanos—Mexicans native to Texas—to invite Anglo-Americans to settle there. Importantly, Stephen F. Austin, considered by many to be the "father of Texas," subsequently brought three hundred families to settle there. Relations between those new settlers—known as Texians—and the Mexican government grew tense over the years, especially when Mexico abolished slavery and the Texians wanted it to continue. In 1835, when Mexican president Gen. Antonio López de Santa Anna abolished the 1824 constitution, effectively ending the Mexican provinces' autonomy, violence broke out in a number of them, including Texas. Texians soon forced out Mexican soldiers from San Antonio and surrounding areas, including in the Battle of Béxar, when San Antonio was captured from the Mexican army commanded by Gen. Martín Perfecto de Cós, Santa Anna's brother-in-law.

Santa Anna then decided to march into Texas with a large force to put down the Texian revolt, first and foremost by retaking San Antonio. As is well known, this led to the Battle of the Alamo, which took place over thirteen days ending on March 6, 1836, when a grossly outnumbered Texian force holding up in the Alamo, composed of Anglos and Tejanos, was eventually defeated, with nearly all of the almost two hundred defenders being killed. This battle became a rallying cry for remaining Texians: "Remember the Alamo." Soon thereafter Texian troops under the command of Sam Houston surprised Santa Anna's troops, defeating them in the brief Battle of San Jacinto, which also resulted in the capture of the Mexican leader and surrender of the Mexican armies. With that decisive victory, Texas became an independent republic later that year. This independent country of Texas lasted until 1845, when it was incorporated into the United States, leading to the 1845–48 Mexican-American War. Winning that war helped to enlarge the United States again at Mexico's expense. Finally, despite some communities like San Antonio opposing separation from the Union, a flag of the Confederacy flew over San Antonio during the Civil War (1861–65), after which the Stars and Stripes have remained—the longest any nation has held this region and this city.

While San Antonio was the landscape for the pivotal conflicts over Texas rule and identity, beginning in the 1830s and lasting through the remainder of the nineteenth century, migrants arrived from all over the world. A large number came from Germany (or what would become Germany later in the century), seeking sanctuary from political and religious oppression. That German influence in the city's metropolitan area is unmistakable today. Beyond their names, surrounding towns like Fredericksburg, Gruene, Boerne, and New Braunfels have the best Octoberfests and Wurstfests. Wurzbach Road, Huebner Road, Jones Maltsberger Road, and many other San Antonio streets remind drivers of our heritage. German migrants influenced cuisine, culture, and language, with something called Texas German, a dialect of German still spoken among some of those original settlers' descendants. In fact, for much of the 1800s this region of the state had no single predominant language; English, Spanish, and German were spoken in equal parts.

The city continued to grow at a steady rate, experiencing the progress and adversity that other American cities did, from the World Wars and Great Depression in the early to mid-twentieth century to the Vietnam War and the civil rights movement of the 1960s.

We have had our ups and downs, but we have persevered. Today we are widely known as a visitor destination, with more than forty million people a year from all over the world coming to enjoy the people, history, culture, and sites—from the Alamo and the River Walk to our eleven-day citywide Fiesta celebration, theme parks, the San Antonio Spurs, Final Fours, the San Antonio Stock Show and Rodeo, and more. The list of attractions is endless. Many people from Mexico come here to shop, and others visit San Antonio en route to shopping in Mexico (the city is less than two hours from Laredo, the country's busiest land port). Visitors drive in, and increasingly they fly. As a side note, for nearly forty years planners and politicians have wrung their hands trying to figure out how to expand or relocate the diminutive San Antonio International Airport. I sent them all home when I became mayor and appointed a group to come up with a plan to build the airport of the future where it sits today (in the heart of the city, ten minutes from downtown; more on this later).

We also proudly carry the title of Military City, USA. In fact, in 2017 the phrase became a trademark of the city, used on logos and promotional material. It's not a slogan, though; it's our heritage, an ethos, and a call to action. From the Plaza de Armas and the barracks at the Alamo to Fort Sam Houston, the U.S. Army outpost after the Civil War, to the building (and consolidation) of air force bases in the twentieth and twenty-first centuries, the military presence in the city has grown and become further embedded in the culture. Despite the closure of Kelly and Brooks Air Force Bases in the 1990s, San Antonio still has the largest military presence in the homeland of any place outside of the Washington capital region, where the Pentagon is located. Joint Base San Antonio is the largest joint operation in the U.S. Defense Department, comprised of Lackland Air Force Base, Randolph Air Force Base, Fort Sam Houston (containing Brooke Army Medical Center, the only Level 1 trauma and burn center in the Defense Department), and Camp Bullis (the only field-training base located in a major urban area). Besides being at the core of our community's cultural heritage and forming the foundation of national security, the military, along with tourism, was the bulk of San Antonio's economy.

With more than 80,000 active-duty personnel in the region, along with 322,000 veterans, the military creates an impact of $55 billion annually across the state. It is intertwined with the burgeoning

VOICES OF SAN ANTONIO

Ret. Gen. Edward A. Rice Jr.

After I served in the U.S. Air Force for thirty-five years, my wife and I decided to make San Antonio our home. While there were many reasons for this decision, a major one was the strong sense of community we had felt when we were previously stationed there. As I thought about how I would spend my time in retirement, I set a priority on getting meaningfully engaged in the local community.

Shortly after he was elected to his first term as mayor of San Antonio, Ron Nirenberg called to ask if I would serve on the Airport System Development Committee. As he explained it, the committee's purpose was to help determine the city's future aviation given its rapid population growth projections. Although I had never met the mayor, I quickly accepted his invitation because I felt strongly that our growing city needed to stay ahead of the infrastructure curve. Moreover, the fact that Mayor Nirenberg was forming this committee so shortly after his election was a strong indication that he was a forward-looking leader who was ready to take big swings at big challenges.

Everything I have experienced since that first interaction with Ron has reinforced my first impression that our city made a wise choice in selecting the right leader at the right time to help guide us into the future.

For example, when San Antonio, along with the rest of Texas, experienced a record-breaking winter storm in early February 2021, leaving millions of people across the state and hundreds of thousands in San Antonio without power for several days in freezing temperatures, Mayor Nirenberg provided exemplary leadership in organizing

health care, cybersecurity, and manufacturing industries. But over the past three decades, since the closure of Kelly and Brooks, each of those sectors has emerged and grown into a powerhouse, as companies like Toyota, Boeing, Navistar, and Standard Aero have the city's resources to restore essential services and give emergency assistance to those in need. Additionally, after the storm he had the wisdom and courage to establish a Community Emergency Preparedness Committee to provide transparency in assessing the events before, during, and after the storm and to determine how the city could better prepare for its next emergency. I served on this committee and was impressed with Mayor Nirenberg's willingness to take a critical look at what he and his staff could have done better. I admire leaders who take accountability for the areas they are responsible for, even when the outcome is not always favorable. Ron Nirenberg has demonstrated time and again that he is such a leader.

Whether it was leading the adoption of an equity framework for the city's budget to more effectively address socioeconomic disparities, undertaking a vast update of our transportation infrastructure, or championing an ambitious workforce development initiative, Ron Nirenberg put San Antonio in a position to create greater economic opportunity while compassionately addressing the needs of *all* of our community members.

During my time in the military I had the privilege of serving with a number of outstanding leaders. At the top of this list are those individuals who provided the vision and force to create change that successfully drove the institution into the future. San Antonio has been fortunate to have had a leader in Ron Nirenberg whose vision and drive created the conditions that will result in a brighter future for us all.

RET. GEN. EDWARD A. RICE JR. was commander of the Air Education and Training Command at Joint Base San Antonio–Randolph, where he oversaw U.S. Air Force recruiting, training, and education.

established major operations, while others like USAA, the Southwest Research Institute, and Texas BioMedical Research Institute have expanded. Today San Antonio's population and location have made it a formidable player in the life sciences and cybersecurity

Walking with (*from left*) Imam Omar Shakir, Live Oak mayor Mary Dennis, Jonah, and Erika, along with some three hundred participants, during the fiftieth annual Martin Luther King Jr. march, January 15, 2018. Photo by Jonathan Alonzo.

industries and a key link in the trade and advanced manufacturing corridor between North, Central, and South America.

This was the amazing city—with all its heritage and potential—that I was ready to lead in 2017. Coming out of a bruising election for mayor, I was excited to get to work and laser focused on restoring the vision and momentum I felt the city was losing under the Taylor administration. There was so much potential, and the city was growing so fast, I told voters. If the arc of our universe was indeed long, it was up to us to do some bending—to make the policy changes and investments necessary to reverse festering socioeconomic inequities, protect our natural resources, and stimulate the economy. We needed to start acting like the seventh largest city in the country.

What I quickly found out, however, is that this is easier said than done. While my election was viewed as nothing short of a mandate, since I had beaten the incumbent decisively (the first time that had happened in San Antonio in twenty years), the work of governing was waiting on the other side of a brief postelection honeymoon. That meant harnessing a calcified city bureaucracy resistant to change and confronting the increasing political polarization (even in local government) that had gone into hyperdrive with the rise of Trump in 2016.

When you enter a new job, you have certain expectations for what it will be like. I certainly had expectations for what I wanted to do as mayor and the types of opportunities and challenges that lay before me. With two terms on the council under my belt, I also had enough experience to know you can fight city hall, even as mayor. But there's really no playbook—a new mayor just has to expect the unexpected and learn when and how to use the authority of the office to get things done and when and how to use the soft power of being "Mr. Mayor."

A new mayor inherits ongoing programs put in place by previous administrations—and much unfinished business that, in some cases, needs to be cleared out expeditiously before the real work of change can begin. In my first term this was the ongoing contract dispute between the city and the firefighters' union that had gotten extremely ugly, as well as a bumbling effort to celebrate the city's tricentennial in just a few months. I quickly learned how to control the inevitable chaos and, when necessary, to create a little bit of it.

This was certainly the case in my first council meeting as mayor. I wanted to send a message—to the council, to bureaucrats, and to the public—about the values from which I would lead my administration. I wanted to make sure people knew we weren't going to waste any time. I am certain some council members did not take me as seriously as they perhaps should have, instead seeing me as some sort of interloper who undeservedly got lucky in the election. There were also six brand-new council members, one of whom—Greg Brockhouse—had become a self-styled populist, taking pages straight out of Trump's playbook on how to generate outrage and distrust of government.

The best public policy comes when the community's diverse viewpoints are considered equitably, so dissent is good and helpful. If ideas are not tested, checked, and refined in genuine deliberation, the public loses. But the kind of grievance and outrage that populism (and Brockhouse) peddled only gave the illusion of debate. It is untethered to the facts, distorts any shared reality, and plays to the basest emotions of fear, anger, and hatred in order to assign blame. By 2017 this kind of polity was on the rise globally, and Trump was its standard-bearer. Here in San Antonio, it was Brockhouse.

One of the challenges of a two-year election cycle, established since the first edition of the city charter, is that council members, whom a mayor has to work with to advance the interests of the city, often have the office of the mayor in their sights. Phil Hardberger counseled me that "it is true for all mayors. Everyone on the dais thinks they can do your job better than you." I've talked to a lot of mayors over the years, and it seems to be true in every city.

I wanted to make sure we started on the right foot, clearly and decisively. On June 22, 2017, at our first council meeting, I placed two items on the agenda that I intended to set the foundation for the next eight years. The first was a resolution adopting a Charter for Compassion and authorizing registration in the International Campaign for Compassionate Cities. It passed unanimously without much discussion.

The original Charter for Compassion is a document written in 2009 that recognizes a universal human value of compassion in all cultures and belief systems. It calls for centering our actions, especially as public servants, in reciprocity: treat others the way we wish to be treated and don't treat others the way we wouldn't. In other words, the Golden Rule. Often used interchangeably with "empathy," compassion is different; not just passive understanding, compassion is empathy in action. It is treating people with basic fairness and with dignity and respect. In public policy terms, it means working collectively to solve the most urgent challenges people in the community face. When we are at our best, people in a community view solving those challenges—whether it's an issue as mundane as street improvements or as serious as childhood poverty—in the best interest of each of us as both individuals and members of a community.

The whole world would come to see this clearly during the COVID-19 pandemic, when we were all reminded that "we are all in this together." That kind of mindset has serious implications for public policy—locally and globally—from environmental protection to economic opportunity to social justice, and I had immediately gravitated to these concepts when I first learned about the charter several years before. It's really about centering the work of government in people, in improving lives. For instance, what good is economic development or improving infrastructure unless the community's residents are better off as a result? Thanks to the council's vote, San Antonio's Charter for Compassion became the first official document I signed as mayor, underscoring my deep belief that compassion is the root of all public policy.

The second item I placed on the agenda declared that San Antonio would adhere to the goals of the Paris Agreement by implementing a plan to reduce carbon emissions and bolster our local resiliency in the face of a changing climate. After taking office, President Trump kept his foolish campaign promise to withdraw from the accord, which had been signed in Paris in 2015 by 195 countries, including the United States under President Barack Obama. The resolution on day one of my administration was designed to make it clear that San Antonio recognized the local and global impacts of climate change—which fall hardest on the most vulnerable residents—along with the responsibility we share to do something about it, for the sake of ourselves and future generations. There was considerable bluster and handwringing by the two conservative members of council (Brockhouse claimed it wasn't fair to put something like this on the first agenda, and Clayton Perry denied that we had any agency in climate change, if it existed at all), but the vote was unanimous in support, minus an abstention by Perry.

I would come to learn that bluster and handwringing are the language of the luddite, and it should not be needlessly entertained. Their goal is delay, and then death, of progress, so you have to push through it. And we did. With that, two foundational values for my tenure—compassion and resiliency—were set in place.

After the excitement of inaugural parties, swearing in, and jitters of the first official proceedings of a new administration, the council is immediately plunged into the process of assembling the annual city budget. Texas municipal governments are bound by state law to pass a balanced budget each year, which in San Antonio goes into effect on October 1. The learning curve for new council members is steep and the stakes are high, since the budget is where one's priorities (and campaign promises) can be realized. For me, the fiscal year 2018 budget would be my fifth time experiencing this, and I was ready to start building on the foundation we had just set.

With city manager Sheryl Sculley's support, we scheduled a pre-budget work session for city council to be briefed by Christine Drennon, an urban studies professor at Trinity University who had become a leading researcher in historic socioeconomic trends in San Antonio. I had worked with Drennon's class during my first campaign in 2013 and again in 2016 to examine how infrastructure and basic services correlate with socioeconomic status in our city. The students produced a report, "The Demographics of Public Funding in San Antonio," that found significant differences in the quality of infrastructure in the city. Essentially, the regrettable legacy of redlining in San Antonio had only gotten worse. Not only was basic infrastructure on the West, East, and South Sides falling farther behind; that trend was also almost perfectly correlated with higher poverty, lower income and educational attainment, and poorer public health outcomes. To me, it was important that we have a public conversation about this before we started talking about budget allocations; if we were to live up to our stated values of compassion and resiliency, we had to start rectifying the inequity in basic services. It's simple fairness: every member of our community deserves to be treated with respect, so every member should expect quality service. At its most basic level that includes decent streets and sidewalks in one's neighborhood, regardless of which side of town one lives on.

In that conviction I found a kindred spirit in Shirley Gonzales, the third-term council member who represented the most impoverished areas of the city's West Side. Shirley had just completed her own analysis of street conditions and showed that the city's most dilapidated streets were indeed in her district. I remember leaning over to South Side council member Rey Saldaña during the presentation and saying, "Today, everything in our city has changed." He agreed.

For the first time in our city's history, we had an official, public discussion about how the city budget has contributed to the socioeconomic inequities felt by San Antonio families. We were just talking about infrastructure investment at that point, but we all knew it was about so much more. Usually, when we allocate resources, each of the ten council districts expects a roughly proportionate "equal share" (basically, 10 percent of the budget goes to each area). But if some parts of town, as a result of past actions—most notably redlining and segregation—are way behind the starting line (and fall further behind every year because they are also the ones where environmental, economic, and social conditions are worsening), those neighborhoods will never catch up.

In fact, when we continue with business as usual, it's not just streets that suffer; cycles of generational poverty continue and community health conditions decline. The entire city suffers, as had been the case in San Antonio for too long. It was already a well-known fact that life expectancy was more than a decade longer for children born on the city's North Side than in the East, West, and South Sides. Compassion—and a desire to improve the city as a whole—required us not only to understand that but also to act on it to improve the outcomes for people who always get left behind. It was in everyone's best interest that we do.

In the wake of that discussion, I called for an "equity lens" to be applied to our budget, starting with infrastructure. We became one of the first major cities in the country to do this. Since then, every budget during my tenure used and refined the equity framework, which is now applied across nearly every city department. Initially introduced as a method for allocating resources for streets and sidewalks, today the principles apply to social services like public health. In fact, as we would later learn during the COVID-19 pandemic, health outcomes and vulnerabilities are the places where inequities are most easily seen and where change can be most impactful over the long term. I cautioned the council and the community then, and I do now, that these inequities were not created overnight; neither would they be rectified in a single budget (or a single mayor's tenure).

While the term "equity" has become politicized by some and abused by others, I'm proud that during my time as mayor, we did not succumb to that kind of irrationality. Equity is basic fairness—giving people an equal shot and not necessarily an equal outcome—and that's what compassion calls for. In budget terms, it's putting our resources where they are needed the most.

In all of this, I worked closely with San Antonio's city manager, Sheryl Sculley, and with her successor, Erik Walsh. Sculley, who had been city manager since 2005, was an outsider recruited to the position with the help of a generous contract by then mayor Phil Hardberger soon after he came to office. By the time I reached the mayor's office, Sculley had more than a decade of experience as city manager, after serving as assistant city manager in Phoenix for fifteen years and city manager of Kalamazoo, Michigan, before that. She had pretty much reached icon status among local government observers by 2017, regarded by many to be the best city manager in the country. I worked well with her, right up to when she retired in 2019. We had our disagreements, some larger than others, but we worked them out privately and presented a united front in public. That's so important in building trust and confidence in the city's leadership. Knowing the political and administrative landscape so well, Sculley was key to getting my agenda off the ground from the beginning.

With a foundation of values affirmed for my agenda moving forward, it was time to get to the heart of the work. The bedrock of any community's economy, and therefore the basis for socio-economic mobility, is housing. That much had been made clear as I walked the city's neighborhoods over the previous five years. While homelessness was the most visible example of a person in distress, tens of thousands of families were struggling to keep a safe and affordable roof over their heads. Older homes were falling into disrepair on the West Side, where homebound seniors on Social Security could no longer afford basic maintenance. Rising rents were pushing families out of revitalizing areas. Homeownership was becoming an ever more distant dream for younger families as wages sagged and housing costs skyrocketed.

These were the stories of San Antonio, and if we were to continue on our path to becoming a prosperous city they could no longer be ignored. While every city in America reckoned with this underlying economic reality during the pandemic—millions of American families were one missed paycheck from financial ruin—the irony of San Antonio, where two former mayors had gone on to become secretaries of Housing and Urban Development (Henry Cisneros under President Bill Clinton, and Julián Castro under Barack Obama), is that we still lacked a comprehensive housing policy or plan. There had been fits and starts over the years, but all of the task forces and blue-ribbon committees had amounted to little movement on the issue of affordable housing.

Following through on my campaign promise to deliver a com-

Meeting with the Mayor's Housing Policy Task Force at city hall: (*clockwise from top*) Ron Nirenberg, Noah Garcia, Gene Dawson Jr., chief of policy Marisa Bono, María Antonietta Berriozábal, Jim Bailey, policy adviser Victoria Gonzalez, and chair Lourdes Castro Ramírez, 2018. Photo by Jonathan Alonzo.

prehensive and compassionate housing policy for the city, in August I appointed a task force led by former HUD deputy assistant secretary Lourdes Castro Ramírez. At the outset I spent considerable time going around the city and explaining the focus on housing, the scale of the problem, and the consequences of housing insecurity in San Antonio—homelessness, lack of employment, poor health, and crime, all of which cost the entire community in a multitude of ways. Along with community banking executive Noah Garcia, former council member and housing advocate María Antonietta Berriozábal, architect Jim Bailey, and Pape-Dawson Engineers president Gene Dawson Jr., the five-member task force spent the next twelve months meeting with the community, listening to residents, and analyzing the housing landscape locally and nationally to create a Comprehensive Housing Framework so that "all San Antonians, regardless of income, can find a safe and affordable place to call home within city limits."

Among the major recommendations, the framework called for streamlining the public decision-making process, aligning the myriad housing organizations and development departments toward the same efforts, changing the city charter to allow for bond financing of affordable housing, and establishing a stronger partnership with the private sector to increase the supply of housing at all income levels. The city council ratified the framework, and we developed a ten-year action plan called the Strategic Housing Implementation Plan (SHIP). As of this writing, the framework and the SHIP combined have made San Antonio's affordable housing strategy a national model at a time when nearly every city in the country is trying to figure out its plan to address the housing affordability crisis. We have since connected the housing effort to our homeless response system for an even more holistic response to myriad challenges in order to ensure that the most basic building block of economic security—a stable, affordable home—is attainable for everyone.

Nearly concurrent with the housing strategy, I announced the creation of ConnectSA, an effort to finally bring mass transit to San Antonio for the first time. Along with housing, transportation is another leg of the three-legged stool for economic mobility and our desire to end generational poverty in San Antonio. Transportation costs are second only to rent or mortgage in terms of the financial burden every family faces, and in San Antonio, where the only alternative to owning a car is an underfunded, under-resourced bus system (VIA Transit), there aren't good options for the working family. Because bus routes are so infrequent, getting to school or work on time means hours of travel time between waiting for the bus, catching the right transfers, and so on. I met an elderly caretaker, Irasema Cavazos, whose weekday fourteen-mile commute took two and a half hours each way. A meager paycheck meant leaving at 4:30 a.m. and arriving back at 8:30 p.m.

VOICES OF SAN ANTONIO

Lourdes Castro Ramírez

Shortly after returning home to San Antonio from my service as a presidential appointee at the U.S. Department of Housing and Urban Development, I received a call from Mayor Nirenberg regarding his plans to bring together five local leaders to develop a housing plan. The call came in when I was at a department store, and I scrambled to find a quiet place to hear more about what the mayor had in mind. The more I heard, the more interested I became in joining this effort, and I accepted his invitation to chair the Mayor's Housing Policy Task Force.

This was 2017, and Mayor Nirenberg was keenly aware that the city was growing rapidly. San Antonio was gaining sixty-six residents a day that year and leading the country in population growth. The mayor was committed to ensuring that, as the city grew, we were doing everything possible to facilitate equitable development and a high quality of life for all San Antonians, regardless of income or zip code.

The mayor assembled an impressive group of public and private sector experts, beginning with the first Latina to serve on the city council, social justice champion María Antonietta Berriozábal; Jim Bailey, associate principal at Alamo Architects; Gene Dawson Jr., owner of Pape-Dawson Engineers; and Noah Garcia, senior vice president at Vantage Bank.

The charge to us was simple: develop a framework for a comprehensive, compassionate housing strategy where every San Antonian, regardless of income level, could enjoy the opportunity to access quality affordable housing, and include protections for local residents amid this historic growth.

Housing was still not recognized as a high policy priority at the state or national level. But Mayor Nirenberg had the foresight to know that housing needed attention. He entrusted us with this monumental effort to develop housing policy interventions and gave us full autonomy to develop the process and level of community engagement.

As we wrote in our final report, "Our homes have deep emotional meaning. For many of us, our homes are the backdrop to childhood memories—the places we played, cried, laughed, argued, and dreamed. When things went well, our homes grew with us. We found stability."

Recognizing this fundamental shared experience, our task force set out to engage the community in developing a housing policy framework with actions that would allow all residents to afford housing, live in dignity, and age in place.

We developed a mission statement and adopted core values focused on transparency and accountability in decision-making, and we made it clear that our process would be data driven and bottom up, meaning that community engagement and input would be fundamental in shaping our recommendations.

We quickly determined, through a review of the data, that San Antonio was experiencing more severe affordable housing problems than it had in the past. We anticipated that, when combined with population growth and declining home production, it would exponentially get worse without interventions. This finding essentially validated Mayor Nirenberg's assumptions.

For almost twelve months the task force led a robust policy-making process grounded in data, best practices, and commitment to inclusive community engagement that would engender trust. Like many cities across the country, San Antonio, with its high poverty rate, historical racial and economic segregation, and aging affordable housing stock, made this effort challenging. All the more reason community engagement was critical.

We listened and reflected on what we heard from more than five hundred residents in every corner of our city. They shared the many pressing issues affecting their lives—from reduced homeownership rates to the lack of affordability in rental units, from homelessness to the regulatory barriers impacting affordable housing construction, and from an aging housing stock to concerns over property taxes.

Throughout this process the mayor lent his support, ensuring that we had the necessary staffing resources and consultants to create technical working groups that included more than a hundred residents to develop concrete recommendations in five key areas: protecting neighborhoods, removing barriers, creating a transparent and coordinated system, funding and finance, and special populations.

We concluded that housing is as essential to the city's economic well-being as water, energy, and transportation. Housing is infrastructure. We doubled down on the belief that every San Antonian should have a place to call home and that housing must be decent, safe, affordable, stable, and delivered through a coordinated system.

The mayor and city council accepted and adopted our detailed report with five key actions: develop a coordinated housing system; increase city investment in housing with a ten-year funding plan; increase affordable housing production, rehabilitation, and preservation; protect and promote neighborhoods; and ensure accountability to the public.

As the chair of the task force, I am grateful to Mayor Nirenberg for having confidence in us, in our process, and in the final product, which continues to guide the city's overall effort. I firmly believe that we created a model for the country on how to proactively address and engage the community. I am also appreciative of the many people who shared their inspiring stories and solutions, which challenged us to be bold.

LOURDES CASTRO RAMÍREZ is the president and CEO of the Housing Authority of the City of Los Angeles and previously served as president and CEO of the San Antonio Housing Authority (now Opportunity Home) and as a principal deputy assistant secretary at the U.S. Department of Housing and Urban Development.

I appointed former mayor Henry Cisneros to lead a small group to approach our transportation modes—from roadways to bike paths to VIA to sidewalks to scooters and ride share—and create a comprehensive, multimodal plan that would culminate in the introduction of bona fide mass transit (i.e., light-rail or something equivalent) and give us a strategy to fund it.

The group brought together every entity that deals with transportation in the city, and about eighteen months into the effort they delivered the plan. I had anticipated and was ready for what it called for in terms of funding: reallocating a one-eighth-cent sales tax from aquifer protection and greenway trails development (the two most popular voter-approved initiatives in city history). I had previously campaigned on those two initiatives, and I had led the campaign to renew them in 2015, so I knew we could not discontinue them, as they are vital to our water security and green space preservation. A sales tax was the only sustainable way, however, to fund public transportation, so I was ready to have some tough conversations with the public and the environmental advocates. I promised a new life for aquifer protection and the greenway trails using different sources of funding (bond financing without any increase to taxes), and I announced a plan to call an election to assign that one-eighth cent to public transit in perpetuity.

The second finding from ConnectSA was that light-rail was not suitable in San Antonio, at least not yet. The city was just too sprawling, and the lack of population density meant it would have been impossible to start a mass transit system of any length significant enough to reach the population that needed it, let alone the population that would want it. The expensive infrastructure requirements of light-rail, coupled with the lack of funding options, led to a state of paralysis on the issue every time it was considered. Not to mention the fact that San Antonio voters had rejected light-rail on multiple occasions, most recently in 2015 when anti-transit activists successfully petitioned to add a provision to the city charter prohibiting any form of rail being built without a public vote. That action had been fueled by the outrage over costs and delays in an effort to build a two-mile streetcar project in downtown a few years prior.

A streetcar. Two miles. Oy vey.

So I accepted the recommendation of the ConnectSA team that San Antonio would be best served by Advanced Rapid Transit, essentially light-rail on wheels. This system would allow us to extend a nearly ten-mile route north-south and a ten-mile route east-west for a fraction of the cost of rail. The service itself would feel like rail to the user, with a dedicated lane infrastructure separated from traffic, at-grade entry of vehicles with cashless, app-based payment, and scalable and (soon) autonomous vehicles. A step above "bus rapid transit," this type of system would allow us the flexibility and cost scalability to build a real mass transit system and make it useful to more people immediately. With my backing of the plan, we secured public approval in November 2020 to reallocate funding from the aquifer and greenway trails sales tax, along with the federal transit administration approval (and additional grant funding) to start building the north-south "green" and east-west "silver" lines. These are the first bona fide mass transit lines to be built in San Antonio. After voter approval, the city council also agreed to my plan to use municipal bond proceeds in order to continue the extremely important aquifer protection program and greenway trail development.

The third and final leg of economic mobility (in my view it's just an academic way of saying "the American Dream") is the dignity of a good-paying career. In today's economy that requires more than a high school diploma, whether that means a professional trade, a college degree, a technical certificate, or some other postsecondary education. Unfortunately, for hundreds of thousands of families in San Antonio, and for millions of American families, that is simply unattainable. They are locked in cycles of poverty, often working multiple jobs that pay low wages to make ends meet, if they can at all. They are increasingly likely to be dependent on some form of public assistance. There is no money to pay for additional training or education, and even if there were, there is no time, no childcare, no health care coverage in the event of illness. Study after study shows that children in these situations are stunted in their own educational attainment and are likely to end up in the same cycle as adults. Thus, poverty grows.

My friend Mike Flores and I had been discussing the power of free community college in breaking those cycles when he was appointed president of Palo Alto College (part of the Alamo College District) on the city's South Side and I was still in District 8. He encouraged me to look into the first college promise program in the country in Kalamazoo, Michigan, and what it was doing for families. I was impressed. Flash forward a couple of years; I was now in the mayor's office, and Mike was being considered for the chancellor position of the Alamo system. I committed to him that I would be a champion to bring the program to San Antonio as one important part of breaking the grip of poverty on our city. "Whatever it takes," I told him.

Mike had already amassed an unparalleled record as a young administrator, rising from vice president to president of Palo Alto and helping the college achieve elite status with its first-ever Aspen Award for Excellence. There was no surprise when the board selected him as the youngest chancellor later in 2018. With Mike leading the Alamo system and me leading the city, we worked together as cochairs of the Alamo Promise program steering committee, along with Bexar County judge Nelson Wolff (in Texas, we call the county's chief executive and highest elected official "judge"), to build community support and initial funding to launch a pilot program. We called it the moonshot to end cycles of poverty in San Antonio and took several dozen business leaders to Washington, D.C., to visit with Martha Kanter, former Obama undersecretary of education and director of the national organization College Promise, to learn more about how these programs worked in other communities. Back in San Antonio, I pushed my council colleagues and city manager Walsh to provide funding to match the business and philanthropic support. "If we had one dollar to spend in our city, education would be the most important place to spend it," I told them.

The first phase launched in 2019, with twenty-five eligible high schools and 3,500 enrollments, providing tuition-free enrollment to eligible high school graduates to any of the five Alamo Community College campuses. The essential benefit to those students, however, was not tuition assistance; it's the counseling and support each received, especially when times got tough, which they inevitably do. The program is a commitment from the community to the student and from the student to the community that they will finish school. "Why should I care?" I'd sometimes get asked. "I don't have any kids, so why do I want my tax dollars paying for someone else's education?"

"Easy," I would say. "Postsecondary education leads to a good job with a good wage, and that means less need for public assistance, the ability to afford a home, and better health outcomes. All that means better public safety for you, too. You want to prevent crime? Give people good jobs."

The Alamo Promise program includes businesses, nonprofits, academic partners, and neighbors committed to providing support if and when needed: financial, transportation, health care, whatever life might require when an obstacle must be overcome in order to keep that student in school. Today Alamo Promise is going strong and growing, having been expanded to all graduates of a Bexar County high school. In 2024 more than sixteen thousand students were enrolled in the program. Other area universities have started their own versions.

The most powerful impact of breaking cycles of poverty—and reigniting the American Dream—is the transformation that can occur from one generation to the next. Just as children who are born into poverty have statistically diminished educational outcomes and are much more likely to be raising their own children in the same cycle, the opposite is also true when that cycle reverses. Imagine the opportunities now afforded to children whose parents are able to help them with homework because they don't have to work extra jobs to pay the rent. This is why we believe Alamo Promise—and workforce training generally, which I would soon stake a tremendous amount of political capital on—is our moonshot. If we were to build a city where everyone had an opportunity to thrive (which is good for all of us), we needed to create pathways to economic mobility, and that meant an investment in education at all levels. All of this was part of my vision for the city upon coming into office, and we got started immediately.

My favorite adage about public service is a Greek proverb that I continuously remind myself of and have repeated to our community whenever there is an opportunity: "A society grows enlightened when old men plant trees under whose shade they will never sit."

I have become known for taking the long view. Most of these initiatives would not reap immediate rewards, nor were they intended to. I sincerely believed that a systems approach that in many instances would take years to bear fruit was in the entire city's best interest. As I always said, the real measure of my worth as a public servant would be decades from now, when Jonah was my age. In San Antonio, it was time for a long-term vision toward equitable growth and a reasoned transition from what was in many ways a great city whose focus needed to rise higher on the horizon. We needed to address intractable poverty and lack of opportunity that, for growing numbers of residents, cast a shadow over our progress and was the source of most of our significant challenges.

I will always be frustrated by the slow speed of the bureaucracy and the all-too-frequent backbiting nature of politics. But we were able to navigate through both. What I am most proud of is that almost all of the major initiatives I proposed went through some form of public approval at the ballot box and were supported overwhelmingly; affordable housing, early childhood education, workforce training, and public transportation have all been supported by large margins. So I knew we were doing the right thing, reaffirming along the way that San Antonio is a place where people reach out to help one another. You can't help but fall in love with this city.

BACK FROM THE BRINK

The job of mayor is all-consuming. As Phil Hardberger warned me, "work–life balance" sounds like a noble goal, but there is really no such separation. It is as much a kind of life as it is type of job; you are in it when you wake up, when you go to sleep, when you're at home, at the gym, or at the movies. It can't be turned off. Every day, a new set of challenges. The impacts of the decisions you make are direct and immediate, and the feedback from those who are impacted—our neighbors—is direct and immediate too. For someone who loves their city, loves to work under pressure, and enjoys being around different people every day, it is a dream job. For me, in fact, it seemed that the longer the day—or the more challenging the situation—the more energy I got from the job. I loved the unpredictability of it all.

It's not a normal life, especially for the mayor's family, and surviving it intact requires an understanding and patience that is nothing short of saintlike. Thank God for Erika and Jonah. During my first term in office, Jonah thought it was cool that I was the mayor. Barely nine years old, he had just started to learn about presidents, governors, and mayors in class, and he recognized the additional attention the family was getting. His Nirenberg genes really started to come out. He became a junior comedian when we were together in public; if I had a microphone, he would take it from me and tell the audience that "my dad is awesome; vote for him." Sometimes he would sing random songs. Riding on floats during parades along the River Walk and meeting players from the San Antonio Spurs—it was all pretty cool for him, although it seemed like a consolation prize for the fact that he had to sacrifice so much for a dad who was working all of the time.

Although a salary had finally been instituted for council members and the mayor in a 2015 city charter amendment election, Erika still had to take on the vast majority of parental responsibilities—such as driving Jonah to school, teacher meetings, lunch prep, doctor appointments, emotional meltdowns, and overall raising him—in addition to her full-time job. It got a little easier as he got older and more self-sufficient, but I don't blame her when she says that for many years she felt like a single parent. It hurt me to hear that, but she would remind me that she and Jonah loved me and saw that I was trying; they just wanted me to try harder. I did what I could, when I could, for the household: laundry, washing dishes, fixing stuff around the house—everything I could when Jonah and Erika were sleeping. Erika and I arranged date nights every few weeks, but they frequently got postponed because of some city issue.

I won't pretend it was easy. It tested the strength of our marriage and my relationship with my son on many occasions. But somehow, as a family, we all grew up and grew together during my time as mayor. I sometimes think about what we would be like as a couple, as a family, if I hadn't gone into politics. There's no doubt we'd be different. But I thank God he put us together just as we are, because we are quite loving and grateful for each other.

Time was ever scarce, because in addition to the job of governing, sometimes being mayor was simply about showing up. As the representative of the entire city—and *all* its people—the mayor's presence makes a statement: "this place, these people, matter to our community." Beyond the usual ceremonial events and commemorations, I always thought it was important to show up where people needed to feel the presence of others, to feel that they weren't alone: funerals of people I barely knew, birthdays in senior living homes, Veterans Day remembrances at VFW posts, the first day of school for a new class of prekindergartners. I never wanted to be one of those public officials who either did not show up at all or made only a brief appearance before leaving, and I was surprised that this is what most people expected. I never felt comfortable doing that, even though there were many evenings when I attended multiple events. I made an effort to spend time at each function meeting people, looking them in the eye, and talking to as many as possible. I put in eighty-hour weeks on the council when there was no salary, so I had already gained a reputation for showing up in my own district. I knew I was going to give even more as mayor in a place as large and diverse as San Antonio.

Early in my tenure people would recognize me when Erika and I attended events together, but many thought she was part of my staff, not the First Lady of San Antonio (she has a theory about that, which is quite interesting and based on society's patrician expectation of beauty—ask her). She often took advantage of it by slipping away and letting me deal with the crowd. By my second or third term, people began to recognize her, and she no longer enjoyed the benefit of relative anonymity. What really made Erika happy, though, was when young kids or teenagers recognized me and wanted to talk with me and take photos. Some said they remembered when I spoke at their school during one of my monthly Kids Town Halls. Others said they were learning about me in their lessons on government. For Erika, this took some of the sting out of our lack of family time because it reinforced why she agreed to let me run to begin with: to make our city a better place for Jonah and the children of his generation who would inherit San Antonio one day. She always volunteered to take the pictures herself in those instances.

The deeper cost of public service at a personal level became more apparent during the mayoral campaign of 2019, when I was seeking election to a second term. My main opponent was council member Greg Brockhouse from the far west suburban area of District 6. He was a sharp-tongued populist with a knack for telling people what they wanted to hear; soon after his election to council in 2017 he declared that he was already evaluating a run for mayor. He seized on the kind of divisive rhetoric that newly elected president Donald Trump was successfully using to garner attention, tailoring it for the San Antonio community and attacking property taxes, government waste, and the "liberal" city council that was blindly supporting my agenda of housing, transit, equity, and climate resiliency. His goal was to sow distrust and erode support in local government, just as Trump was doing at the national level, and to position himself as a plain-speaking everyman who wanted to protect citizens' money and their families from politicians' pursuit of power. While Brockhouse was seen as champion for conservatism, he managed to gain support from some on the far left by speaking out of both sides of his month and attacking institutions they thought were better rebuilt than reformed.

Despite trying and failing in a previous run for city council, Brockhouse gained traction by becoming a political consultant for the fire and police associations during an increasingly adversarial collective bargaining negotiation that started in 2014, when I had just joined the council. City Manager Sculley convinced Mayor Julían Castro and the council that San Antonio's spending on police and fire union wages, health care benefits, and pensions could not be sustained. Unless this was changed, public safety expenses—driven primarily by benefits unmatched in the industry (such as 100 percent health care coverage for employees, retirees, and all dependents)—would continue to grow faster than city revenues, crowding out all other city services.

The framework had been established in 1989, when a contract with the San Antonio Police Officers' Association was hammered out hastily and approved by the city council without long-term fiscal analysis. After the contract was approved, a fiscal impact analysis was completed that spelled out extremely hard financial times for the city as a result. The report was leaked to the media, and the city's finance director was fired. Business leaders and watchdog journalists had decried the issue for years, calling it a ticking financial time bomb. Sculley had tried unsuccessfully to get every mayor she worked with to address the issue since her arrival in 2005, but now, with the two associations' five-year collective bargaining agreements set to expire in 2014 and Mayor Castro likely leaving for the Obama administration, the time had come. Public safety spending already took up 66 percent of the city's general fund budget, which obviously limited the city's ability to fund other important public sector projects like basic infrastructure, homeless shelters, parks, and libraries.

Before negotiations began, Sculley organized the business community and released a report predicting that unless the contracts changed, public safety costs would consume 100 percent of the general operating fund by 2031. What was meant to be a sober presentation of data to begin the collective bargaining process only sparked outrage among first responders and association leaders, who said she was essentially blaming first responders (and retirees) for a looming city bankruptcy. Sculley, along with anyone who openly supported reforming the agreements, including me, became a lightning rod for attacks, which included posts on social media and a one-million-dollar advertising buy on local television attacking city leaders and Sculley personally.

With all the action happening everywhere except for where it counted (at the bargaining table), both contracts expired without a resolution in September 2014. In a fatal mistake that seemed like the only way to get things unstuck, the city sued for relief, seeking to have the evergreen clause—a feature of the contracts since the 1980s that kept the contract terms in place for ten years after they expired—declared unconstitutional. This didn't help. Instead, the heat turned up even more and eventually the offensive against the city turned to opposition at the ballot box. With Brockhouse as a political consultant, the San Antonio Professional Firefighters

Walking with district chief Eloy LaQue (*left*) past fire union members gathered at city hall on the way to the city council chambers for a briefing on the quickly deteriorating contract negotiations, February 2014. Photo by Billy Calzada, *San Antonio Express-News*.

Association, seizing on increasing public resentment over a proposed downtown streetcar project, led a successful campaign to adopt a city charter amendment that prohibits light-rail from being built in the city without a public vote.

Ivy Taylor, now in her first full term as mayor, took the cue, bypassing city negotiators to cut a deal with the police association in time for a 2017 reelection campaign and earning their support in return. Meanwhile the dispute between the fire association and the city deepened. The fire association declared that they would not negotiate until the city dropped the evergreen lawsuit, which at that point was making its way through the courts.

The pressure peaked after I defeated Mayor Taylor and the new city council—which included Brockhouse and six new members—took office in 2017. As Brockhouse looked for ways to attack Sculley and me from inside city hall, the fire association—led by president Chris Steele—declared war on the city, launching an approximately one-million-dollar drive to gather signatures to place another city charter referendum on the November 2018 ballot. The referendum was split into three proposals. Proposition A would make it easier for voters to overturn city council decisions by allowing a referendum on budgets, taxes, utility rates, and zoning and would have lowered the number of signatures required to overturn an ordinance by petition voters from seventy-five thousand to twenty thousand. Proposition B would put an eight-year term limit and a salary cap on the city manager position, a direct rebuke of Sculley, who would ironically be grandfathered and unaffected by the measure. Proposition C would grant the fire union unilateral authority to declare an impasse in contract negotiations and send it to binding arbitration by a three-person panel.

All three propositions were aimed at weakening the city, and we quickly sounded the alarm, working with community and business leaders—along with all living former mayors except Taylor—to launch a two-million-dollar campaign to defeat them. Proposition A, which the *San Antonio Express-News* called "ridiculous," fortunately failed (54 to 46 percent). It would have significantly impeded the city government's ability to function, subjecting any action by the council to a possible referendum, including adopting an annual budget. Proposition B passed by a large margin (59 to 41 percent), as the four years of public attacks on Sculley had taken its toll, and proposition C passed (51 to 49 percent), narrowly winning after a huge election day push by firefighters stationed at every polling site in the city. After the dust settled a few months later, still feeling the sting of proposition B, Sculley announced her retirement, a bitter end for one of the most revered city management careers in the country and in San Antonio's history.

Although the firefighters association claimed proposition C

as a victory, it came back to haunt them. After they failed to get Brockhouse elected mayor in the next election (as you'll read later), they declared an impasse, and an arbitration panel was appointed. Despite a great deal of pressure from Steele and the association, the panel did not believe the city was being unreasonable. Instead, it produced a five-year contract with a 5 percent signing bonus for the remainder of 2020 and more modest increases than the city had proposed over the next four years. Health insurance benefits mirrored the deal the police union had accepted, and the association lost a lot of bargaining leverage since they were now not on the same negotiating cycle as the police union. In the future the two associations would not be able to cull their resources when negotiating a new contract. Overall, for rank-and-file members of the union, the binding, court-ordered contract was more austere in terms of salary and pension benefits than what their leadership had promised them over the previous six years of conflict. Unsurprisingly, Steele was soon replaced after eighteen years as the association president.

The referendum ended with mixed results: we staved off the most serious damage to the city by proposition A, but the harm was done. A handicap was put on our ability to hire and retain the city's most important executive position—the city manager, who oversees all of the operations of thirteen-thousand-plus employees; our credit rating was downgraded, and institutional relationships were damaged, perhaps for years to come. Both sides spent a lot of energy and emotion on something that really did not have to happen. I replayed those months and years again and again in my head, thinking about how we could have defused the situation instead of continuing until it overheated.

But there was no time to dwell on that. In the run-up to the charter election, Steele, caught on a recording at the fire union hall, laid out his master plan not only to win the charter vote but also to essentially control the mayor's office. Rallying association members and detailing his strategy to destabilize city government and attack the city manager, the final blow and pièce de résistance would be to unleash all union resources and execute a campaign, Steele said, to "put our own guy in the mayor's office, which would be Greg Brockhouse" in the May 2019 elections. It was a bold, if not disturbing, articulation of seizing control of city government; Brockhouse ("his guy") would do whatever they wanted, Steele said, including with their collective bargaining agreement.

Brockhouse soon made his intentions known. After eighteen months on the city council, he was running for mayor, making it official at a Trump-like rally featuring a cast of people convinced that they were aggrieved and that city government was to blame. Accordingly, the firefighters association announced their full support and commenced spending more than one million dollars from their PAC, aided by an increase in membership dues specifically for the purpose. Thousands of yard signs began popping up emblazoned with the union logo, and firefighters began going door-to-door. The police association soon followed suit, as did the local Republican Party, for reasons I'll describe later. Admittedly these were lonely days. I read all of the biting criticism and insults on social media. I was angered by the anonymous attacks—even on my wife and son. It felt like I was getting crushed by a tidal wave, and what made it worse was that I deeply respected San Antonio's firefighters and police officers. Some were my friends. I knew they were strongly supported by the same public I served—as a group, much more popular than any politician—and they earn our admiration for good reason: police and firefighters are there on our worst days. They are known everywhere as heroes, guardians of our families' safety and security.

But I remembered my father's early lessons about being a statesman and not a politician. If being honest and fair, even when negotiating police and fire association contracts, meant I had to sacrifice popularity, so be it. I steeled my resolve to move forward one step at a time (or, in the case of this election, one door at a time).

There were some flashpoints in my first term as mayor that complicated the election even more than the issues with fire and police, turning it into more of a partisan political exercise and less of the nonpartisan election it is supposed to be. The long shadow of Trump that started at the top of that escalator in 2015 had been fully cast over our nation's political discourse by 2017, and the poison quickly spread to the local level. Things got a bit raucous, if not ugly, especially as some of these flashpoints received national attention.

The first occurred around the removal of a Confederate monument from the middle of Travis Park downtown that summer. I had signaled my desire to remove the monument in my spring 2017 campaign, and city council voted to approve its removal by September. Right before that happened, violent demonstrations in Charlottesville, Virginia, brought racial tensions locally and nationally to a fever pitch, and our statue became the site of increasingly dangerous armed protests and counterprotests. Right wing groups showed up, brandishing their long guns, marching outside city hall and around the park, and trying to intimidate us from doing what I already knew we had the votes to do. It was long past time to take the "unnamed Confederate soldier"—this glorification of slavery that towered over one of the most diverse cities in America, a city that had voted against joining the Confederacy's rebellion—from our public park. After two required public hearings, I quickly scheduled a vote and took the monument down seventy-two hours later, with a crane at the ready on the night of the vote, before any protesters could get organized and create unrest. It worked. No violence ensued, but it didn't endear me to any of those who cried foul and sued (unsuccessfully) to have us put the statue back.

The next issue that gave fuel to those ready to attack me came from retail giant Amazon, of all places. That fall Amazon, which today makes more ad revenue than every newspaper in the world combined, announced that it was going to build a second headquarters, dubbed Amazon HQ2, with some fifty thousand jobs and, through a press release, invited every city in the country to "bid." I hadn't been on the job for more than a few months, and my next move, as the guy who said being mayor was the job of "salesman-in-chief," would be closely scrutinized. Mind you, the press announcement from Amazon was akin to the company telling every community in America to "show me the (tax) money," since economic development deals of that size usually feature huge taxpayer subsidies. The way other cities responded unofficially through media stunts and overtures of affection for Amazon was really unbecoming.

I knew—and our economic development teams agreed—that for a company as advanced as Amazon, with the kind of resources and research it commands, incentives would probably be a deciding factor. The site selection would almost certainly be based on the community's fundamentals: the health of the labor market, air connectivity, the local transportation system, the cultural and educational environment, and so on. I reasoned that if we wanted to get Amazon's consideration, we needed to tell them why we wouldn't play the incentives game; we would instead use our resources to invest in and improve all of those fundamentals and make San Antonio the best place to raise a family or build a business. On October 11, 2017, Judge Wolff and I jointly authored a letter to Amazon CEO Jeff Bezos withdrawing from the open bidding process but inviting his consideration. We stated that although San Antonio offered many competitive advantages, the reason it was the best place for Amazon was that we wouldn't mortgage our future by compromising investments in education, transit, air service, and all the other things that would make the company's business thrive. "Blindly giving away the farm isn't our style. San Antonio has had a long history of successfully attracting and retaining global companies by smartly finding the right mix of incentives and opportunities to make our community the perfect location for long-term investment. It has to be the right fit; not just for the company but for the entire community," we wrote.

Some local elected officials and members of the business community came unglued. Even though they admitted we did not stand much of a chance compared with the cities under consideration, they said that we gave up. They said that in their eyes, being seen bidding seriously would have indicated that we were in the game, so to speak, open for business for other potential large corporations to relocate here. They weren't wrong about that, but I vigorously defended our response, reminding them that we did not say no to Amazon, just no to incentives for Amazon. We laid out the reasons we thought the company should consider our city. In retrospect, I should have brought other council members (and Judge Wolff should have brought other members of the court) into the decision before it went public, so that the message was clear and we could garner support beyond our small circle.

Nevertheless, time ultimately proved that we made the right decision. Not only have we continued to bolster our fundamentals and made San Antonio a much more desirable city for business and families (as I write this, the city is poised to set a record for business growth and relocation investments in the area, with more than five billion in the fiscal year—in contrast to our previous best of six billion over five years), but also, after Amazon HQ2 was eventually awarded to northern Virginia, the commitment turned out to be grossly overstated, with only a fraction of the jobs promised. But the whole situation put another arrow in my critics' quiver in the short term.

This was nothing compared to the wrath I summoned by saying no to the Republican National Committee that winter. This is another issue that, in hindsight, I would have handled a little bit differently, even though time proved us right again. Anticipating a Trump reelection campaign in 2020, the GOP wanted San Antonio *bad* for their convention. So bad that they prepped some Republican stalwarts in the local business community who invited me to a meeting to discuss the hosting opportunity with the site selection chairman of the Republican National Committee. Phil Hardberger was also invited to the closed-door meeting, along with about a dozen key business and chamber leaders, where the RNC proceeded to tell us how great hosting would be for the community in terms of economic impact and media exposure, and how great it would be for me politically. They acknowledged Trump's unpopularity (especially in urban areas like ours) and how polarizing he had become but said they needed "vocal support from the mayor" to move forward. Before I could say anything, Phil said the quiet part out loud: they were asking to hold a party coronation in San Antonio for someone who had spent the past two years demonizing Hispanic people—two-thirds of our population—as rapists, murderers, and thugs. A celebration of the same person who said he wanted to build a wall between us and Mexico—friends and neighbors to San Antonio, and for many, family—and make that country pay for it.

After a brief moment of slack-jawed silence in the room (and a few head nods from the courageous ones), the RNC's pitchman acknowledged that controversy would accompany the 2020 Trump convention but stressed that the benefits to our city would be far greater. He claimed that, along with the eyes of the world being on San Antonio for five days, our hosting the event would generate approximately two hundred million in economic stimulus. Clearly we were getting sold. To slow his roll, I told him there were plenty of post-event analyses from previous national party conventions that proved those claims false and, in fact, led to communities holding the bag.

Later on, after a predictably brief conversation with the city council, I announced that we would not pursue a bid. To explain our position, in a *San Antonio Express-News* op-ed I wrote that national political conventions aren't the great deal for cities that parties and their advocates want us to believe: "Not pursuing the convention isn't a partisan decision. The same downsides apply to a Democratic National Convention as well. Neither is a good deal based on the commitments required of the city and of local taxpayers." It was no surprise that only one city was aggressively pursuing the convention and that San Antonio had not pursued a bid for either party's national convention in more than two decades prior to this. The GOP wanted a roughly seventy-million-dollar guaranty agreement up front from the host city. I did not want to put this on the backs of local taxpayers since the host committee guaranty would be in the form of a letter of credit with earnest money deposited, and taxpayers would have to make up the difference between private-sector contributions and the full commitment. Further, the RNC said they needed exclusive use of portions of our convention center—one of our major economic drivers—for up to six months, which would disrupt major events already in the works.

Many local politicians and columnists lambasted us. Right wing talk show hosts said it was because San Antonio was run by liberals, and Brockhouse claimed that Republicans were not welcome in our city because of me. Trump's campaign manager said we had "made the business community (our) enemy." They suggested that, just like with the Amazon deal, I wasn't swinging the bat for San Antonio. I was accused of playing partisan politics since most of the council members were seen to be politically left of center.

None of that was really true, but the episode reloaded the guns that were pointed at me during the 2017 election. Those groups had not gotten over the fact that this upstart council member hadn't bent a knee to the establishment power brokers and had still become mayor of their city. "Liberal Ron" was now mayor, and the RNC situation brought their campaign caricature of me into full color. Looking back, I should not have allowed them to carry on convention discussions with me or anyone else behind closed doors. Rather, we should have demanded that those talks take place in the open, in full view of the taxpaying public. The most vocal Monday morning quarterbacking was done by politicians who knew—but wouldn't admit—what taxpayers really thought of their hard-earned tax dollars going to elaborate political conventions. It was a lesson learned, but I am as confident now as I was then that it was the correct decision.

The last flashpoint, which took place ahead of the 2019 election, was the most challenging and the most absurd, and it involved Chick-fil-A. If there was a local election equivalent to the October surprise, this was it. For most people in the country, Chick-fil-A is the name of the most popular fast food chicken sandwich around. In San Antonio it is synonymous with a political near-suicide. After a multiyear run-up to awarding a new concessionaire contract for the San Antonio International Airport (subtext: every lobbyist in town was banging on the doors of council members trying to gain favor with their client-bidders), in March the award was scheduled for a vote. The week of the vote the winning proposal was revealed, including which restaurants and retailers would be coming to the airport. That included Chick-fil-A, the fast food chain based in Atlanta, as a new eatery in the airport. The city council voted six to four to approve the concessions agreement, but council member Roberto Treviño added the requirement that Paredes Lagardère, the concessionaire, find a replacement for Chick-fil-A. Doubling down, he said that the reason was the company's "legacy of anti-LGBTQ behavior." The campaign season had just begun, and the controversy became the hook conservative media needed to claim the trifecta of grievances: bad for business—check; bad for Republicans—check; bad for traditional Christian values—check.

"Going viral" would be an understatement; the issue soon became the subject of two lawsuits and a federal investigation against the city. A local anti-LGBTQ, anti-abortion group claimed religious discrimination, and famed megachurch pastor John Hagee came to pray for the city council at the invitation of Brockhouse, who was absolutely delighted to get a political boost by voting against it. Suddenly a chicken sandwich was the biggest issue not just in the local election but in Texas politics.

Trump-aligned Texas governor Greg Abbott signed a bill defending Chick-fil-A and religious freedom in June, at the end of the 2019 legislative session, and far-right Texas attorney general Ken Paxton opened an investigation to determine whether San Antonio officials had violated federal law by denying the location to Chick-fil-A based on the owner's religious beliefs. This stemmed from a remark made by Chick-fil-A then-CEO Dan Cathy, when he said that his company backs "the biblical definition of the family unit." Paxton also requested that the U.S. Department of Transportation launch a probe, which prompted the Federal Aviation Administration civil rights division to investigate the dispute. The issue quickly spiraled out of control, and conservatives from all over the country condemned the city's actions. Brockhouse, of course, latched onto the dispute's increasing visibility to further win over conservative and religious support in the city—and perhaps some in the business community.

For me, however, it was never about LBGTQ rights or religious beliefs. In fact, the idea that Chick-fil-A was a holy meal or that denying the restaurant a space at the airport would somehow fight LGBTQ discrimination was absurd. There was a reason to support the decision to exclude the restaurant, however, and that was economic. Chick-fil-A's founder, S. Truett Cathy, was a devout Southern Baptist who decided to close the company's restaurants on Sundays. I argued that because Chick-fil-A was closed on Sundays for religious reasons (though it could have been for any other reason, for that matter) and our airport was not, the city would lose valuable, scarce space to serve the public in our very small terminal. At the airport, Sunday is a heavy travel day and we do not have concession space to spare. In response to a local reporter's question about whether I supported the council's decision because of LGBTQ discrimination, I said, "No, the issue is making sure we have a restaurant that's going to serve seven days a week, because travelers come in every day of the week and we know that 15 percent of volume in the airport happens on a Sunday."

In the end, Chick-fil-A decided not to pursue a location at the airport (at the time it had thirty-two other locations across San Antonio, all of which didn't require passing a TSA checkpoint to get to), but Brockhouse and his supporters certainly made hay of it in an attempt to paint me as a far left-wing liberal. The controversy waned slowly, but it never fully died down. In fact, to this day, saying "Chick-fil-A" in local political circles may cause some post-traumatic stress.

With a full quiver of arrows to sling my way, the fire and police unions, along with Republican groups around the country, started spending big money to unseat me and put a so-called conservative in the mayor's office. What was supposed to be a disciplined reelection all of a sudden became a fight for my life. But the election's increasingly higher stakes also led to more scrutiny of the candidates, including Brockhouse. Soon his past alleged domestic violence incidents started to surface. In a county that has suffered from the highest rates of domestic violence in the state, the more his record came to light, the worse it got. After months of calling a report of an incident in 2009 false, Brockhouse admitted that police were, in fact, called to his home. The *San Antonio Express-News* printed a copy of the supposedly expunged police report and also discovered that the police were dispatched to the Brockhouse home on another occasion, in 2006, to respond to allegations of domestic violence involving a previous wife.

Certainly, the public began to sense that there might be a pattern (and lying). Indeed, Brockhouse's ex-wife, who was born and raised in San Antonio, had remarried and moved to Washington, D.C., and was quoted as saying that she was afraid to return to see family, "especially if that man [Brockhouse] is going to be mayor. I'm going to have to wait four years to come home." It cut to the heart of Brockhouse's character at a time when he was attempting

Shaking hands with District 6 council member Greg Brockhouse after a mayoral debate, April 17, 2019. Photo by Matthew Busch, *San Antonio Express-News*.

to define himself as a Chick-fil-A choir boy supported by public safety associations.

In the initial election in May 2019, I received 48.67 percent of the vote to Brockhouse's 45.56 percent. It meant another runoff. I remember walking to our election night watch party. I felt shell-shocked. What was I going to say to our supporters? I felt like I was flying a plane that had taken so much flak it could barely stay airborne. Now we had to keep it in the air for another month and somehow land it in better shape than we were in right now. I already mentioned how hard it was for me to give the speech to my staff and supporters after my first runoff in 2013. *How am I going to do this again?* I thought. If you're an incumbent pushed into a runoff, you're in serious trouble. It means that more than half of the voters wanted someone else. In my case, not only did I fail to get to 50 percent, but Brockhouse was just three percentage points away. Politically I was a dead man walking, and now I had to, once again, walk up to the podium. I had to ask everyone to dig deep and give their all one more time. To their credit, they did. As more information came to light regarding Brockhouse, it became a fight for the city of San Antonio, and we could not let this guy win.

About a week after the May election, one of my policy advisers, Ivalis Meza Gonzalez—daughter of beloved grassroots organizer and Chicana activist Choco Meza—invited me to meet with two young campaign organizers who said they had information they wanted to share with me. Ryan Garcia and Zack Lyke were both barely thirty, but they were seasoned in politics by then. They proceeded to tell me how much they wanted me to win and how bad Brockhouse would be for our city. Zack then unfurled a giant spreadsheet of voter precinct data, down to the ballot boxes, that showed how each street had voted in the May election. He explained exactly where he thought I left votes on the table and—surprise!—that these votes were in largely conservative areas where progressive candidates don't typically tread. The conversation was a bit surreal, almost like the scene in *Moneyball* when Billy Beane is relearning how to win baseball games by playing the data.

It was a glimmer of hope during an otherwise bleak few weeks. If these guys showed me the play we needed to run, I'd execute it and we could win. I told myself I would not be outworked. I brought the two of them in to energize the campaign, and they did. Ryan organized the field staff (door knocking, phone banking, etcetera), and Zack worked with Bert Santibañez, our data analyst, to develop the strategy. Zack had already done the impossible in 2017—leading the campaign to get John Courage, a liberal Democrat who had run for office unsuccessfully countless times over the course of three decades, elected (and reelected) to District 9, the city's most conservative area. I left our meeting convinced that Zack was a savant—passionate and knowledgeable about the data science and someone I definitely wanted to have on board. He would later become my chief of staff.

Along the way Zack, Ryan, and Bert pulled us back from the brink, and despite the army of political operatives now campaigning for Brockhouse, we stayed one step ahead, sometimes literally. On one occasion they called me into the campaign office for an emergency meeting around midnight and said they'd figured it out. Earlier that day one of our canvassing teams had been visiting homes on a particular street and encountered a group of door knockers from the Brockhouse campaign. Zack, Ryan, and Bert said they had uncovered a pattern based on previous elections, and they could predict which homes our opponents would target, why, and when. If we could get to those homes first and "inoculate" them with our message, we had a good chance of converting those voters to our side. It worked; data analysis after the runoff showed that they had indeed figured it out, and the votes from those streets were the difference in the election.

I won the runoff on June 8, but it was a nail-biter until the last ballots were counted late into the night. I won 51.11 percent to Brockhouse's 48.49 percent, with the turnout ticking up from May. The night was very emotional; I remember hugging Jonah and Erika and many tears being shed. It was an ugly and difficult campaign that took everything out of us. My victory speech at the Friendly Spot—one of my favorite downtown icehouses, in the middle of the King William District—was more like a coach's postgame scrum. I stood in the middle of a crowd of several hundred friends, family, and supporters, everyone beat up and weary after leaving everything on the field. The light was dim, provided mainly by what was mounted on television cameras, and there was no stage. I told the audience that this campaign had changed me as a public official and that I intended to spend more time in the community and less in the office. I felt like I had peered over the edge of the abyss and taken a step back, that I had been given a great gift of recognizing the temporary nature of the job, and I was determined to make every moment count.

Several columnists later described me as a tarnished victor—a mayor without a mandate—noting that I narrowly won a runoff as an incumbent. I would be unable to govern, they said. Even on the city council I was seen as vulnerable, and the jockeying for the 2021 mayoral election began almost immediately.

After the too-close-for-comfort win, I knew I had to make some changes and bring a higher level of urgency to the mayor's office. I hired Jim Greenwood as my new chief of staff. Jim had a long career in government affairs in Congress and as an executive at Valero, a Fortune 500 energy company based in San Antonio. I had gotten to know Jim over the years and was impressed by how easily he seemed to navigate the politics in local, state, and federal offices. He was universally respected and treated everyone kindly, which I came to learn were uncommon traits in the government affairs business. And despite the fact that he worked in the oil and gas industry, Jim had gained a reputation of being an environmental advocate, bringing Valero to the table to assist in land conservation efforts and, later, emissions reduction plans.

When I hired Jim, I told him I needed someone who would beat down the doors of the city hall bureaucracy to get my agenda moving in the second term. Erik Walsh was our new city manager, and my chief of staff needed to be an ally on the one hand but also a pain in the ass on the other when necessary. He did exactly that, and he also knew how to build an effective team. We brought in Zack Lyke as a full-time assistant to communications manager Bruce Davidson, and we elevated Ivalis Meza Gonzalez to Jim's deputy chief of staff. On the political side, I parted ways with Kelton and brought in consultant Gilberto Ocañas as a political adviser, and later, James Aldrete. I also shuffled my political cabinet, bringing in East Side community advocate Dwayne Robinson, labor leader Linda Chavez-Thompson, and Gordon Hartman, a friend and prominent businessman and philanthropist

VOICES OF SAN ANTONIO

Jim Greenwood

Two days after winning reelection, Mayor Nirenberg asked me to be his chief of staff. While surprised, I wasn't shocked. For the six months preceding the election I volunteered for him. I came into the office most days and pitched in where they needed help. Ron enjoyed introducing me as his intern. It usually generated a laugh, mainly from him.

Business leaders said I was crazy to do it, and progressives were either befuddled or just plain pissed off. No doubt Ron understood the optics of hiring me, a former oil industry executive, past San Antonio Chamber of Commerce chair, and someone who had worked for Mayor Ivy Taylor, whom he defeated in 2017.

What most didn't know was that for eight years I worked in D.C. for two Texas Democratic members of Congress, progressing from answering phones, meeting constituents, and managing committee assignments to becoming a chief of staff. After Capitol Hill I joined Valero Energy Corporation, one of the nation's largest manufacturers of transportation fuels. My job there centered on building coalitions to preserve the clean burning fuel's section within the 1990 Clean Air Act Amendments, and as chair of the Chamber of Commerce I worked to advance Mayor Julián Castro's signature Pre-K 4 SA initiative.

I was not an obvious choice, and despite significant community pushback Ron held steadfast in his support of me, expressing unwavering confidence in my ability to manage the office. If he were willing to take the political heat, how could I say no? It was one of the best decisions I've ever made.

who had founded the first fully accessible amusement park in the country, Morgan's Wonderland.

I made it clear to everyone that the mayor's work was in the streets and that I needed to get out of the office. They needed to handle the administrative and political aspects of the job more

On my first day on the job, instead of moving into the "chief of staff" office, I shared space with Ivalis Meza Gonzalez, the mayor's new policy director. My desk was positioned in line with an open door, and I was seen by anyone passing, always accessible to the staff and the city manager's office. The mayor also brought on Zack Lyke, the campaign's social media savant, to push out the mayor's priorities. Most important, I followed the lead of the mayor's scheduler, who has the hardest job in the office.

Day two began with a series of meet-and-greets with those local nonprofits that knocked on doors for Ron and did a ton of work to secure his thin margin of victory. Ivalis joined me in these meetings, and I'm certain that due to her connections to grassroots organizations and her support of me, they took a wait-and-see approach, which is all I could ask for.

As the office staff worked as a team, each understanding their important role for advancing the mayor's priorities, I set three goals: help the staff reach their potential, secure council approval of the mayor's Climate Action Plan, and position him to win a third term. We stayed focused, we embraced the opportunities we were given, we worked long hours, we built bridges, and we laughed a lot. The foundation we laid during the initial seven months of the mayor's second term proved indispensable as we approached the unpredictable—the COVID-19 pandemic's arrival with passengers of the *Diamond Princess* disembarking in San Antonio.

JIM GREENWOOD retired from Valero Energy in 2016 after twenty years as a lobbyist and later vice president of governmental affairs.

fully. I kept recalling the election night scrum and my promises to be a mayor of the people, which is how I got elected in the first place. Jim posted a map of the city down the hall from my office so that everyone on my team could see it. The staff used push pins to track wherever I went: a red pin for neighborhood meetings, green for community events, blue for political rallies. Within weeks the map filled and the pins spread out all over the city. A few months into the second term, after a brutal reelection, it felt like I was finally having fun again and like I was back in command of the job. That was always the case; no matter how challenging or complex the situation was politically, the cure was always hitting the streets, getting out and talking to neighbors about how I could better serve them.

After the arbitration panel rendered its decision on the fire union contract, which quietly vindicated the city's position in the six-year dispute, it felt as if the dark clouds over city hall—including from the reelection battle—had finally been lifted. But the scars would linger. There is an unseen cost to being an elected official and public servant, and this is especially true for families. Inflamed by the bitter and growing division in Texas and across the nation, politics in 2019 had turned nasty. Besides what was targeted at me directly, Jonah—eleven at the time—began to get it at school too. As if middle school isn't terrible enough for kids already. One day he came home and was particularly bothered. It took a while, but Erika finally got him to open up. Another student had told him, "My dad is going to shoot your dad with his gun." The teacher quickly got everything under control, but it was very hard on all three of us. That moment, whatever last wall existed between innocence and politics—the image of Mr. Smith going to Washington—came crumbling down. Jonah had begun to realize that some people wanted to hurt him simply because of who his dad was.

Even with the rampant disinformation put out by my opponent and his supporters in my first city council campaign, it had never gotten this ugly. It had never gotten personal with Ivy Taylor either, although things ended bitterly. But the 2019 election was a different animal altogether. Even Erika lost her cool a bit, which was understandable and warranted; emulating Trump, the only thing those kinds of politicians like more than being the bully is playing the victim. As a result, we had all become even more energized about the campaign; there was no way we wanted someone with that type of moral compass in office representing the city.

For her part, Erika had always looked at my previous races in a practical manner—how is this going to affect the family and our livelihood? In 2019, she said, "It hit me. My husband goes through this every day and doesn't tell me about it. He doesn't tell me these emotions. He doesn't tell me about these attacks. For the first time I was really put in his shoes, and it was then that I thought, okay, as First Lady, I'm your partner now. No more avoiding the pain." All of this brought us that much closer together.

I got past the contentious election with a new team, a renewed focus and sense of purpose for San Antonio, and I was back to enjoying the grind. It felt like I had both hands on the wheel again. We were already moving on my agenda more aggressively. But unbeknownst to me, the biggest challenge of our lives—one that would upend the entire world—was lurking right around the corner.

PANDEMIC

The World Health Organization (WHO) office in China received news in December 2019 of what was thought to be an isolated outbreak of a pneumonia-like virus in the city of Wuhan. The developing cases of high fever and shortness of breath at first appeared to have been connected to an outdoor fish market in Wuhan, which was closed down by emergency order on January 1, 2020. Chinese authorities reported no evidence of significant human-to-human transmission at that time. The WHO identified a novel type of coronavirus similar to the SARS virus that hit Asia from 2002 to 2004 and called it SARS-CoV-2 (severe acute respiratory syndrome coronavirus-2). Little did I know that this was the start of something that would place San Antonio on the frontlines of a global pandemic and come to define my tenure as mayor.

Officially, the first person in China died from the disease on January 11, 2020. Since then, the exact origins of the virus have been vigorously debated, with one theory being that the virus jumped from infected animals to humans at the Wuhan market; others tend to believe that the virus escaped from the Wuhan Institute of Virology, a research lab that was studying coronaviruses. Whether it originated from either of these or some other source in China, the situation got caught up in already frayed U.S.-Chinese relations and unfortunately led to a heightening of anti-Asian prejudice in the United States—stoked all too eagerly by President Trump.

The first reported case of what the WHO would soon classify as coronavirus disease 2019 (or COVID-19) in the United States occurred on January 18, 2020, near Seattle, Washington. A number of Americans had likely contracted the disease before this time but it was either not properly identified or they did not know they had it. The first confirmed death in the United States from COVID-19 occurred on February 6, 2020, but it was a severe outbreak at a nursing home in suburban Washington that infected a large number of patients and nurses that finally made COVID-19 a household word. By March all fifty states in the country had reported at least one positive case, and nearly everyone had gotten the disease from "community spread" rather than contracting it while traveling abroad. On March 11 the WHO officially declared COVID-19 a global pandemic.

The COVID-19 pandemic easily became the most disruptive global event since World War II, affecting virtually the entire world's population beginning in early 2020 and claiming more than 7 million lives worldwide over the next few years. Deaths in the United States from COVID exceeded 1.1 million, nearly twice the death toll from the 1918 flu pandemic. In official terms, the pandemic ended in 2023, when President Joe Biden signed a bipartisan congressional resolution bringing to a close the COVID-19 national emergency status. But the pandemic's wide-ranging effects will be with us for many years, if not decades, to come.

As in most other cities nationally and internationally, it hit us pretty hard in San Antonio. It was an unprecedented health crisis with significant economic, social, political, and even psychological ramifications. There was no playbook for what we would deal with, and it would test our mettle and resolve, as it did for every civic leader in the world. From the outset I knew my first responsibility was to the health and safety of the people in my city. Everything else would be secondary to trying to save lives. And while our response in San Antonio wasn't perfect and we sometimes made mistakes, in the end, we guided our community successfully through the maelstrom. My office's actions were significantly influenced by the disease's evolution and the disjointed—to put it mildly—national and state government responses during that time. I recommend reading *The Mayor and the Judge: The Inside Story of the War against COVID* for then–Bexar county judge Nelson Wolff's perspective of our partnership in San Antonio during those challenging times.

Health officials at the Centers for Disease Control and Prevention and the National Institutes of Health prepare for pandemics, so initially a general national plan was put into place once the gravity of the situation became clear. Governments and businesses at every level in the United States and abroad took emergency measures to prevent the virus's spread. Travel was restricted, and schools and other public places began to close. Businesses and offices, except for those deemed essential, such as hospitals and grocery stores, were shuttered. By early April 2020 more than 316 million Americans were under stay-at-home or shelter-in-place orders, during a time when the virus was spreading exponentially and there had already been more than a thousand deaths and a hundred thousand cases in the country. The virus especially preyed on vulnerable people, including the elderly and people with preexisting health conditions or lack of adequate medical care. The CDC recommended using face coverings in public, to thoroughly and frequently wash hands, and to socially distance. In those early days the measures were met with acceptance and understanding—sometimes reluctantly—by the general public. We accepted the responsibility we had to protect one another, and communities from coast to coast began to repeat the mantra "We're all in this together." Leaders at every level of government were constantly reminding people that their actions not only protected themselves and their families, but that they were also important for the health of others. Republicans and Democrats at the local and state levels seemed to be on the same page. Texas governor Greg Abbott, an increasingly strident conservative firebrand, publicly lauded San Antonio's response in the early weeks, which at that point was focused on preventing the spread of the disease and operating mass testing sites once that resource became available. Alongside Judge Wolff and the governor at our Emergency Operations Center, I announced new measures to prevent community spread by limiting public gatherings.

The unity didn't last long. By April, while thousands of Americans—especially immunocompromised and older residents—were dying in hospitals that were increasingly over capacity, President Trump was downplaying the virus, undermining CDC recommendations and saying that the virus would magically disappear. In 2017, like a privileged child defying his parents, he was photographed looking straight into a solar eclipse, flouting the advice of scientists (and optometrists) to protect one's vision. In 2020 the consequences of his childlike behavior were more deadly. He stated that masking was voluntary and that he would not wear a mask himself. This drew the entire field of public health into the country's existing political divisions, hampering the national response to COVID-19, with blue states and cities tending to more aggressively apply CDC recommendations and red states and areas tending not to do so. Blue cities in red states found their public health authorities stymied and their local governments preempted with an increasingly heavy hand by their legislatures and governors (like Abbott). The end result nationally was a health crisis that was deeper and longer lasting than it would have been if everyone cooperated, with corresponding social and economic impacts that were much more severe than they should have been. To make matters worse, those impacts landed hardest on communities that were the most socially vulnerable. By this I mean those with prevalent poverty, health disparities, and inequitable access to services—the same fundamental, long overlooked challenges in San Antonio that we were finally addressing. This political and

Lending a hand at a San Antonio Food Bank drive-through distribution at Toyota Field during the COVID-19 pandemic, April 2020. Photo by Josie Norris, *San Antonio Express-News.*

cultural dynamic played an important role in the nature of our response locally.

With the virtual shutting down of society when the virus started raging, including short-term business closures that were ordered locally first, then hours later by governors and the Trump administration, the economy tanked. From early February to March 23, 2020, the Dow Jones Industrial Average lost 37 percent of its value while the S&P 500 was down by 34 percent. Unemployment skyrocketed, especially in the service sector, where restaurant, hotel, and retail workers were hit particularly hard. By April 2020 the U.S. unemployment rate was 14.7 percent, the highest rate of unemployment since the Great Depression almost a century earlier. While businesses began opening up, lost jobs, lost wages, and overall uncertainty had already swept through American households. Food insecurity became a serious issue. By July 2020, 30 million Americans reported that they did not have enough food to get through the week. In San Antonio, 120,000 area families a week were coming to food bank distribution lines. Broken or nonoperating supply chains for products, including those getting food into grocery stores, exacerbated the problem. People of color, especially Black, Hispanic, and Native American, suffered disproportionately compared to white Americans, further highlighting the health disparities between racial and ethnic groups in the country, driven primarily by inequitable access to health care. The White House and Congress authorized a series of COVID-19 relief packages in 2020 and 2021 in an attempt to prevent complete economic collapse. This included sending stimulus checks directly to American families, which soon enough had the unintended effect of helping to fuel an inflationary trend.

The Trump administration's Department of Health and Human Services and the Department of Defense launched Operation Warp Speed, providing billions of dollars in a public-private investment to condense the usual ten- to fifteen-year timeline required for pharmaceutical companies to complete clinical trials, gain FDA Emergency Use Authorization, and begin manufacturing while still mitigating risk. By December 2020 the first vaccines developed by Moderna and Pfizer became available and were given mostly to health care workers and elderly residents at nursing homes (notably, the critical development and testing of the Pfizer vaccine was performed at the Texas Biomedical Research Institute in San Antonio). But by spring 2021 vaccines had become available to all American adults, with priority for those who were older and deemed more vulnerable. Indeed, by October 2022, of the 1.1 million deaths in the United States, 72 percent were individuals ages sixty-five or older.

It was a traumatic time for most Americans—and most San Antonians. We had to act quickly and wisely to address a situation that was unexpected and potentially devastating.

San Antonio was thrust into the coronavirus conversation for the first time in late January 2020, when we received word that Americans would be evacuated from the Hubei province in China, the epicenter of infections at that time. It was not a surprise to anyone here that these evacuees would be brought to San Antonio—particularly Joint Base San Antonio–Lackland (JBSA-Lackland). After all, we are a disaster response hub for an eight-state region, frequently staging first response teams like Texas A&M Task Force 1 and hosting evacuees from other emergencies across the southern United States. With Brooke Army Medical Center (the Department of Defense's only Level 1 trauma and burn center), along with POW and hostage repatriation facilities, JBSA is the place Americans come to when they experience trauma abroad, whether it's physical or psychological.

There were plenty of nerves when our community got the call to step up during the pandemic's early days. Outside of the base, we wanted to make sure our residents were protected, but as I've said many times, there are no fence lines in San Antonio when it comes to the esprit de corps between our military and civilian populations. Hosting Americans fleeing from a deadly pandemic seemed like patriotic duty.

At this time, on a previously scheduled trip to Washington, D.C., for a mayors summit that had become much more urgent, I met with Texas senator John Cornyn and members of San Antonio's U.S. House delegation, including Will Hurd, Henry Cuellar, and Joaquin Castro, to discuss what was going on specifically with regard to evacuees to JBSA. These included the possibility of more than a hundred Americans from the *Diamond Princess*, a cruise ship that had been touring Southeast Asia in January when passengers and crew began coming down with COVID. Huntsville, Alabama, was also named as a possible location to receive evacuees, but Alabama senator Richard Shelby vehemently came out against evacuees being sent to his state. In fact he bragged about diverting these Americans elsewhere, writing that "I just got off the phone with the President [Trump]. He told me that his administration will not be sending any victims of the Coronavirus from the Diamond Princess" to Alabama. He added, "Thank you, @POTUS, for working with us to ensure the safety of all Alabamians." Mimicking some of Shelby's harsh language, even a few public officials in San Antonio came out against relocating the passengers to JBSA.

It's not like I wasn't also concerned about the well-being of our local residents and Texans in general, but even though we were entering uncharted territory we couldn't abandon our duty to fellow Americans. I wanted to make informed decisions and better understand the parameters of the process so that we could be prepared for whatever came our way. All we knew at the time was that the virus was spreading rapidly and that it was deadly. Apart from those facts, mixed signals were being sent from the federal authorities, including an increasingly dismissive President Trump. So I chose to base my actions on what the medical experts, not the politicians, were telling me.

On February 5, 2020, the CDC announced that a plane carrying Americans from Wuhan was headed to JBSA-Lackland, located about ten miles west of the city center. From that point on, the coronavirus news cycle took off like a rocket locally and abroad. On February 7 a plane holding some 250 evacuees from China's Hubei province landed at JBSA-Lackland, with national news cameras awaiting its arrival. On February 13 I held a press conference with CDC officials to announce that one of the evacuees had tested positive for COVID-19. At the time this was the first known case of the virus in Texas. Medical experts at this point started getting much more precise with their language, using "COVID-19" to specify the particular kind of coronavirus that was spreading. On February 15 it was announced that Americans on the *Diamond Princess* off the coast of Japan would also be sent to JBSA for quarantine. A charter flight carrying 177 passengers, including 7 who had tested positive for COVID, arrived early in the morning of February 17. The press conferences were becoming more frequent, and I could feel the anxiety in our city ratcheting up, as it was all across the country. While cases started accumulating in other places, San Antonio was looking like the front lines in the fight against the virus.

Complicating matters even more, the first of two planes together carrying more than three hundred passengers from another cruise ship in East Asia, the *Grand Princess*, landed at JBSA on March 10. It was a chaotic period, to say the least, and we were all working with incomplete information and haphazard protocols coming from the Trump administration. The national press started to recognize the increasing urgency local officials were operating with as we tried to gird our communities against what the WHO had now declared was a global pandemic, while our president downplayed warnings from public officials. I told the *Washington Post*, "It's disconcerting. Throughout the course of this, what I've seen is that the lack of coordination at the highest levels of this president's administration is simply stunning." San Antonio had been thrown onto the front lines of the first pandemic since the 1918 Spanish flu, and requests from public health authorities—including those within Trump's own CDC—were being met with disinterest. We needed personal protective equipment for our health workers and emergency responders and tests for people who were being evacuated into our community. Instead, for almost two months, we essentially had to fend for ourselves.

While this was happening, I convened all of the hospital CEOs and the head medical officials of the Southwest Texas Regional Advisory Council (STRAC), the regional trauma and emergency health care system for the twenty-two counties in its jurisdiction, including Bexar. This group could tell us what the experts were saying about COVID-19, what to expect, and how we needed to best respond. What they shared I couldn't really fathom at the time. They suggested that, at the rate of spread that was occurring globally, our entire country was going to be affected within months, with virus cases growing rapidly in waves until at least September, perhaps even into the following year. Depending on how lethal COVID-19 turned out to be, and how quickly tests and vaccines could be developed and distributed to the population, many thousands of Americans would die.

After that meeting everything on my agenda became secondary to protecting our community from a potential onslaught. I started convening situation reports with public health authorities, including city management, our city's medical director, the fire chief (who also directs EMS), Judge Wolff, and STRAC leadership. At those meetings we were able to share the latest information from inside the hospitals, get advice from medical professionals, and strategize about our collective response.

Though most evacuees were confined to the military bases for a fourteen-day quarantine period, those who tested positive for COVID-19 had to be transported by local emergency crews to nearby hospitals, as unbeknown to us, Department of Defense policy prohibited any evacuee who had tested positive to be housed on base. We had been assured by then that all evacuees, while being observed for any sign of infection, would be confined under tight quarantine at the base, therefore posing no risk to residents in the event that anyone was carrying the virus undetected. For the hospital transports, we had to quickly locate specially equipped ambulances and assign a dedicated infectious disease response team to staff them. STRAC scrambled to find beds at a hospital equipped to treat the patients, finally settling on Methodist Hospital, located in the north central part of San Antonio. As assistant city manager (and our former health department director) Colleen Bridger said at the time, "We took [the Feds] at their word." But after we were suddenly told to have seven ambulances and seven isolation rooms waiting for infected patients, she added, "Don't we get to say no? What happens if we say no? They told us, 'This is happening, so figure it out.'"

We had a lot to consider on short notice. In addition to the isolation rooms, we needed special chambers with negative air pressure to prevent airborne particles (such as virus cells) from escaping. State officials offered the Texas Center for Infectious Disease, a tuberculosis hospital in southeastern San Antonio with twenty-two negative-pressure rooms. Ten cruise ship evacuees who had tested positive but were asymptomatic were transferred there. We were not happy with all of this. Judge Wolff and I wrote letters to Secretary of Defense Mark Esper complaining that the beds should be reserved for the sickest of our patients. Republican congressman Chip Roy, who represents some areas of San Antonio, also wrote a letter to Esper as well as Alex Azar, secretary for Health and Human Services, asking whether "the extra transportation and movement of sick patients put San Antonio at risk," further saying, "I'm pretty ticked about it." As the pressure and politics in Washington ramped up, getting CDC officials to talk was like getting a diamond out of coal. CDC and other officials in Washington continued to point their fingers up (in other words, the White House). They weren't being empowered to make the necessary decisions.

It all came to a head on March 1, a Sunday. While picking up groceries that morning, I ran into city manager Erik Walsh at our local H-E-B, something that had never happened before. We were in the middle of the cereal aisle talking about the upcoming week when we both got the news: the CDC had mistakenly authorized the release the day before of an infected woman from JBSA quarantine. At the time CDC protocol required three negative tests after a fourteen-day quarantine in order to declare someone free of COVID. The woman had apparently tested negative twice, but before the third test had come back from the lab (which, early in the pandemic, took forty-eight to seventy-two hours), she was released. The third test came back positive. According to a detailed timeline assembled by the San Antonio Metropolitan Health District contact tracers, the woman checked into a Holiday Inn Express near the San Antonio International Airport and boarded a hotel shuttle to North Star Mall, a few minutes away. She stayed there for about two hours, visiting the Dillard's department store, a Talbots clothing store, and a Swarovski crystal shop, followed by the food court. She was located and rushed back into isolation. We were flabbergasted. This was exactly what we had assured the community would not happen.

After this fiasco, I called a press conference to inform the public. "Local health professionals, in whom I have the utmost confidence," I said, "are working very hard to prevent the spread of this virus here in San Antonio, and we simply cannot have a screw-up like this from our federal partners." Even Governor Abbott, a staunch supporter of President Trump, issued a rare rebuke of the administration in a news conference, calling the CDC's actions "unacceptable" and "a case of negligence." North Star Mall was closed for twenty-four hours so that everywhere the woman had been could be carefully sanitized.

Thankfully, a potential outbreak was averted. My staff and I went out to lunch at the mall the next day in an effort to reassure the public that it was still safe in San Antonio.

On March 2 Judge Wolff and I issued local disaster and public health emergency declarations for Bexar County and San Antonio, activating our emergency response protocols, which allowed us to take "actions necessary to promote health and suppress disease, including quarantine, examining and regulating hospitals, relating ingress and egress" from our jurisdictions. Even though the federal officials charged with keeping two hands on the wheel of the pandemic response were unable to do so, we wouldn't abandon our responsibility to protect residents.

As outbreaks appeared in other states, the pace of decision-making and planning accelerated. We had to mobilize local government, health officials, nonprofits (particularly the San Antonio Food Bank), and businesses to begin preparations for what looked like a prolonged health issue. But nothing prepared us for what started to unfold on March 11. That day local universities and colleges announced an extension to spring break. In no way did they want students coming back from all parts of the country, indeed the world, possibly infected (students soon adapted to remote learning for what turned out to be the rest of the semester, as did primary and secondary schools, all of this reflecting what was happening nationally). That evening I was at a meeting in La Cantera with my deputy chief of staff, Ivalis Meza. The Spurs pregame was on television in the background. All of a sudden news broke that in every arena across the country, players were called back into their locker rooms. The NBA was suspending the rest of its season.

We were in disbelief. In the United States, professional sports are a symbol of our collective spirit and resiliency. I watched when the Giants and the Athletics resumed the 1989 World Series just days after a deadly earthquake devastated the Bay Area, and I remember the uneasy adulation of fans when NFL teams took the field after 9/11 and nearly every stadium was on heightened alert for terrorism. This was uncharted territory. The NBA shutting down injected a new level of fear into the COVID-19 situation that we had never experienced before.

From that point on, our public health team sat shotgun with my staff and me as we navigated the first global pandemic of our lifetimes. Within twenty-four hours of the NBA shutting down, large public gatherings of any kind were deemed at risk of becoming "super spreader" events. We were already experiencing community spread of the virus, and it was clear that crowds with people in close proximity were COVID powder kegs that would explode in the days and weeks to come if we didn't act decisively. One day into the Tejano Music Awards Fan Fair in downtown San Antonio, which drew annual crowds of more than a hundred thousand, I ordered its cancelation. Understandably, the musicians and vendors were not happy (they were notified as they set up for the second night of performances), but they understood and complied. We also announced the cancelation of the Saint Patrick's Day river parade, which sees upward of seventy thousand visitors and residents lining the green-dyed water along the River Walk each year. Each of these decisions fell to me alone but was preceded by intense deliberation with our public health authorities and debate among my staff about the economic ramifications. There was a lot of information and "analytical noise" in my head at the time, but I always fell back to my number one responsibility: protecting the lives of my community.

On March 13 the biggest shoe dropped in San Antonio. After discussions with Fiesta Commission leaders, we came to an agreement to postpone the upcoming Fiesta San Antonio celebration. The annual eleven-day celebration of San Antonio culture and heritage, with high attendance events occurring across the city, started in 1891. It generates hundreds of millions of dollars for our economy along with a good portion of the annual operating revenue for more than two hundred of the city's nonprofit charitable organizations. One of the world's largest and most attended outdoor festivals, it had been canceled only in 1918 during World War I and from 1942 to 1945, during the height of World War II. We called it a postponement at first, and I really thought we could reschedule it for the fall. It was 2020, in the United States—surely we had the wherewithal and command of medicine to deal with this virus by then. But by summer we knew the celebration would be canceled altogether. The press conference at the Fiesta Commission headquarters was a mix of muted optimism, anxiety, and somberness. Mostly it was a realization that the world, from our perch in San Antonio, was now truly turned upside down.

By this point we were effectively no longer operating as a council-manager form of government. By law and necessity, in times of crisis the mayor is the emergency operations director, so I could execute orders quickly and mobilize local resources to respond to any situation. Being able to act in a timely way was critical, and bureaucracy is the enemy of crisis response. The virus was spreading rapidly in virtually every city in the world and was already killing by the thousands.

It was increasingly evident that the crisis would be a long-term one. This meant we needed to consider how to engage our other elected colleagues meaningfully to keep essential services—beyond crisis response—working effectively. We also had to redefine what those essential services were, at least for now, and to triage every function of government.

In San Antonio, and in cities across the country, the economic impacts were starting to be felt. Service sector jobs went first, and the most vulnerable members of our community, those who were already the working poor with no financial safety net, were hit the hardest. People were running out of food and basic supplies, and overnight the lines at San Antonio Food Bank distribution sites doubled. *San Antonio Express-News* photographer William Luther captured an aerial photo of a drive-through distribution event on the South Side that showed thousands of cars lined up, end-to-end and side-by-side, as far as the eye could see, some of them occupied by parents who had lined up the night before. It was a devastating image of my city and its people. The photo became the iconic image of the pandemic and a call to action for leaders everywhere to address the fundamental inequities of our economy that put so many vulnerable families in those lines so quickly. The *New York Times Magazine* reprinted Luther's photo on the front page and wrote that "San Antonio's mayor, Ron Nirenberg, believes the worldwide attention focused on his city...ought to prompt a long overdue reckoning. 'That it took a pandemic for us to stop and assess just how precarious the economic conditions are for millions of American families is unfortunate, but let's not waste the moment to address it.'" That photo still haunts me. And it will grace our home as a reminder of what really matters if you're a public servant.

I remember getting a call from the panicked San Antonio Food Bank director, Eric Cooper, the morning of that South Side distribution event. He said he had no way to serve that many people. It wasn't that they didn't have enough supplies; they didn't

A drone photo captures the scale of need during the pandemic as thousands of cars line for a San Antonio Food Bank grocery distribution, April 9, 2020. Photo by William Luther, *San Antonio Express-News*.

have enough people to work the lines, mobilize additional trucks from the warehouse to replenish supplies, and maintain safety. With thousands of hungry, anxious families, if we didn't handle it appropriately, we would be dealing with an entirely different kind of emergency. City manager Erik Walsh activated several departments and sent them to work logistics at the distribution site (for instance, we didn't need to keep libraries open at that time, so librarians became food bank staffers). Many of our own direct reports were also activated, and San Antonio police monitored safety while also helping to distribute the food.

The basic functions of our city government had clearly changed in the face of this crisis. Primarily, we had to figure out how to keep people fed who were without money for groceries and keep people housed who were without money for rent. I called Judge Wolff and told him we should effectively consolidate and restructure our bureaucracies. Rather than having unnecessary meetings on issues that were now on the backburner, our city council and Commissioners Court should be focused and activated in the areas where we needed their collective muscle. He agreed, and we suspended all existing activities and committees and appointed five "COVID-19 Community Action working groups, which [would] act as strike teams focused on immediate areas of impact within our community." Three centered on addressing the community's basic needs (food and shelter, business and employment, and social services) and two were charged with identifying support and financial resources to help us fill those needs (federal and state government advocacy and philanthropy). We asked Gordon Hartman to be our COVID-19 working group coordinator, organizing the meetings and keeping them on task so that the judge and I could stay focused on the now near-constant pace of emergency developments and public briefings.

It was clear from the beginning that Judge Wolff and I would need to operate as a single unit to meet the challenge ahead of us, if only to provide consistent direction to our community and show a united front in an effort to maintain the public trust amid so much chaos around us. We had some initial disagreements, especially when I recommended fully closing bars and restaurants. On that decision, I spent hour after hour combing over the data, talking with restaurant owners, and debating with our public health officials. Just a day before, we had briefed the news media that such establishments would remain open, with mandated distance between patrons. But at that stage the pandemic transformed at an almost hourly pace, and I concluded, based on all of the data and input, that closure was necessary for the community's safety. I called the judge, and he was not pleased, giving me his opinion on it in the colorful R-rated drawl that had endeared him to so many over the course of his five decades in public service. After a brief but heated exchange, I told him we'd be fighting on the same side of the next battle. He quickly apologized, and we agreed to disagree.

Beyond seeing all of the death, suffering, and trauma in the city, holding that news conference on March 18 to announcc the closures—essentially, at that moment, an indefinite shuttering of a huge portion of our hospitality industry—was the pandemic's lowest point for me. It was almost like radiation therapy for our entire city, and I knew it would not be without consequences. But the number of COVID cases in San Antonio was doubling, and the disease and death were accelerating throughout our community and the country at a frightening pace.

About ten hours later Judge Wolff came to the same conclusion about the closures and asked me to join his press conference to announce them. From that point on, and for the next two years through COVID all the way until Wolff's retirement from public service in 2023, any question about disunity between the county and the city disappeared. Judge Wolff and I and our entire teams, with exceptions that were always ironed out behind the scenes, stayed in lockstep. Mayor Nirenberg and Judge Wolff, San Antonio and Bexar County, were one team.

Governor Abbott followed the next day with similar measures statewide and declared a public health emergency. During this period, web conferences (Zoom, WebEx, and others) became our modus operandi for meetings, including official ones like city council sessions. We all learned as we went ("you're on mute"), and while they were less than ideal, virtual meetings opened up new possibilities to stay connected and coordinated. I started having regular, sometimes daily, meetings with the mayors of the state's big cities. We talked about how things were progressing in our localities, what we were doing, and how we could work together. And we started planning some of our actions together. On March 23 all of Texas's largest metros—cities and counties—issued "Stay Home, Work Safe" emergency orders, directing nonessential businesses to close and residents to remain in their homes unless commuting or carrying out essential services. It was the most sweeping effort to break the virus's contagious chain by physically separating

VOICES OF SAN ANTONIO

Nelson Wolff

There comes a time in life when a public official is confronted with an unexpected crisis. How he responds to that crisis will test his character and his willingness to make difficult decisions. His actions will define him for the rest of his life.

The global COVID-19 pandemic was the world's most terrible ongoing crisis since the flu epidemic of 1918. More than seven million people across the world, including one million Americans, perished from the fast-spreading virus.

On a daily basis I saw how effectively Mayor Ron Nirenberg responded to the pandemic. In our 319 daily broadcasts to our citizens, Nirenberg's calm, clear, and articulate voice overcame the emotion, fear, and confusion our citizens faced.

He stood up to state and federal leaders when they refused to take measures to protect our citizens from the deadly virus. He was willing to issue controversial emergency orders. Together we issued thirty of these, such as the ones to close nonessential businesses and to limit gatherings during the first stages of the pandemic.

He carefully reviewed the 616 daily situation reports that included the number of people who had contracted COVID-19, how many were in hospitals, and how many vaccinations were given. He led more than four hundred health care conferences during the pandemic that determined what actions we would take.

I enjoyed the many personal visits we had as we planned our strategy to make the most difficult and important decisions of our lives. Ron Nirenberg exemplified the character of a leader that we all needed in the terrible crisis we faced.

NELSON WOLFF served as mayor of San Antonio from 1991 to 1995 and as Bexar County judge, presiding over the Commissioners Court, the governing body of Bexar County, during the COVID-19 pandemic.

infected people from healthy ones. Public health officials and scientists suggested that if the population actually did this simultaneously, the virus would have nowhere else to go within the incubation period of twenty-one days, and it would recede. Similar orders came out from the state and across the country, and by the end of March the brief but extremely traumatic era of lockdowns was in full effect.

This is when Judge Wolff and I started daily news briefings, carried live on all local television networks, radio, and social media and covered by the daily print news media. From March 27, 2020, until the pandemic's end, we updated the community on what was happening, what we were doing about it, and how people could protect themselves and their loved ones. We did more than three hundred live briefings during the first year, starting seven days a week and slowing the pace as the crisis subsided. As the *San Antonio Express-News* stated after our final briefing, it had become "an evening ritual that even hardened political cynics agree helped unite a community in crisis." Every night at 6:13 p.m.—a time local television news directors favored because it had the most viewers, immediately after the weather and before sports (what little there was at that point)—we met in the city's public access broadcast studio in the basement across from city hall, along with members of the press, socially distanced and masked, who were able to ask us questions after the routine briefing. As Judge Wolff was quoted as saying during our last broadcast, some two years after it started, "It was a frightening time. We were all scared. But it was important that we all be on the same page. Openness. Honesty. Giving people facts."

Each broadcast lasted about seven minutes, with a round of questions lasting another ten to fifteen minutes (or none at all), depending on whether reporters had follow-ups. I began by reviewing the numbers—infection rate, hospitalizations, deaths, available ventilators and intensive care unit beds—but always reminded people that behind every number was a family member, a

With Bexar County judge Nelson Wolff during a daily televised briefing on COVID-19, June 2020. Photo by Kin Man Hui, *San Antonio Express-News*.

friend, a coworker, a "life well lived and lost too soon." And I always asked people listening to keep those we lost—and the people they left behind—in their prayers. After that I gave updates on city functions or policies and handed things off to the judge. The judge, being the folksier political veteran, often told a personal story from a nursing home, neighborhood, or person he knew. It took a week, but we settled into an on-air rapport that nearly everyone we ran into positively commented on, thanking us for our efforts. I was the play-by-play person, usually wearing a traditional face mask, and Judge Wolff the color commentary, wearing a signature bandana. As you would imagine, when updates were especially grim or when either of us had a personal story to relate, our emotions could not be held back. I agreed with the judge, who thought it was a good thing. As he later said, "I think that's important to see in our leaders. He [Mayor Nirenberg] got emotional about these issues. I'm proud of the mayor, and we developed a close partnership in the briefings and learned from each other."

In the darkest moments of a crisis, people need confidence and trust in the people leading them. With COVID increasingly politicized as the pandemic wore on, honesty and sincerity were what the public appreciated from us most, and that honesty saved lives. That meant also admitting when we'd made mistakes or when new guidance contradicted old actions. I remember when the data emerged that cloth masks were ineffective against transmission of COVID. After wearing them for several months, we explained the new data and how, as the data around the virus got more precise, our response to it should change too.

At each briefing, after the judge finished his remarks, I usually turned the report over to a guest, who, depending on what the update required, was a member of our public health team—epidemiologists, respiratory therapists, the fire chief, hospital administrators, etcetera. They offered any medical guidance and rationale directly, so that our efforts as political leaders remained visibly in lockstep with health experts. We wanted, as best we could, to depoliticize the situation and avoid the rhetoric and division happening at the state and national levels. Christian Archer, a longtime political consultant in Texas, said that the judge and I "showed a common purpose and inspired confidence that there was a path forward...there was no thumping of the chest politically. And because of that, there's absolutely no doubt in my mind that people listened and those two men probably saved thousands of lives."

When the first live briefing aired, there were 120 COVID cases and 5 deaths in San Antonio and Bexar County to report. By the time of our last broadcast, nineteen months later, there were a total of 322,454 cases and nearly 5,000 deaths. As the days wore on, people from across the state tuned in because we were one of the only places they could get consistent, updated information close to home. Increasingly, we began to receive phone calls and email from around the country. Residents in other cities were tuning in to our online broadcast, grateful to see "guys at the local level" offering transparent, unbiased information directly from public health officials. They said they were tired of the politics.

The judge and I issued many emergency orders over the coming months, closing gyms and sports facilities, requiring face masks, and so on. Most of these establishments were able to resume limited business by late April, some with drive-through or curbside service. Gyms, exercise facilities, and personal care services were allowed to reopen under new standards on May 18. On May 1 it was announced that all retail stores, restaurants, movie theaters, and malls in Texas were allowed to open as long as they maintained at only 25 percent occupancy and followed distancing guidelines. Health care professionals were also allowed to resume services under similar guidelines.

While the judge and I worked fairly well with Governor Abbott at the beginning of the crisis—setting up testing sites and appearing at press conferences to prohibit large gatherings—in late April, we began to deviate on some important matters. The pandemic response was becoming increasingly divisive, and the governor, like many of his Republican peers, was getting a lot of pressure from politicians, science deniers, and businesses who were seeing their profits evaporate. Their cause was fueled by high-profile politicians around the globe who were caught violating their own orders of lockdown. The 2020 presidential election cycle, in full tilt (virtually), added fuel to the fire, as did the fact that, on top of the chaos and death all around us, COVID had tanked the economy. Conspiracy theories emerged quickly and often spread faster than the virus itself.

First we differed with the governor on the reopening of nonessential services: too soon, the medical experts warned us. Of course, there was a significant uptick in COVID cases and deaths across Texas when businesses and other establishments started to open back up per the governor's orders. We wrote Abbott urging him to reconsider, to no avail. "You don't cut off your parachute just because you've started to slow your descent," I explained during our daily briefing.

Then we disagreed on the issue of wearing face masks: they don't work unless people use them, and the governor wanted only to "encourage" them. We attempted to work around his rules—not conflicting with them but finding loopholes, for instance, issuing an order that all people over ten years old must wear a face mask and requiring businesses to have a health safety plan that posted a face mask requirement. But the dividing lines in the COVID response further deepened. Eventually Abbott issued an emergency order declaring any local order more stringent than his to be null and void. It was absurd, but that's where we were in Texas amid a deadly pandemic that became a political war: the governor used his emergency powers to prevent local communities from managing the emergency. We sued and won in district court and in the Texas Court of Appeals, but we had no chance in the Republican-controlled Texas Supreme Court.

Despite our desire to show a united front, our goal was to save lives and protect the health of our community, and Abbott's orders defied the science and medical guidance of public health authorities at the time. We believed they would not go unchallenged. Ideally federal, state, and local governments would be on the same page, especially during a crisis. But this proved impossible in such polarized times heading into a Trump reelection campaign when COVID drew a dividing line in our politics. Most of the mayors, Democrat and Republican, agreed on the policies and worked together to respond to the crisis. When they occurred, the disagreements were with state and federal politicians who were eager to put those divisions on the front page and on social media, to score points with their supporters and favor with Trump himself.

Needless to say, I did not get much sleep for more than a year. I often got up in the middle of the night to jot down notes and ideas or to research something I couldn't get off my mind. If I couldn't do that, I went to the garage to exercise. Erika, of course, did not get much sleep either. And I am sure I was tested for COVID more than any other person in San Antonio during the pandemic, as I had to show up for work and attend meetings and gatherings; time and again I had to make sure I tested negative.

Meeting with Gen. Charles Q. Brown, air force chief of staff, at the Pentagon, October 2020. Photo by Eric Dietrich, U.S. Air Force.

I also went to my fair share of funerals. At these funerals there was tremendous shock and sadness, but there was also a lot of gratitude. People were grateful that San Antonio, at least, seemed to be an oasis amid the division and turmoil about COVID that was played all over the news. Our residents couldn't get away from the pandemic, but every evening at 6:13 p.m. they felt like someone cared about them and their families. And they felt like we were doing what we could to protect them and their loved ones. Oftentimes a family member recounted to me someone they had lost, and they never expressed anger. Allee Wallace, a good friend of mine and a photographer and historian of the city's annual Martin Luther King Jr. march for more than four decades, lost his wife, Doris, early on to COVID. She was the first recorded fatality of the pandemic in San Antonio. I used to recall her name often at the daily briefings.

The world kept turning during those days, even though it felt like everything was standing still. In retrospect, some of our policies to reduce the spread of COVID did not produce much impact, and we made some mistakes. I ordered a curfew during the Thanksgiving holiday weekend in 2020, when I was reminded that students coming home would flood local bars and that alcohol would make it much less likely for commonsense health measures to be observed. We took a lot of heat for that. And of course, it has been shown that school closures by district officials across the country, which we praised at first, were not beneficial for children; in fact, extended closures were harmful to their social and intellectual development. Despite the American Academy of Pediatrics suggesting that schools could reopen in June 2020, many stayed remote or hybrid, and we should have been more forceful in our support of those that did open; many faced serious pushback from well-meaning but misguided public health advocates. But I realize that hindsight is twenty-twenty. When it came to our mission, we were following the best public health guidance in order to save lives. We were making the best decisions we could at the time based on the information available to us, and when we erred, it was on the side of caution.

In the final analysis, facing an existential global health crisis—the worst in our lifetime—we pulled together and got through it. Many thousands of our neighbors died, among them seniors and those with health vulnerabilities, especially those who lacked access to adequate medical care. The pandemic became an indictment of the inequity of our critical systems, like health care and housing, upon which we have built American communities for generations. It exposed the incomplete foundations of our economy, and that's why the pandemic became a catalyst for change. In San Antonio it was a clarion call that brought immediacy to our ongoing work on resilience and economic mobility. As I wrote in the foreword to *The Mayor and the Judge*:

I remember in April 2020, as the magnitude of the pandemic just became clear, being asked by *San Antonio Express-News* Editorial Page Editor Josh Brodesky, "What keeps you up at night?"

My mind went to the photo taken a few weeks earlier by veteran *Express-News* photographer William Luther of the staggering lines of cars filled with residents seeking food at a San Antonio Food Bank mass distribution site on the south side of San Antonio. That image, an aerial shot of the sea of cars which got reprinted and reproduced in *The New York Times* and publications and TV shows across the nation, was transcendent.

Some 120,000 families in a week's time—twice as many as in the days prior to COVID-19—needed food donations to feed their families. That meant that in my community, where we had 3 percent unemployment, where major employers were relocating their headquarters, where the economy had some of the best momentum in a generation, sixty thousand families each week would still be unable to put food on the table if not for the charity of the San Antonio Food Bank.

But that is not just San Antonio's story. That picture was America. In our new gilded age of economic disparity and segregation, millions of American families were one event—a health event, a lost job, an accident, a pandemic—away from economic devastation, and many others were already there. COVID-19 became that event for those millions.

My answer to Brodesky's question of what keeps me up at night is the same today as it was in April 2020. I hope we are not content to go back to the way things were: that same "normal" that had so many millions of Americans so close to the brink.

GETTING IT DONE

Phil Hardberger has a way with words, and when the occasion calls for it he'll coin a phrase that combines his love of world history, nature, and our shared human condition with straight-off-the-farm West Texas simplicity. While our talks became less frequent as my mayoral tenure continued, he always managed to connect at just the right moment, when I needed perspective from a judge, mayor, skipper, and amateur historian.

"It's easy to be a good captain in calm waters," Phil told me during one of those occasions.

Well past the worst days of the pandemic, that one has stayed with me. It was a reminder that the real value of leadership—and whether I'm worth my salt as mayor—is being able to guide my community through the inevitable storms while delivering on the agenda I was elected for. San Antonio is a big, dynamic city in a big, complicated world; expecting a clear road with no distractions would be pure fantasy.

One such fantasy occurred in 2017. Erika had worked so hard to get me three days away from work on Labor Day weekend. It was our first time off as a couple in more than two years, and she had booked a room at a rustic hotel in the middle of the Hill Country. She selected this place carefully; Wi-Fi was limited, and there was a chef on site, so there would be no temptation to work or leave. She had even reserved a sports massage for me at the hotel, again curtailing any excuse to leave and get distracted by city business. It was her birthday weekend, forty-eight hours, to be exact. All she wanted was time.

About six hours into our stay, a call came to her cell, not mine.

"Can he talk?" Trey Jacobson, my chief of staff at the time, asked gently.

"Why?" Erika said, somewhat bluntly.

"It's an emergency...again."

We had just escaped the worst of Harvey, an intense hurricane that barely missed the Gulf Coast's major population centers. What could have been a major emergency response in which San Antonio always serves as an evacuation center and launch point for disaster recovery turned out to be a successful stress test of our emergency systems—and by default, my first disaster response as mayor—and we had both passed. So when the storm knocked out some of the fuel refineries along the coast and we were told that supplies were intact, only delayed slightly, we were confident that the public would heed our official messages: "Gas is available for everyone. Please continue normal use."

Unfortunately that's not what happened. Within thirty-six hours, aided by social media and panic-buying videos, a full-on gas crisis ensued. Local news stations led with images of cars stretched around the block at nearly every gas station in town. Viral twitter posts showed some idiot filling an oil drum in the bed of his pickup as the pumps started running dry. It was a run on gas, and I spent the next twenty-four hours sitting in a small corner of the hotel manager's office—the only place where Wi-Fi would work—talking with fuel suppliers about getting additional trucks to San Antonio while crafting messages with my staff in an attempt to quell the panic. The Gas Panic of 2017 ended after a few days, but not before it canceled Erika's forty-eight-hour birthday wish, a reminder that the job of mayor doesn't work according to your family's schedule.

When a crisis hits, it often comes when you're already dealing with another one (or more). That certainly was the case throughout the depths of COVID-19, which stretched on for nearly two years. In late May 2020, while we were pretending to enjoy virtual graduations and drive-by birthday parties, the world was once again seized, this time by the horrific video of Minneapolis police officer Derek Chauvin kneeling on the neck of George Floyd, a forty-six-year-old Black man arrested for allegedly passing a fake twenty dollar bill at a local retailer. Struggling to breathe, Floyd cried out for help repeatedly as Chauvin and others looked on with cold indifference. After nearly ten minutes of being pinned to the asphalt, Floyd lost consciousness. He suffered cardiac arrest and was pronounced dead at a local hospital an hour later. It was a shocking video that immediately opened up old wounds and created new ones across America.

Almost instantly, sustained demonstrations broke out in cities from coast to coast, especially in places where cases of police brutality had been demoralizing communities for decades. Rather than losing steam over time, the demonstrations continued to grow in intensity throughout the summer. Many devolved into violence and destruction, but the marches kept going and gaining in strength, with an extraordinary cross section of Americans of all ages and ethnicities calling for reforms. Governments, corporations, media, churches, nonprofits—nearly everyone was forced to confront the issues being raised by the Black Lives Matter movement. For cities, those issues were centered on the culture of policing and the persistence of racial bias in our political and economic systems.

The first days of protests in downtown San Antonio began peacefully, with police and other law enforcement keeping their distance despite taunts directed their way. But late into the night one evening, small groups of people began agitating the crowd, and taunts gave way to projectiles, including glass and frozen water bottles thrown at police. Vandalism, broken store windows, and looting followed. To disperse the crowd, law enforcement deployed tear gas and nonlethal projectiles, including "cork plugs" that ended up injuring two local journalists. The tension escalated from there. I called a press conference to impose a curfew on the downtown business district and address the situation with crowd dispersals. "The vast majority of folks we saw out there today and this evening were there to peacefully assemble, which this city has a great tradition of doing," I said. "We can't let a few folks ruin it." Police chief William McManus also issued a statement that police would not disperse crowds unless projectiles were used by the crowd, and even then only on his direct command.

Tensions remained high as protests continued each day and violent scenes from other cities played out on television and social media. And although it was no surprise that demonstrations took place in San Antonio—throughout history the city has been a confluence for people organizing for labor rights, civil rights, and equal justice under the law—what stunned people was that the first few nights of protests descended into violence. That was new. And disturbing. But in typical San Antonio fashion scores of people from all over the city showed up unprompted the next morning to clean up the mess and get business owners back on their feet. Members of the San Antonio Spurs were even among them, as guard Lonnie Walker IV showed up, removing graffiti and passing out water to volunteers.

In spite of the disruptions that accompanied nationwide protests, the calls to confront systemic racism and reform the American criminal justice system were not new. They simply reached a crescendo and a new level of urgency, including in San Antonio. They were at the heart of our efforts to address long-neglected socioeconomic inequities (so visible in the city's rate of entrenched poverty among Latino and Black families) and the police collective bargaining agreement, which at the time often led to significant reductions in the discipline issued to police officers suspended or fired for misconduct.

With all of these troubles converging, 2020 was a summer of

peril in San Antonio. Public trust was balanced on a razor's edge, both as we managed through a deadly pandemic and as we simultaneously tried to keep the peace and pursue equity and justice for communities who had lost faith in those same public institutions of political and economic power.

At every meeting protesters filled the city council chambers and attempted to draw attention to their cause. Our proceedings were frequently interrupted, but I resisted having anyone escorted out, which would only spiral into physical confrontations between the police and angry citizens. I didn't want to put anyone in that position and if I could prevent more violence, I would. Instead I gave a wide berth, allowing people to speak, chant, and sometimes yell. Such deep-seated anger and frustration—compounded over generations—had been let loose in the aftermath of George Floyd's murder, and I would rather it manifest itself in a designated public forum than out on the street. But every chance I could, I also reminded everyone that we shared the same goals: a safe city for all people, where residents didn't have to live in fear of each other or the police, where the government was accountable to its people, where public representatives were stewards of the trust and their resources were invested so that quality of life wasn't only for privileged people or certain parts of town.

On June 4, six days into the protests, the marchers asked me to join them as they walked to their rally at the county courthouse. I did, and I could feel the crowd seething as I was handed the bullhorn. Similar scenes had played out in other cities, and it was almost invariably a setup to have a politician fall flat on his face. I was wary of making promises we couldn't keep or setting false expectations. Instead I wanted the protesters to feel that they were being heard and that there was an appropriate place to direct their frustrations, and as the head of the city government that staffed, equipped, and trained our police, that meant me.

"We hear you," I said. "We know there needs to be change. I will be working every single day until everybody goes home and feels like they don't have to fight for something that God gave them to begin with, which is the freedom to feel safe in their own community, to feel protected by the people who work for them.... I'm asking you to hold me accountable, nobody else. Because I'm the mayor of this goddam city and we're going to make change together, okay?"

In that moment I was overwhelmed by the feeling that our beautiful, historic, compassionate, destination city had some dark shadows that we needed to bring into the light. The reaction was swift as local news aired my comments constantly and the *Express-News* put them on the front page. Up to that point in my career, I had gotten a reputation for being very measured when speaking. But while I was walking to the courthouse, I imagined the many marches throughout history—and the many broken promises of reconciliation—that had already taken place in our city and across the country. The protest song "Mississippi Goddam" by Nina Simone started playing in my head (at KRTU, we played it each year, broadcasting live along the MLK march route, despite pushback from donors and university administrators, to remind listeners of why people still marched):

> Alabama's gotten me so upset
> Tennessee made me lose my rest
> And everybody knows about Mississippi, goddam
> ...
> All I want is equality
> For my sister, my brother, my people, and me

I wanted to return the protests' focus to the place where we had common cause, so that rather than breaking store windows or attacking our local police, the pressure would be on policymakers—starting with the mayor—to fix what needed to be fixed. And I knew that creating a place where everyone had an opportunity to live a healthy and prosperous life was about much more than policing.

We needed to improve neighborhoods that had been neglected

for years, where redlining and highway construction had cut off access to basic services and left crime and crumbling streets in their wake. We needed simple things like bus stops and improved public transportation so that working families—teachers, nurses, laborers, the people we had been calling essential workers during the pandemic—could afford to live in the city where they worked. We needed better housing. The reality for much of our community is that while two out of every three dollars in the city budget went to public safety, more than 20 percent of the city's residents were living in poverty, and many of them didn't feel safe at all.

In San Antonio and around the country demands for police reform continued to grow, from calls to change tactics and equipment to pleas to "defund the police." Some politicians jumped on the "defund" bandwagon, and a few communities even did so before reversing course. There was tremendous pressure to do the same in San Antonio as we approached the September 2020 budget adoption, but "defund the police" was clearly a bad idea if taken literally. Rather, I saw it as a grievance about the reality experienced in our city and across urban America: families worked hard, scrimped and saved, and paid their taxes, and after all that they still found it harder to barely get by each month. To make matters worse, while city budgets kept going up—including police, the largest department budget in most cities—potholes filled their streets, sidewalks crumbled, and the parks their kids played in fell into further disrepair.

Shouldn't we be doing as much to prevent crime as we do to respond to it? If we did, we'd see adequate investments in housing, streets, parks, libraries, and other city infrastructure. That's not what I heard just in summer 2020. I'd been hearing it since I chose to run for city council the first time. And it was the agenda I ran on and was elected mayor to implement: "The City You Deserve." We needed to stick to the vision. It would take time and continued commitment. "Defund the police" wasn't a budget directive; it was an indicator that patience about managing the public's precious few resources to improve their lives—what every political campaign since the dawn of time has promised—had worn out a long time ago.

In the face of those protests, in the September 2020 budget we increased the police budget by $8.9 million (believe it or not, a more modest increase than most years), angering many activists. But we stuck to the plan, including significant new investments in housing, job training, transportation, and public health (more on that in a moment). We are a growing city, and we have growing needs, and that includes public safety and emergency response. We also worked with the police department and the Metropolitan Health District to improve response protocols, including the expansion of mental health training and the addition of clinical experts for the thousands of calls the city receives for mental health emergencies each year. We worked with the University of Texas at San Antonio to establish a violent crime prevention program built on data analytics to increase police presence initially and then direct the appropriate investments in neighborhood infrastructure and youth outreach. And we worked with neighborhood leaders and former gang members to disrupt cycles of retaliation through Cure Violence, a program that treats violent crime like the contagious yet curable disease it often is.

This all happened while a new collective bargaining agreement was hammered out peacefully with the police association under the new leadership of longtime patrol officer Danny Diaz, who, unlike his predecessor Mike Helle, was much more interested in improving our city than he was in his own political career. Working with the police association, we strengthened the disciplinary process and finally did away with decades-old provisions that shielded the behavioral records of disciplined officers.

In the aftermath of that summer's turmoil, we ultimately bolstered the city's ability to fight crime and respond to emergencies while demonstrating the importance of the equity agenda. A nationwide spike in violent crime followed the pandemic, but we rebounded quickly to historic lows, and the crime rate continues to decline sharply, among the lowest per capita in big U.S. cities. By the time I left office in 2025 we had a fully funded police department focused on smarter, data-informed policing, and our violent crime rate had dropped to the lowest point in more than a decade. A new collective bargaining agreement, which was reached without the rancor of years past despite a sea change in accountability and transparency, was both enabled by and proof of increased public trust and confidence.

When summer turned to fall and fall to winter in 2020, it seemed like every time we were finally out of the woods with COVID-19, another surge or a new variant hit us broadside. I had a virtual office set up in our dining room at that point, with two computers (one for supporting documents during council sessions and one for handling the parliamentary procedures, like voting, as I presided) and an iPad (for the camera and video screen). It was basically the cockpit I sat in for countless virtual meetings, or when I was taking press interviews after hours. So there I sat as I convened our emergency operations teams—including public works, the fire and police departments, the water and energy utilities, and homeless services—to go over preparations for a cold snap we anticipated in the days leading up to Valentine's Day in 2021. While a polar vortex was descending over most of the country, meteorologists and state emergency management officials were not predicting anything out of the ordinary for our region, just freezing temperatures and precipitation, which meant that we needed to get our roadways conditioned for ice and make sure the public was getting ample warning about possible road closures. We coordinated with Texas Department of Transportation personnel and our own city crews. We were ready.

A day later forecasts predicted light snow, which is easier to deal with than ice, and when it started accumulating enough to make snow angels for the first time in more than a decade, residents were excited. Social media abounded with videos of San

Antonians playing in a local winter wonderland. There seemed to be a collective joy that had been missing ever since COVID came to town.

Then, in the dead of the night that February 13, at about 3 a.m., our full-size boxer named MuMu climbed onto the bed and curled up on my pillow, on top of my head. She woke me up, shivering, and I heard incessant electronic beeping coming from a downstairs surge protector. All of the lights were out; we had lost power. Not a big deal. It was inconvenient, to be sure, but I was confident that our CPS Energy utility crews would be able to get electricity on in short order, as usual. I grabbed my cell phone from the nightstand to check how widespread the outages were, and that's when I realized there was a problem. Just after 2 a.m. the Electric Reliability Council of Texas (ERCOT), a governor-appointed entity that manages the energy system for 90 percent of the state's population, had gone from Threat Level 1 to Threat Level 3 in a matter of minutes. Basically statewide electrical capacity plummeted so rapidly that reserves were not enough to meet demand for an indefinite amount of time, and ERCOT was forcing utilities across the state to reduce usage, which meant shutting off circuits. Within moments 4 million Texas households—370,000 in San Antonio—were without power as temperatures dropped into the single digits. The snow was coming down in sheets. Everything was shut down, even some local cell towers. Winter Storm Uri had arrived with a size and fury we had not seen in Texas in a long time.

For several hours I could not get information in or out. By sunrise, in order to prevent total collapse of the energy grid, ERCOT had demanded more reductions, extending blackouts across the state. Circuits that included hospitals and the San Antonio Water System (SAWS) pumping stations were shut down throughout San Antonio, as water pressure dropped so low that water was no longer flowing in several areas of the city. When I was finally able to place a phone call around midmorning Monday, we were able to assess the situation, and it was dire: electricity was out for a large portion of the area's residents and across the state, and there was no estimate for when it would be restored. We wouldn't be thawing out for several days; temperatures were expected to remain in the low teens and even single digits. With our emergency response team, we held an impromptu media call to relay what we knew about the situation, and I headed downtown to my office, where there would be backup power so I could oversee emergency operations and communicate consistently with area residents.

Within the next seventy-two hours it went from bad to worse. There was no relief from the cold, and pipes were bursting in homes across the city. Frustrations went through the roof as people naturally looked to assign blame. I knew there would be plenty of time for that, so I stayed focused on what we needed in the immediate term. Because we were still in the midst of our COVID response, the connective tissue between our city, county, emergency response, and social service teams was in good shape. In addition to starting regular press updates and public communications through every channel available (including door-to-door), by Tuesday we were up and running with a mass shelter at the convention center, along with food and water distributions throughout the city. The military commanders at Joint Base San Antonio deployed their personnel to help us, and scenes we had become too familiar with during COVID played out again, this time against a backdrop of snow: families lined up, cars for as far as the eye could see, relying on their San Antonio neighbors to get the basic necessities to keep their families going. Community health workers and other volunteers conducted wellness checks on senior living facilities, and we moved several people to safer shelter, including some who had lost power to their critical medical equipment. I teamed up with businessman and philanthropist Gordon Hartman once again, along with the San Antonio Area Foundation, to create an emergency fund to help residents with basic plumbing repairs.

It wasn't until Thursday that we saw a glimmer of hope.

ERCOT's rolling blackouts had finally stopped, so all of the electrical capacity CPS Energy could muster was staying in our service area to power up residents' homes rather than going to other parts of the state. By the weekend the vast majority of the city was up and running, as crews continued to make repairs to some severely damaged lines and circuits. That's when the heart-wrenching stories about what families endured during Winter Storm Uri really began to emerge from all across the state. A Houston area man died from hypothermia as he slept in his truck to keep warm. A woman in Austin froze to death after she slipped on her icy driveway and was unable to get up. Dozens died from loss of power to critical medical equipment and from carbon monoxide poisoning as they tried to use their vehicles for warmth.

Uri turned out to be one of the worst natural disasters in Texas history: 246 lives were lost across the state, including 16 in Bexar County, and the economic damage was estimated to be between $80 billion and $130 billion. A University of Houston report found that 69 percent of Texans lost power for an average of forty-two hours during the storm, many for far longer than that. It was no surprise that the public, already reeling from twelve months of COVID disruptions, was livid and looking for people to blame. As details emerged about what had transpired as the lights went out in Texas, I was livid too.

More than a decade's worth of empty political rhetoric on emergency preparedness and weatherization in the state, coupled with lack of enforcement, came home to roost when Uri arrived. After a smaller winter storm in 2011 knocked out power in parts of the state, the legislature passed toothless laws requiring electricity market operators (particularly natural gas producers and distributors, which account for the majority of Texas energy) to be fortified for cold weather, leaving the Public Utility Commission—appointed by the governor and responsible for implementing those laws—ineffectual to prevent a future weather-induced shutdown. Coincidentally, according to the Texas Ethics Commission, oil and gas companies spend between twenty and thirty million each year lobbying Texas lawmakers for favorable legislation. As Uri tightened its grip on the state, gas turbines, storage facilities, and other equipment froze up, and more than a third of electricity the state expected to generate from gas was knocked offline.

To make matters worse, we later learned that in the days leading up to the storm, many natural gas operators began spiking their wholesale prices by as much as 16,000 percent in anticipation of increased demand from local utility companies like CPS Energy—versus an only 39 percent increase on average in the rest of the country (they say everything is bigger in Texas). An investor earnings call during the week of the storm painted a clear picture of who was getting rich while Texans froze: "This week is like hitting the jackpot with some of these incredible prices," said Roland Burns, chief financial officer of Comstock Resources, a Texas gas producer owned by Dallas billionaire and Cowboys owner Jerry Jones. "I mean, frankly, we were able to sell at super-premium prices for a material amount of production." A few weeks later the Dallas Cowboys gave an NFL record $66 million signing bonus to its quarterback, part of a $160 million contract extension.

ERCOT, charged with regulating the market price of electricity and ensuring adequate power generation on the grid, accomplished neither. As the winter storm accelerated and capacity was forecasted to be tight, they simply raised wholesale rates to the maximum allowed by law (from around thirty dollars per megawatt hour to *nine thousand* per megawatt hour) in an attempt to lower demand. Electric companies, captive in the Texas energy market and connected to the state's grid, had no choice but to pay these prices if they wanted to make sure they had enough power to keep their customers' lights on through the storm. But ERCOT's plan didn't work; blackouts rolled across the state anyway, and instead they left prices artificially inflated for several days. Even Governor Abbott recognized that his agency had failed spectacularly, saying that "they downplayed the severity of [the storm and its impacts], at the same time telling me and the public that they were fully prepared for it."

When the dust settled, nearly every member of the ERCOT board had resigned by summer and the CEO was terminated. The Texas chairwoman of the Public Utility Commission stepped down under pressure as well. The independent market monitor appointed to oversee ERCOT concluded that the council had failed in its responsibility to control the market, resulting in sixteen billion dollars in electricity overcharges when prices were kept artificially high. It recommended that the charges be reversed, but the Public Utility Commission declined to do that, saying it would be too complicated to correct. In an interview with Bloomberg News, I said that the actions of inept regulators resulted in "the most massive wealth transfer in Texas history. Energy market participants took full advantage of the declared disaster, or did not take the appropriate steps to stop the exorbitant and unconscionable prices." I promised that we would fight on behalf of our own residents and those across the state. That fight continues in the courts.

A handful of Texas energy utilities companies declared bankruptcy in the aftermath of Uri, and to this day CPS Energy is still litigating against gas companies in an attempt to keep its residents from having to pay the full cost of Texas's energy market freezing them to death. So far, although details have not been disclosed since cases are ongoing, several settlements have been reached, chipping away at the public's overall financial burden. A separate lawsuit against ERCOT over their sixteen-billion-dollar mistake was dismissed by the seven-member Texas Supreme Court, which ruled that ERCOT is a government agency and is immune from lawsuits. Four members of the court at the time were appointed by Governor Abbott. Convenient.

In the immediate aftermath I also wanted to assure the public that we would look inward to find out where failures occurred locally. "It is our duty to report to the community how our emergency response operations and public utilities got into this situation and what can be done to prepare better for the future," I said. "Our community deserves answers." I appointed a Select Committee on Emergency Preparedness to conduct a thorough investigation into the city and our utilities' emergency response to Uri and report back to the public what we could do to be better prepared in the future. The committee was chaired by Reed Williams, a former oil and gas executive who had served two distinguished terms on the city council. Among their recommendations: CPS Energy should reconfigure "critical circuits" so that essential facilities (like water pumping stations) would not be subject to rolling blackouts ordered by ERCOT; the city should establish resiliency hubs throughout the area where residents can go for shelter and supplies during a crisis; and the public utilities should work together to identify locations for large-scale generators to be used during a prolonged outage. The full report was delivered publicly to the city council and to the boards of CPS Energy and SAWS, each of which incorporated the recommendations into their operations.

Predictably, the effects of Uri kicked climate science denialism into high gear in Texas, as conservative lawmakers and the governor suggested that overdependence on solar and wind energy led to the loss of power. In subsequent legislative sessions, under the guise of grid resiliency, the state adopted new subsidies and reduced regulations for oil, gas, and coal energy while pushing restrictions on renewables. But the facts were clear: the Texas electrical grid suffered a massive market manipulation and failure, and lack of regulatory enforcement led to the loss of capacity from every energy segment the state was relying on, most specifically natural gas. Even ERCOT was smart enough not to plan on solar and wind power during overnight hours (when the grid failed) because—go figure—there's no sunlight, and minimal wind, at night. Blaming renewables was just dumb, but these types of climate change–induced challenges and crises are here to stay if we keep doing dumb things.

Each time a new crisis hit, it brought San Antonio's existing vulnerabilities—many of which we knew about and were working to address—into sharper relief. Uri did too. On the first day of my tenure as mayor, just weeks after President Trump formally declared that the United States would withdraw from the Paris Agreement of 2015, I signed the resolution—approved by the city council—that committed San Antonio to the local goals of the accord and commenced work on our first Climate Action and Adaptation Plan (CAAP). I also agreed to serve as a member of the steering committee of the bipartisan Climate Mayors network, which represented nearly four hundred cities across the country that were committed to similar efforts. With technical assistance and funding from Bloomberg Philanthropies, we worked through the next two years to create a plan that was actionable and affordable—not just a bunch of platitudes.

By then Michael Bloomberg was special envoy to the United Nations and, using his vast network and resources, was helping cities solve some of their most complex challenges by bringing mayors together with leading international experts in infrastructure planning, finance, climate mitigation, and countless other fields. Programs like the City Leadership Initiative, the City Data Alliance, the Local Infrastructure Hub, and the American Cities Climate Challenge proved invaluable to us. Bloomberg paid a visit to me in San Antonio, where we held a press conference in early 2019 to talk about the importance of climate change to our residents' health and pocketbooks. "This is one of the fastest growing big cities in the nation. You are growing your economy, and you're investing in sustainability, which I think is very smart," he said. "Mayors get it, even though the White House clearly does not. But you can have responsible climate action and economic growth at the same time."

The CAAP was finally ratified in October 2019, and despite significant controversy and pushback initially from some business associations surrounding its targets and strategies (carbon neutrality in 2050, accelerated use of renewables in CPS Energy's portfolio, introduction of mass transit, and elimination of urban "heat islands"), the plan's most powerful aspect was in the first few pages. The same vulnerable communities that were at the heart of our work to address San Antonio's history of disinvestment and socioeconomic inequity—lower-income families, elderly and isolated residents, those with limited access to basic services because of language or other barriers—were also the ones most adversely impacted by both climate change and the actions intended to mitigate it.

Winter Storm Uri underscored all of that. Lower-income families who lived in poorer neighborhoods were more likely to have lost income during the pandemic, so energy bills that had already started piling up got even worse as residents tried to keep older, often poorly weatherized homes warm during the freeze. The cumulative health impacts, especially since those families had far less access to adequate medical care, were devastating during the pandemic and now, as the winter storm roiled Texas. Once we showed that we could meet our CAAP goals affordably (in fact, it would be less costly than inaction), even some of the sharpest critics got on board, albeit reluctantly.

Uri reinforced the CAAP's urgency and compelled us to push forward. More extreme weather at both ends of the spectrum (heat waves have become more prolonged and intense in the summer as well), regardless of the cause politicians assigned, was taking a toll on our city and its people. And while we didn't have a clear line of sight on every long-term strategy needed to reach our aspirational goals, I was confident that the public would be behind us on increasingly aggressive actions as long as the costs weren't dumped onto already struggling families. After all, it's hard to be resolute about tomorrow's cleaner air, a more resilient grid, and better built homes if you can't afford to feed your kids today. "We don't have to choose between the protection of our environment and the strength of our economy," I said at my mayoral campaign announcement in 2016. The ensuing five years proved that true; in fact, we could either do both or none at all.

The backbone of those efforts would always be our public utilities, CPS Energy and SAWS, and there were many board meetings where I reminded my fellow trustees that the public were our utility owners, not simply our customers. (CPS trustees are nominated by the board and ratified by the city council, while SAWS trustees are nominated and approved by the council; the mayor serves as ex officio on both.) Therefore resiliency was not just my priority as mayor; I was entrusted by voters to make sure we got it done, affordably.

As the first shadows of Uri began to fade, CPS Energy, under the leadership of its new CEO Rudy Garza, spent the next two years pulling itself out of the ditch. It formed a partnership with SAWS and CEO Robert Puente on large-scale generators that would provide emergency power to critical water facilities during an outage while also sending additional energy to the rest of the Texas grid if ERCOT requested it. An advisory committee of citizens that I pushed trustees to form in 2019, also chaired by Reed Williams, worked with CPS Energy executives to create a balanced generation plan that aligned with the CAAP and shored up its long-term finances, which had taken a significant hit during the pandemic and the winter storm.

Since then, the utility has been transformed. San Antonio became the state's top solar producer (fifth in the country), CPS acquired additional natural gas and nuclear reserves to stay ahead of a sharp rise in demand, and the utility has made significant investments in battery storage along with a second phase of the successful Save for Tomorrow Energy Plan (STEP) that conserved more than 800 megawatts of electricity in the previous decade, the equivalent of an entire energy plant. The second phase of STEP, now called the Sustainable Tomorrow Energy Plan, aims to conserve another 410 megawatts by 2027, weatherizing sixteen thou-

Shaking hands with President Joe Biden at a dinner hosted by Biden and First Lady Jill Biden, the White House, Washington, D.C., April 2023.

sand homes along the way and reducing carbon emissions by 1.85 million tons. These milestones were all part of the community-driven plan that trustees formally approved in 2022, in which CPS Energy will end its use of coal by 2028, nearly three decades ahead of schedule, lowering emissions and saving substantial money. As a result, in the face of great uncertainty in the energy industry, CPS is among the best prepared electric and gas utilities in the country and San Antonio residents continue to have some of the lowest energy bills among the nation's big cities, less than any other major city in Texas.

Meanwhile the city council approved an annual fund, using its dividend revenue from CPS Energy, to execute additional CAAP strategies such as reducing the urban heat island effect through cool pavement coatings and improving energy efficiency at area schools. And since we secured voter approval in November 2020 to (finally!) improve public transportation, President Joe Biden included in consecutive annual budgets the federal match funding necessary for construction of VIA's green and silver Advanced Rapid Transit lines, making up the north-south and east-west backbone of the city's first bona fide mass transit system. Construction has begun, and the first portion (the green line) is set to open in 2027. This was a key pillar of our CAAP strategy and the work to improve physical and economic mobility in San Antonio.

Indeed, the November 2020 election was an important moment in our efforts to reverse cycles of poverty in San Antonio. I asked the city council to send three separate propositions to the ballot that would redirect how we spent a portion of sales tax already being collected by the city. All three focused on creating a more equitable and resilient economic foundation for our community that could withstand future crises. Proposition A asked voters to extend the Pre-K 4 SA early childhood education program for another eight years and expand eligibility to three-year-olds and middle-income families. Results of the first eight years were conclusive: Pre-K 4 SA earned plaudits nationally for improving long-term social and learning skills—particularly reading and math—for the thousands of participating students since the program launched in 2013. Proposition A passed with 73 percent of the vote.

Proposition B, San Antonio Ready to Work, was approved by 77 percent of voters. It called for roughly two hundred million of future sales tax collections to be invested in workforce training to help thousands of adult workers train for and get placed into higher-paying jobs in a variety of in-demand sectors, including manufacturing, construction, technology, and health care. After four years of sales tax collection for Ready to Work, with voter approval of proposition C (by 67 percent), a portion of sales tax revenue would be dedicated to VIA's new transit operations. Most training is conducted by designated providers like the Alamo Colleges, Workforce Solutions Alamo, Restore Education, and the nationally acclaimed program Project QUEST, which was created more than thirty years ago in San Antonio and provided a model for Ready to Work. The providers also conduct career counseling and job placement while connecting individual participants with wraparound support they might need to complete training successfully. Two years into the program nearly ten thousand people had enrolled in training—some of them for professional certifications like welding or vocational nursing and others for degrees like data science. Nearly three thousand had completed training, and more than two thousand have been placed in new jobs.

It wasn't all smooth sailing with Ready to Work. With any publicly funded program, there is a natural inclination to judge its impact by fixating on the scale of impact, and by that measure, two years into the program, Ready to Work was falling short of our initial expectations. I made the mistake of repeating analysts' early estimates of how many people could be trained with four years' worth of sales tax revenues. They estimated that it would be enough for ten thousand trainees per year of funding, and they assumed that given the scale of the problem, the resources would be spent as fast as they came in. But for prospective participants life wasn't so simple, and the program started frustratingly slowly; the numbers were far below estimates in the first year of implementation. We hired Mike Ramsey, a workforce development expert from Tampa, Florida, to coordinate the program's advisory board, community advocates, training providers, and businesses, and quickly learned that it takes longer and is much harder to assist each individual through the program, from initial assessment to completion of training to placement in a new job. After all, we are dealing with real people with real lives and unique challenges that lock them into a cycle that leads to underemployment and, often, poverty. The program's initial slow pace was not because its operation was moving too slowly; it was because life—specifically, changing the circumstances of life for people enduring poverty—didn't move so fast.

But that's where Ready to Work comes in. Like Alamo Promise, which is now available to every high school graduate in the area and provides wraparound support to help with life's unexpected challenges so students can stay focused on completing their degrees, the real power of Ready to Work is not what happens in the classroom but rather what happens outside the classroom to help participants stay in it. "Life be lifin'," I heard one counselor say as she described a Ready to Work participant who was faced with the choice of dropping out or getting another job to help her sick mother, who she took care of, pay for her medicine. Participants are trying to improve their lives while life's difficulties are coming at them full speed. Breaking that cycle—staying in training and on track to a better job and a life free from the impossible decisions that poverty presents—could simply hinge on connecting a single parent with childcare if she has children at home, making sure she's getting medical care for her mother's illness, or helping with a car repair.

With a year's worth of real-time experience in what trainees need to be successful, the estimate of how many people would be served was revised to twenty-eight thousand over the life of the Ready to Work program. Because some training lasts two months while other training could last two years, and because the average job placement takes less than two months but some industries take painfully longer than that, it will take approximately eight years to reach those total numbers. Critics use those differences from the original estimates like a bludgeon. "Mayor Ron Nirenberg Urges Patience for Ready to Work, as Program Crawls Forward," read one headline from the *Express-News*. "Tax-Funded Ready to Work Falls Short on Key Jobs Goal," read another. It was a constant drumbeat.

Here's the thing: civic leaders, activists, pundits, and journalists in every city in America like to talk about poverty. Some like to study it. A few even campaign on it. It's usually used as a backdrop to describe what ails a community. Rarely, however, do we see an earnest effort to do much about it. And in my view, if we

With U.S. Department of Labor secretary Marty Walsh at a Ready to Work roundtable discussion in San Antonio, August 2022. Photo by Joey Palacios, Texas Public Radio.

are sincere in wanting to break cycles of poverty, we should either do something about it or stop talking about it. Ready to Work, Alamo Promise, and the other pillars of our approach to creating pathways to economic independence and mobility—like public transportation and housing—are doing something about it. We have been told by officials at the U.S. Department of Labor, who took an interest in Ready to Work and made additional investments in the program, that it is the single largest investment a local community has made in workforce development in our nation's history. Both former U.S. secretary of labor Marty Walsh and his successor, Julie Su, became fervent champions of our efforts. Because San Antonio is a community that stands together time and again when the lives of our neighbors are on the line, I believe there is not a city in America that needs a program like this more or that is more poised to make it a success.

After all of the handwringing about numbers and whether Ready to Work met expectations, this is what I do know: When we can help one person acquire the skills necessary to get a better job with a better wage, she no longer has to work two or three extra jobs to make ends meet and instead can spend time with her children, help them with homework, nurture them. Imagine what that means for those children when they grow up. Statistically, we already know they are much more likely to grow up and fulfill their own educational goals and get a better job with a better wage, as will their children after that. Just as the cycle of poverty expands from one generation to another, breaking that cycle for one person has an impact that expands generation after generation. Communities are healthier, safer, and more prosperous. And that's good for every resident.

I say "she" and "her" because while there is no "average" story when dealing with real people and real lives, the "average" Ready to Work participant (based on intake data) is a single mom raising children in a household with income of less than fourteen thousand a year. When she finishes the training program and gets placed into a job, she has a career-building credential and earns forty-four thousand a year. With benefits. (A job only meets Ready to Work standards if it is full-time, pays a living wage, and comes with benefits like health insurance, standards that are being met by all nine-hundred-plus employers who have already hired our graduates.)

Take, for instance, the case of Patricia Saldivar-Lopez, as recounted in the September 2023 Ready to Work newsletter. At fifty-seven years old, she was heading back to work and a life of financial independence after a decade of caring for her ailing mother as well as a husband who had undergone liver transplant surgery. She applied to Ready to Work after seeing it advertised on Facebook, a decision that changed her life, and she went on to obtain her certificate from Texas A&M–San Antonio, a partner in the program. As Saldivar-Lopez commented,

> Ready to Work helped me build my self-esteem while at the same time giving me the opportunity to make better money and support my family.... There was a light at the end of the tunnel for going back to work and getting out of low income status. Now I'm excited to be able to take family vacations once in a while, go out to eat, go to the movies—simple things that I couldn't do before. When you're on a limited income, it all goes toward bills, so the last part of the month we really struggled. Things like going out to eat will be a real treat and luxury for us now.

Saldivar-Lopez's story is just one of many like it, and as of the time of writing this book, three years into the Ready to Work program, there are thousands more.

When I think about Ready to Work, I imagine what a neighborhood will look like decades from now if we are able to break the cycle of poverty for ten families who live there, or what a district will look like if we can break the cycle for a hundred families. I think a lot about what our city will look like thirty years from now if we can break the cycle of poverty for ten thousand families or more. And when I hear complaints about the numbers, I remind myself of what Jonah asked me each day when I started ("Have you made the world a better place?"), and how I thought I should measure success by what kind of city we'd leave our children when they are our age, thirty years from now.

We will keep the program for as long as there is funding available for it. By current estimates, since the sales tax revenue shifts permanently to fund VIA's mass transit system in 2026, we still have a few years of funding left to sustain the program, after which time I am hopeful that the ecosystem of workforce training we've built in San Antonio—the connections between training providers and businesses, career counselors, and prospective participants—will be maintained by future leaders. Hopefully they will continue these generational investments that are transformational in their impact. It's hard work—excruciatingly slow for critics who are still counting widgets. But breaking the cycle of poverty for one family is far less expensive than the social assistance they'll need now and in the future, if we don't.

I'm proud that today, as a result of public support and our residents' belief in the potential of each person in our community, San Antonio has one of the best coordinated and resourced education and workforce pipelines in the country, from the youngest children in pre-K to every high school graduate in the county to adults who need training for a good-paying career. We have created a pathway to a good job for any San Antonio resident who seeks a better future, and we will be there to help them navigate it every step of the way. We are helping businesses fill jobs and industries grow, and at the same time we're helping families reach independence and fulfill their version of the American Dream.

Because San Antonio is a community that stands together time and again when the lives of our neighbors are on the line, I believe the city needs programs like these, and we are poised to make them a success. That was demonstrated yet again in May 2021, only three months after we thawed out from the trauma of Winter Storm Uri. I was up for reelection to a third term, and the circumstances were much different this time around. Over the course of two years, navigating San Antonio through some of the most challenging times of our lives, I knew I had earned the trust of the community. Brockhouse came back to mount a nominal challenge that I largely ignored, and on election night I was reelected with 62 percent of the vote.

On the same ballot, voters also approved a change to the city charter, paving the way for the city's first-ever affordable housing bond ($150 million), which they approved a year later in 2022. Safe, affordable housing was becoming increasingly out of reach in our city, and I had formed the Mayor's Housing Policy Task Force just a few weeks into my first term five years prior so that we could start down the path of addressing that most fundamental aspect of family economic stability.

VOICES OF SAN ANTONIO

Edward Whitacre Jr.

Most citizens like me are aware of the issues affecting their city, but they don't know all of the details. We want to trust our elected officials to handle these matters because they are supposed to understand the specifics and facts. Our trust in them is earned by their leadership and the results they accomplish. The mayor's job in a city as large and varied as San Antonio is complex, with challenging issues such as budgets, sports franchises, labor negotiations, immigration, infrastructure maintenance, and, perhaps most importantly, the unexpected, such as the COVID-19 pandemic that hit us in 2020. The list could go on and on.

How did Ron Nirenberg score on the trust and leadership scale? How effective was he as mayor of the seventh-largest city in the country? I give him a solid A grade.

In addition to the issues I mentioned, he did a very good job managing the utilities infrastructure, including electricity and water demands in an extreme climate, as well as changes in the makeup of the city council and the city manager's office, labor issues, and engaging with groups and businesses across the political spectrum. He considered a multitude of factors and was not afraid to make hard decisions when necessary, especially those that would contribute to the city's long-term health and growth. And he did all of this while keeping the San Antonio community well informed. His decisions overall showed compassion and thoughtful concern for the city and its citizens.

EDWARD WHITACRE JR. is the former chairman and CEO of General Motors and the former chairman, CEO, and president of AT&T.

Those plans turned into actions as San Antonio voters reaffirmed our commitment with the most significant steps needed to implement the ten-year housing plan. We are well ahead of schedule in stabilizing, by 2031, a total of ninety-five thousand households experiencing housing insecurity. We are rehabilitating what we can and producing what we need, in partnership with nonprofits and the private sector. In the first three years of the effort, we completed production and preservation of more than five thousand homes, with another four thousand in progress. Not bad for a community that leveraged our own Emergency Rental Assistance program (created by the housing policy framework)—the most successful in the nation—to keep sixty-five thousand families from becoming homeless during the pandemic.

While homelessness has only worsened around the country after all of the economic upheaval, the rate of unsheltered homelessness in San Antonio has been cut in half since 2019. That's in large part thanks to voter-approved efforts to fill gaps in our homeless response system, including the construction of permanent supportive housing and low-barrier shelter that seeks to get people in a safe place first so that they can begin to rebuild their lives and ultimately become independent.

As I look back at my tenure, riddled with crisis after crisis, I'm proud that we were able to navigate through those troubled waters while staying on course to become a city where every family, regardless of their circumstances, has an opportunity to thrive. We haven't reached that destination yet, but I'm more confident than ever that we have found the right path and that the adversity we experienced together was fuel to make us more resilient and determined to reach our shared goals.

REFLECTIONS

In October 2023 I got a call from my brother, Marc, that my mom had been taken by ambulance to the hospital. She inexplicably lost her balance, fell at home, and was unable to get up. It wasn't the first call I'd received like that. She had suffered a massive heart attack in 2018 that forced her to quit a lifelong smoking habit. (Very few people knew I was dealing with that in my first term.) With a new grandchild on the way—my sister, Heather, had just announced that she was having a son, Miles, in the spring—my mom began a daily walking routine and started eating better. But despite that fact that she was a relatively young seventy-one years old, her health was noticeably declining.

Within two weeks she was given a terminal diagnosis: stage four renal cell cancer that had metastasized to her brain. The doctors said she might live two months or, with aggressive treatment, possibly another two years. We were devastated. My mom had lived under a cloud for years, struggling with depression as her kids started their own lives and moved away, and she was still missing her own family in Massachusetts, even after we left them behind decades ago. When Granny and Granpappy and then her younger brother, Conrad, all passed away in the early 2000s, her loneliness intensified. She often struggled to hide her anguish, occasionally lashing out at the people she loved the most: Marc, Heather, and me.

My mom briefly tried radiation treatment, but because there was no progress—only more discomfort—she discontinued it and focused on spending as much time with us as possible and keeping comfortable. I saw a side of my family in the months before she passed that I had been too distracted to see before. For a few hours each week, the focal point of my life as a public servant seemed to shift from the foreground to the background, where it was before I came to San Antonio, before I got married, before the gravity of career and fatherhood made me a more serious man. I saw how honorable Marc had become as an adult, a devoted father to three daughters and several grandchildren, and now the son who spent every last bit of remaining time and energy on ensuring that our mom's final days on earth were lived with dignity. I saw the same look that my mom used to give us in Heather's eyes when she watched her daughter Izzy run around the nursing home.

During that time I also learned that dying with dignity is a luxury afforded to too few people in this country. My mom's final months were spent in a nursing facility, with her only social connection—aside from Marc, Heather, and me—being with nurses and hospice care workers, some of whom tried harder than others to create a meaningful relationship with someone they knew was only waiting for the inevitable hour. And that was with three adult children navigating the maze of insurance, providers, and Medicare almost daily. I recalled how depressed my grandfather, Papa Bernie, had become after Nana Ida passed away and he moved to a nursing home in Massachusetts. Into his eighties Papa Bernie had a wry, gracious humor and never hesitated to express affection for his family. But when he was confined to the four walls of his room, his mind began to fade, and his spirit did too.

In the last few weeks before my mom died, she stopped communicating with words, but I brought a radio to her room and we played her favorite Cliff Richard songs around the clock. I often drove to Austin to sit at her bedside and hold her hand as she slept for a couple of hours. Then I drove home to San Antonio, where my final lap as mayor had just begun.

With ten years (four on council and six as mayor) under my belt and my agenda finally being implemented, I didn't draw any serious competitors in the May 2023 election, which would be my fourth and final mayoral term because of term limits. In that decade of work I had visited with hundreds of thousands of San Antonians, learned about their hopes for their families and their community, the things that concerned them, what they feared, and what got them inspired. I was overcome by a feeling similar to when Erika and I brought a newborn Jonah home. Almost instantly the center of life—the life purpose you feel in your bones—shifts from self to them. I devoted my days and nights—all of my energy—to leaving San Antonio a better place when the next mayor was elected in 2025.

I was poised to be the longest-serving mayor of San Antonio since Henry Cisneros, but each time I visited Austin I was back to being Charlotte's son and saying goodbye to the first person I ever had contact with in this world. It was mid-May 2024, and my mom squeezed my hand as Cliff Richard's "Visions" played in the background.

> When will we meet again?
> When? When? When?
> I remember the days, beautiful days

"This is heaven," she said faintly. Her eyes remained closed. These were the first words I had heard her speak in a couple of weeks. I'm not sure if she was conscious. A week later she was gone. In the obituary we noted that "in place of flowers, the family asks for tributes that honor Nirenberg's lifelong advice to her children: 'Be good to each other and love each other. And throw some Cliff Richard on the record player.'"

My mom taught me to be passionate about life and how you choose to spend it, even in her final days. It was with that spirit—

and my father's constant guidance "to thine own self be true" and to always be a statesman—that I approached my time as mayor through the last moments of my final term in June 2025. I firmly believe that to be a public servant is to run your leg of a relay race as far and as fast as possible before you hand it off to your successor. The race never ends, but if you are doing your job, the aspirations of the families you serve continue to rise higher and higher, just beyond your reach.

"What work did you leave unfinished?" a reporter recently asked me, referring to my time in San Antonio politics.

"All of it," I said.

That's the truth. San Antonio is now on a steady upward trajectory, its growth reflective of a city where people want to raise their children and where businesses see opportunities to invest. There is a palpable optimism about the future of the city. It's illustrated by enthusiasm for projects like the San Antonio International Airport redevelopment, which is—at long last—under construction after I launched the work in 2017 to end a four-decade futile debate about where we should build a new airport. A new ground load terminal will be followed by a state-of-the-art international terminal in 2027. If the work continues, a second parallel runway will accelerate new connections around the world. San Antonio's airport is an "airport of the future" according to ARPA-E federal interagency efforts to pilot new airport technology for energy sustainability. Our plans for the airport include electrification of ground vehicles (and soon, aircraft), along with vertical takeoff and landing capabilities.

There is also excitement about San Antonio's future as it relates to how we are nurturing our history and heritage. One of the unique downtowns in America is getting a makeover, with the launch of mass transit that will intersect not far from where residents and visitors will walk to the River Walk or the Alamo. The redevelopment of the Alamo—aimed at reclaiming the original footprint to honor its rich history, from Indigenous communities

Flanked by city manager Erik Walsh (*left*) and airport director Jesus Saenz (*right*), breaking ground on the $1.2 billion state-of-the-art terminal at San Antonio International Airport, December 2024. Photo by Fred Gonzales, City of San Antonio.

and the 1836 Battle of the Alamo to the 1950s civil rights–era lunch counter sit-ins across the street and beyond—was started and stopped many times. The entire project nearly fell apart (again) around 2020, when redevelopment was caught in the middle of perennial debates about which versions of history (and how much) to tell. We finally got it back on track in 2021 (tell the facts and let people interpret them as they may, I said), with a delicate partnership between the city, the state of Texas, and the Alamo Trust. A new state-of-the-art visitor center and museum, along with restoration of the original buildings, will bring proper reverence and more accurate history to one of the country's most recognizable landmarks. If everything stays on track, the site will reopen in 2027. It is still the only UNESCO World Heritage site in Texas.

In 2018 we announced a partnership with the University of

Texas at San Antonio to build a downtown campus that is now bringing students, faculty, and a vibrancy that had been missing in the city's urban core since its midcentury suburban sprawl began. Academic departments, including the Center for Data Science and the nation's first College for AI, Cyber, and Computing, are being built now, along with new residential spaces, restaurants, bars, and shops. Once a forgotten little brother in the University of Texas system, as a result of its growth and achievements UTSA is recognized as a tier-one research institution by the Carnegie Classification of Institutions of Higher Education, and it is poised to be one of the country's largest universities after a merger with UT Health San Antonio, announced in 2024.

A few blocks down the street from that campus, Hemisfair—the site of the 1968 World's Fair—which has been in various stages of revisioning for the past twenty years, is the focus of our strategy to bring all of these developments together into one harmonious vision for a revitalized center city. That is the essence of Project Marvel, the name we gave to the effort that culminates with the creation of an entertainment district in the heart of downtown. It would be a new focal point for historic downtown San Antonio. The concept, which we presented publicly in late 2024, had initially started to take shape in my mind after UTSA president Taylor Eighmy first approached me and then–city manager Sheryl Sculley about a downtown campus in partnership with the city. A more holistic strategy for elevating downtown San Antonio would eventually include improved street and sidewalk infrastructure, parking, transit connections, recreational areas, residential and commercial spaces, sports and entertainment venues, and park space to bridge across Interstate 37, which divides the Alamodome from the Hemisfair area. (Like many cities that had their urban communities severed by the federal highway system years ago, San Antonio suffered a double dose of it: I-37 on the eastern edge of downtown and I-10 on the west.) Although attention has predictably focused on the proposed new Spurs arena in the middle of all

Watching the NCAA men's basketball championship game with Erika and Jonah, the Alamodome, April 2025.

of all this, Project Marvel was envisioned as a transformation of the urban core that will create reasons and ways for residents to reconnect to the city's original heart. I am hopeful that breaking down the barrier of I-37 on the east will provoke more serious conversations about doing the same with I-10 on the west side, where the highway and the county jail stand in the way.

The proposed district would be anchored by major venues, the most significant being an overhauled Alamodome capable of hosting the country's top sporting events, an upgraded Henry B. Gonzalez Convention Center, and possibly a new Spurs arena to bring the team back downtown where many residents believe they should have stayed all along.

It's a big vision, and talking about big visions publicly brings along plenty of detractors, perhaps because it's easier to point to examples of how we as a city have fallen short of our aspirations in the past. Nevertheless, leading a community, especially one that has so often gotten the short end of the stick, means being willing to bet publicly on it, take risks, and rally the community behind its own ambition for the future. I have always felt that a mayor must insist that we are worthy of our highest aspirations and not let detractors (or history) convince us that these aspirations can't be reached.

Execution is key, of course. Success builds credibility and public trust, which can lead to more success, and that has certainly been the case with the risks we took on the airport, the Alamo, public transit, and any other major initiative while I was mayor. It wouldn't have been possible without the partnership and ingenuity of our excellent city management team, led by city manager Erik Walsh. And it wouldn't have been possible if we were cavalier about the public's support. For instance, there has been significant concern about taxpayers footing the bill for sports stadiums along with the broken promises for revitalization that so often accompany them. We made it clear that a new Spurs arena—just like the much-needed new downtown ballpark for the San Antonio Missions, the Double-A affiliate of the San Diego Padres ballclub, announced in 2024—will not come at the expense of our residents' basic needs and will not be paid for by their taxes.

But beyond all of the grandiose plans, what gives me genuine optimism about the city—and our ability to turn these big visions into reality—is the fundamentals, the foundation we've laid for long-term, inclusive prosperity and the fact that San Antonio voters have resoundingly supported it. Many years ago, when four-year-old Jonah asked if I had made the world better, that's what I imagined: a community where every family could thrive, a city that didn't leave any families behind economically or otherwise. From better transit to safe, affordable neighborhoods to education and training for quality jobs that pay well, thankfully, each and every time I asked San Antonio voters to invest in their neighbors and put their faith in the future of our city (including six bond initiatives, three sales tax reallocations, and seven city charter amendments over the eight years of my tenure as mayor), they said yes, reaffirming our direction and allowing us to sustain progress. As a result, our ten-year plan for a healthy and affordable supply of housing is ahead of schedule, and starter homes being built in San Antonio are once again attainable at the average wage. Thousands of residents are training for new skills to compete for higher paying jobs (and breaking out of perpetual underemployment), while more students are going to college or entering trade schools. Public transit is faster, more reliable, and more accessible to residents who need it (or want it), and we're building and fixing roads and sidewalks (and bicycle lanes!) so that once-forgotten neighborhoods are finally getting their fair share.

Still, as I continued to remind my team and the people I serve, success in public service is not a destination that can ever be reached. There is always more work to be done, more progress to be made, more problems to be solved. In my final year as mayor I was determined to "run through the tape." Part of that was to strengthen governance by reforming several provisions in our charter, a goal that was repeatedly sidelined during my first three terms. In November 2024, despite a toxic political environment that swept out incumbents and brought Donald Trump back to power, San Antonio voters approved six transformational changes to the city charter, some of them building on reforms that Mayor Hardberger and Mayor Taylor initiated. Among the changes, term limits for future mayors and council members will go from four two-year terms to two four-year terms (so that sustained progress is not sidelined by the near-constant campaigning of two-year terms), and their pay will be indexed to area household income (so that salaries for representatives will rise only if and when the standard of living rises for local families). Voters also removed the city manager's tenure and salary caps (a byproduct of the 2014 fire union contract dispute, which handicapped us against other cities when it was time to recruit a future city manager). All of the changes faced some opposition, despite the fact that the citizen's commission I asked to examine them overwhelmingly recommended these specific reforms. Pundits and polling predicted that all six propositions were in trouble—and some were doomed to fail—but once again voters showed their confidence in the direction we were moving in San Antonio by passing all six.

During remarks to the National Legislative Conference of the National League of Cities in 1966, President Lyndon B. Johnson said, "When the burdens of the presidency seem unusually heavy, I always remind myself it could be worse—I could be a mayor of a city instead." Joking aside, he acknowledged that unlike in federal or state government, where politicians are often far removed from the consequences of poor decisions or partisan gridlock, in local government there is nowhere to hide. If a problem affecting people doesn't get solved, even if it's the responsibility of the federal government or the state house, it's the mayors and city council members who receive phone calls. Stuff rolls downhill, as they say. After his quip, Johnson offered encouragement to the audience and talked about the difficult choices local leaders had to make with limited resources: building up opportunities for working people so that the nation could "start up that long road which will place the great American city at the summit of a new stage in the life of civilized man." Mayors are their communities' last line of defense; they have to work across every aisle and every sector to come up with solutions to the problems residents face every day. Collaboration and compromise are essential and so is being anchored to the community's values. It's no wonder why, at a time when public trust in virtually all areas of government has plummeted, it remains highest in local government.

It is with that spirit, focused on the kind of world we would leave my son and his generation, that I approached my time as a public servant: Protect the public trust. Think long term. Find common ground. Lift up those who struggle and fight for the

Meeting with the Dalai Lama, along with Louisville mayor Greg Fischer, at the Dalai Lama's residence in Dharamsala, India, December 2022.

common good. It's not how I thought I'd spend my prime working years, but it became a calling. And as I wrapped up my final days as mayor—at the still (sort of) young age of forty-eight—the two most common questions I got were "What are you proudest of?" and "What's next?"

The first one was easy to answer. My highest achievement as a public servant is that I was able to make Erika and Jonah proud, in spite of the time away from them and unrelenting family sacrifices that had to be made. I frequently referred to them as my toughest constituents (except for, perhaps, my dad, when he moved to San Antonio with my stepmother, Carol, during my third term). When I thought I had all the right answers, they never failed to ground me in the values and idealism that first propelled me into the arena of politics. They remembered the promises I made, especially about

VOICES OF SAN ANTONIO

Erika Prosper

In my vows, I promised Ron to always support his dreams and to always have ice cream sandwiches in the freezer. I've kept the dreams vow alive and well. The ice cream sandwiches eventually became chicken breasts for my protein-loving hubby. He vowed to always seek my counsel before any big purchases, and I suppose buying into a new life counts as such. So I'd say that all in all we've been pretty good about keeping the promises we made on July 6, 2001.

I married my beautiful husband because he was the only person I ever knew who could make me laugh and cry at the same time. He's wickedly funny if you like puns and sharp wit. He's especially effective at being earnest, and you can't help but get sentimental when he pays attention to you. His eyes are kind, his smile is broad, and he has a dignity about him—which he had even at age twenty-two, when I first met him.

Our love story is generally well known. Boy meets girl. Boy immediately falls in love with girl. Girl not so much. Boy woos girl for months until finally she says yes. After one date girl gets smitten, and four months later they are engaged. They marry a year after that. Stuff of rom-coms. But our love story has been far from a fairy tale. Like all young couples, we grew into our own several times over and worked to navigate those changes together. Once a year we go out and update each other on our favorite color, ice cream flavor, and movie. Once a month we try to go on a date. Once a week we try to watch a movie as a family. Once a day we won't leave the house without kissing each other. And always there is the update: I am this person now. Will you still love what I am becoming?

This was especially important when Ron sat me down one day in 2012 and told me what he was becoming: a candidate for San Antonio City Council. He asked for my counsel, asked for my fears, and asked for my blessing. "If you say no, I won't do it," he declared. But I knew my vows were being tested here, maybe not by him but by my own dedication to this partnership. So I gave my counsel, I very painstakingly explained my fears, and in the end, I gave my blessing.

It has been a wild and crazy ride from there. This journey is outlined in the pages you've already read. From being a no-name dad to being mayor of one of the top ten cities in the country, my husband's journey is far from over, but a significant portion of it played out in our beautiful city of San Antonio, a city that will forever guide our outlook on resilience, compassion, and family.

In all transparency, this type of journey also had a fifty-fifty chance of ending our marriage many times over.

Our life has been fraught with long periods apart, milestones, and daily family rituals interrupted, rescheduled, or outright skipped due to meetings, emergencies, or other "I have to get this" situations. It isn't easy to be told you matter most and then be treated like you matter least among a million other residents. And it can breed resentment when you have fostered an egalitarian partnership, only to be referred to as "the wife of the mayor" at every turn. Your spirit gets trampled early on as the focus shifts entirely to who you are married to versus who you are, and your insecurities get amplified as you realize the world can now see the wondrous light within a person that you thought was reserved just for you. Yes, this journey could have indeed led to loss, but instead it gave us renewal.

Like most earth-shifting choices, my husband's political career has also been a time of great honesty and introspection for us as a family. The changes in time commitment gave birth to a realization that many of the activities we were steadfastly holding on to were based on what society expected a woman to take care of, and by extension, a First Lady. It led us to a new philosophy prioritizing boundaries over balance, and focusing on having truthful conversations about what I would no longer do to "keep face" as a wife and mother according to unspoken, outdated "rules" for women in my position. We renewed our commitments to each other in a more fluid and forgiving manner—no longer tied to quantity but quality, no longer judged by what looks right to others, and no longer just my burden to bear.

It also gave us a renewed sense of freedom as we looked at this role as mine to shape and carry out in my own way as I started to see the power of being "the wife." It opened doors to me, amplified my voice, and gave me the ability to talk to children about their worth and the importance of accepting who you are. I got to live out my own advice to them.

To be a family in elected service takes a willingness to humble yourself, to forgive, to recalibrate constantly, and to separate yourself from expectations. Yet I believe that in the losses we faced and in the regeneration of our outlook lie the strength for our family to continue serving—be it as private citizens or, if my hubby chooses, as public servants once more. At this point, after all these years, that sounds like another spirited adventure to me. So bring on the next ice cream sandwiches—and the chicken breasts!

ERIKA PROSPER is a Latina executive, mother, and farmworker, who is educated and proud, and stands next to her husband, not behind him.

being an example for Jonah. Erika always reminded me that one of the reasons I chose to run was to show how an average neighbor could make a difference. Whenever we were out together at public events, she never let me forget to greet families in the crowd and thank them for their trust. And I remember the first time Jonah said, "Dad, I'm proud of you." No accomplishment will ever top that.

While I finished my time in the mayor's office optimistic about San Antonio's future, I joined countless millions of people who are concerned about the world we are leaving to our children and grandchildren. Despite the efforts of many, we have become more divided, not less, drifting away from seeing our own well-being as intimately connected to the well-being of our neighbors, locally and abroad. Fear, anger, and hatred of other people—whether on the basis of politics, religion, nationality, race, or social status—define Trump-era politics, while the United States, the preeminent world economic and military power, has seemingly retreated from its responsibility as the model of healthy democracy for the rest of the globe. We've witnessed unchecked attacks on centuries-old democratic institutions such as the system of checks and balances and freedom of speech, the rejection of longtime global allies, and an obliteration of the guardrails preventing corruption and conflicts of interest. Embedded within the federal government, Elon Musk profits with one hand and demolished the agencies that regulate his companies with the other. Both he and the president conduct personal business openly from their positions of power, even with foreign countries, comingling our national security and diplomatic interests with their own. It's back to the Boss Tweed and Tammany Hall days.

None of this, of course, is helping the average working family. During my time in office, it became plainly evident that, regardless of who is in power, most people's priorities have not changed. They want to feel safe in their neighborhoods. They want their children to get a good education and come back home safely from their schools. They want their roads paved and their trash picked up on time. They want to know that if they put in an honest day's work, they will be rewarded with a decent wage in a job that's stable and secure. And they want to know that if there's an emergency they can count on competent systems and leaders to come to their aid, whether it's as personal as their home or health or as urgent as a natural disaster or our national security. Other than that, they just want government to stay out of their lives.

But the chaos and disorder of the second Trump administration has done exactly the opposite, causing people to feel less safe while destabilizing our economy and the global markets on which it is built, according to economists. As I write this, they have now warned that a global recession is likely. Many families are starting to wonder what will be left for them as they struggle to afford housing, groceries, insurance, and medication while sinking markets drain their savings. Others are looking for work after being laid off by employers looking to trim costs and balance budgets amid the economic instability. And then there are those who have lost confidence because of threats to veteran benefits, Social Security, Medicare and Medicaid, which they've sacrificed so much for and had been told would be there when they needed it. At the same time costs have continued to rise for families and businesses in every sector (predictably, again, as Trump initiated new tariffs and a trade war with our strongest global partners). JP Morgan reports that the costs absorbed by the average household as a result of Trump's tariff policies amount to the largest tax increase since 1968. Meanwhile social safety nets that had been there for struggling families have been dismantled through funding cuts and culture wars being waged against diversity, equity, and inclusion. As if those are bad things.

Here in Texas, where Republicans have held every statewide office along with a majority in the House and Senate for three decades, state leaders have waged their own culture wars, seeking to undo equal opportunity protections, women's health care rights, voting access, and a host of other individual liberties that Republicans used to embrace. While Texas has seen record surpluses year after year, they've managed to underfund public schools (now ranked in the country's bottom ten states for per-pupil spending) and the health system—both core responsibilities of the state. In 2024 Texas ranked forty-eighth in the nation in overall child health, according to the Annie E. Casey Foundation, and had the highest rate of uninsured children and adults. It was also among the bottom ten states in terms of educational attainment.

The question of what's next has never been easy to answer and always requires a lot of meditation and prayer. I feel pretty confident about two things: that my life will still be about service and

Meeting with Claudia Sheinbaum, mayor of Mexico City (elected president of Mexico in 2024), to sign a friendship city agreement, in 2019.

that there will still be problems to solve. What I have learned from being raised in Austin, raising my own family in San Antonio, and eventually being entrusted to lead my community through the most difficult of times is that when people have hope for a better future, they will bind themselves together as neighbors to try to achieve it. In San Antonio, time and again, when we have identified problems to be solved, we have worked together as one team to solve them.

While my plate was always full from the first to the last day as mayor, I added initiatives I believed would bring people together and build trust, bridging political, social, cultural, and even geographic divides. Together with mayors across the Rio Grande

Valley, we founded the South Texas Alliance of Cities, an organization devoted to advocating collectively for our often overlooked communities. As chairman of Sister Cities International, and a member of the U.S. State Department's Assembly of Local Leaders (which includes twenty-one mayors and governors), I leaned into the role cities play in creating people-to-people exchanges that foster civic, educational, and cultural partnerships and pave the way for business development. I led delegations to all of San Antonio's own sister cities and signed new sister city agreements in Germany, the Philippines, Mexico, Canada, and Spain.

Building on the first document I signed as mayor in 2017—San Antonio's Charter for Compassion—with the guidance of my friend Rev. Ann Helmke and backed by our city's interfaith community, we launched Compassionate USA, an education curriculum that has been adopted by organizations and communities across the globe and is aimed at fostering opportunities to bridge differences and treat each other with respect. Not everyone who disagrees with us is an enemy. We can be firm in our values and still learn from each other. No one has to wait for "what's next" to do their part to change the nature of our public discourse and model how we find common cause despite our differences. We can start working on that today.

When the days got toughest and it was hard to stay positive, I frequently returned to a phrase made famous by Martin Luther King Jr. during a 1965 speech in Selma: "The arc of the moral universe is long, but it bends toward justice." It was timeless encouragement to keep moving forward, especially in the fight for equity and giving people a seat at the table. I later learned that King took his inspiration from Theodore Parker, a minister and abolitionist, who wrote in an 1853 sermon, titled "Of Justice and the Conscience," "I do not pretend to understand the moral universe, the arc is a long one, my eye reaches but little ways. I cannot calculate the curve and complete the figure by the experience of sight; I can

Riding through the streets of San Antonio in the Fiesta Battle of Flowers Parade with Erika and Jonah, April 2024. Photo by Jonathan Alonzo.

divine it by conscience. But from what I see, I am sure it bends toward justice. Things refuse to be mismanaged long."

In my life, I have been blessed to be a husband, a father, and a public servant. I do not know what the future holds, and perhaps by the time this book is published it will become more clear. But with whatever remaining time God gives me along the arc, I will keep bending it.

ACKNOWLEDGMENTS

The idea for this book emerged from a brainstorming session at a local restaurant. My coauthor, David Lesch, arranged and moderated these sessions, which were held on a fairly regular basis since my initial campaign for mayor in early 2017. David has an eclectic group of friends, so these small gatherings—typically consisting of a diverse group of eight to twelve business leaders, academics, and community leaders from around San Antonio and across the political spectrum—were fertile ground for spirited discussions about current events in our community and our world. At these dinner meetings we loosely followed an agenda David and I put together that was relevant to matters important to the city at the time. Even though these sessions usually came at the end of a long day at work and lasted late into the night, I relished them and always looked forward to the open and frank discussions. The group of really smart people enjoyed testing my preparation and ability to defend issue and policy positions. Luckily I'm always up for a challenging debate and enjoy being in the hot seat.

At the end of one of these sessions, in late 2019, a number of months after my (heavily contested) first reelection as mayor, David approached me about writing a memoir or biography about my life and political career. At first I balked, saying that I had not done anything to warrant a book-length treatment. David scoffed and said that I was being much too humble and that I had accomplished more than I thought. He added that a book like this would take at least a couple of years to write and publish, so there was plenty of time for more material to emerge.

The idea for the book soon took a backseat, however, as our world—locally and globally—was plunged into one crisis after another, from the pandemic to a reckoning on race relations after the murder of George Floyd to a winter storm that knocked out the entire state. A lot of life happened to me during those turbulent months, as a mayor, a husband, and a father. In late 2022 David approached me again about the book, saying somewhat facetiously, "How about now, Ron?" Of course, he was asking me after I had navigated the city through some of the toughest, most complicated times in its history, and by then I had more than enough material for a book.

The next big question was who would help me write it. I hadn't written anything of comparable length since my master's thesis at the Annenberg School for Communication at the University of Pennsylvania. And with my full schedule as mayor, I definitely needed help—and guidance. David and I discussed a number of writers as possibilities, but after going through the list and making a couple of inquiries, I decided to ask David instead. In all honestly, this is who I wanted to cowrite the book all along, and I was thrilled that he agreed to help me. Not only is David an accomplished academic and author, having published seventeen books, but I trusted him as a custodian of my story. Maybe this was more important than anything else.

Next on the to-do list was figuring out who should publish the book. This was an easy one. We went with Trinity University Press, right here in San Antonio. I am a proud graduate of Trinity, and David has been a professor there since 1992. We arranged a meeting in early 2023 with Tom Payton, then the press's director, and from the get-go he was enthusiastically on board and supportive.

Then we got to work. My wife, Erika Prosper, and I met in the seminar room at Trinity University's department of history with

David and his research assistant, Jennifer Chiesa, for hours of interviews from August through December 2023. It was important for Erika to be there because in many cases she had a more accurate recollection of events than I did, even from my early years before we met. After this series of interviews, David and I continued to meet regularly to fill in the blanks and discuss what to include in the book and what to leave out.

Based on the interviews, documents, and artifacts I retrieved and his own research, David wrote rough drafts of the book's eleven chapters from January to August 2024. He sent the chapters to me as he completed them, after running them past Jennifer Chiesa's considerable copyediting skills. The text was essentially the skeletal structure of each chapter, to which I added the connective tissue, the fiber and sinew, to bring it to life. I expanded, sometimes considerably, upon what was written, using David's first drafts as prompts to include more detailed discussion of aspects of my personal life and professional career, along with more anecdotes that this process compelled me to remember and contemplate with the advantage of hindsight (and David's third-person objectivity). Then I returned the chapters to David for a touch-up before sending the completed manuscript to Trinity University Press for the final review.

I wanted to see this book published for several reasons. Now that we are in the aftermath of my termed-out eight years in office, I think there should be a more detailed accounting of a number of things that happened while I was mayor. Many aspects of the decision-making process are, often by necessity, behind the scenes. I think a more detailed exposition and analysis of these processes will help many officials, public servants, and corporate and community leaders understand better what goes into these decisions and, in particular, the many variables and circumstances I had to consider when making them.

My whole life, personal and professional, helped prepare me for the challenges of public office. This book examines the inflection points that led me to go in one direction over another, accumulate important experiences (good and bad), and develop a value system that helped pave the way for public service. In a way, this book can be seen as my side of the story, but I try to be as objective as possible, admitting some mistakes or in retrospect wishing I had done something differently—and reflecting on some of the struggles that helped shape who I am. I hope what the reader deduces from this account at the very least is that I always tried my best.

This book is something of a love letter to San Antonio. I was neither born nor raised in what we know as Military City, USA, but soon after relocating here for college at Trinity University, I fell in love with it. I often say that I grew up in San Antonio while also gaining a deep appreciation over the years for its history, heritage, diversity, institutions, and, most importantly, its people. This book is another way of sharing my gratitude to San Antonians for having faith in me and entrusting me with the authority to help take care of their past, present, and future.

Finally I have always considered the possibility of writing a book to be a letter to my son, Jonah. This is besides the fact that he and Erika had to put up with so much and gave up a lot while I served on the city council and as mayor. Even though public service was a constant strain on the time we had together, Jonah and Erika were integral parts of this whole adventure, and our collective ride was worth it in the end. Some of the lessons and observations along the way, including some from before they came along, are perhaps best expressed within the written arc of my life.

David and I thank Tom Payton and all of those at the press who took part in the publication process. We also thank David's fabulous research assistant, Jennifer Chiesa, without whom we could not have done all of this (although David did not want me to write this for fear that someone else will hire her away on future endeavors). We also want to thank those who wrote the short Voices of San Antonio essays that appear throughout the book. Their insights and comments certainly add some color and perspective to the narrative, and I am grateful both for these and for their own significant contributions to San Antonio.

David profusely thanks his wife, Judy Dunlap, who he said has always been his biggest supporter; she was the first line of defense for reading our chapters and offering comments and suggestions. He also asked that I include the following statement: "It has been one of my great honors to get to know Ron Nirenberg and to support his efforts in San Antonio. I am privileged to have helped Ron with this book, to get to know him even better than I had before, and to collaborate on what I think is an important work, one to which he committed a great deal of effort amid an already demanding schedule. The world is a better place when people like Ron are in leadership positions, and I look forward to seeing—and supporting—what comes next."

For my part, Erika and Jonah are my north star, my inspiration for a life in public service. Making them proud each day when I get home is what has motivated me to work hard in every job I've ever had. Their love and support have often been the reason I am able to get from one day to the next. The focus of my work has been—and remains—leaving the world a better place for Jonah and his generation and, I hope, inspiring them to do the same for those who come after.

Being mayor has required the entire family to be involved. I thank my dad, Ken Nirenberg, and my stepmother, Carol Noble, for always stepping up for us and (indirectly) for my community. Often this meant babysitting, carpooling, and even volunteering at the polls during the early vote. Sometimes it was just offering a shoulder to lean on. Similarly my mother, Charlotte Nirenberg, although she had limited means, was a source of unconditional love and support from childhood to adulthood, including as I entered politics. When I was very young she told me I could achieve any dream I put my mind to, and she made me believe it. My mom passed away as I wrote this book, and I miss her.

Although my siblings and I started our own lives long ago,

Marc, Heather (McKillip), and I got a lot more time together recently as we took care of my mom in her final year. During that time I was able to see and admire who they have become for themselves, their communities, and their children. The same goes for my stepsiblings Will Wysocki and Anna Brady and their families. I am grateful that they have all shaped my time as a public servant. Thank you also to my in-laws, Pat and Jonah Gray, whose adventures together gave them perfect instincts on how to love their children who are always in the public eye. Thanks, also, to the other side of Erika's family, who accepted me as their own, especially Abundia, the late Tafolla matriarch who lived a life of struggle to make a future in America, Laura and Esperanza, Jamey Sepulveda, and our nephew Julio Garcia.

When I speak to San Antonio audiences, I often repeat the mantra "Nothing good happens without teamwork." I want to thank my two closest mentors, Phil Hardberger and Lionel Sosa, along with my mayor and city council office staffs over the years, especially the chiefs of staff who have served so ably in a job that burns most people out: T. J. Mayes, Rosie Noble Stewart, Trey Jacobson, Jim Greenwood, Ivalis Meza Gonzalez, and Zack Lyke. I am grateful for Bruce Davidson, my communications manager, who agreed to come out of retirement after a four-decade newspaper career (and stayed all four mayoral terms); "the daisies" Alice Aguirre, my executive assistant, and Jackie Bolds, my office manager, who both also eschewed retirement and worked with me for my entire tenure at city hall, both on city council and in the mayor's office; and Victoria Shoemaker, Gabrielle Herrera, Maria Luisa Cesar, Sarah McLornan, Alex Sarabia, Rocio Guenther, Alex Dixon, Teresa Menendez-Myers, Juan Valdez, Michelle Lugalia-Hollon, Marisa Bono, Victoria Gonzalez-Gerlach, Ishmael Abuabara, Ruby Perez, Drew Galloway, Coda Rayo-Garza, Harjot Kaur, Walter Ague, Eloy LaQue, Hudson Kyle, Gayle McDaniel, and Raymundo Garza. Erika, Jonah, and I are also beholden to Chief William McManus, Albert Castillo, Peter Knutson, Joe Serratos, Gus Segura, Stephen Flores, Aaron Del Angel, and all of the police officers who served at one time or another on the executive detail.

I owe a great deal to all of the people who served on my campaign teams over the years. Their main motivation was the same as mine—creating a better future for our community and the world. In twelve years, I was on the ballot in nine elections (including three runoffs), and during that time I initiated ballot propositions for five sales tax propositions, six capital improvement bonds, and seven city charter changes. All were successful. That would not have been possible without excellent political strategy and execution, from my advisers to campaign staff to volunteers to donors. There are too many to name, but thank you specifically to Kelton Morgan, Lionel and Kathy Sosa, James Aldrete, Zack Lyke, Betty Sutherland, Judy Hall, Gilberto Ocañas, Christian Archer, Gordon Hartman, Bert Santibañez, Ryan Garcia, Linda Chavez-Thompson, Frank Dunn, Sonia Rodriguez, Blakely Fernandez, Rebecca Cedillo, Harvey Najim, Jamie Kowalski, Brandon Logan, Berto Guerra, Irene Chavez, Janelle MacArthur, Norma Denham, Pasha Moore, Jeff Goldblatt, Dwayne Robinson, Beth Hudson, Oliva Travieso, Alex Dixon, Colt Osburn, Vanessa Macias, Sonia Jimenez, Johnny Villarreal, Jocelyne Soto, Juany Torres, Natalie Marquez, Austin Dolan, Cole Bowles, Kirby Braun, Rosie Noble Stewart, Noah Howe, Zack Dunn, Jonathan Alonzo, Kazim Fahim, Theresa Canales, Michael Quintanilla, Martha Tijerina, Jorge and Victoria Herrera (and their kids), and Mike and Martha Flores (and their kids), to name just a few. I'm so proud that many of our youngest student volunteers have gone on to successful careers in public service, including elected office, as well as business, law, and many other fields. Some have even started their own companies devoted to getting more people engaged in government. I thank Manny Ruiz and Bonnie Conner, treasurers in my mayoral and council campaigns, respectively, who were able to get an unknown, under-resourced candidate successfully elected and reelected.

I thank several friends and colleagues who have cultivated a passion for particular aspects of service and policy, people I have served most closely with through challenging times, and others who helped through their collaboration and example: Sherry Dowlatshahi, Ann Helmke, Gen. Juan Ayala, Sally Basurto, Erik Walsh, Sheryl Sculley, my thirty-six city council colleagues over the years, Amir Samandi, Rabbi Chaim Block, Archbishop Gustavo García-Siller, the South Texas Alliance of Cities (especially my fellow cofounders), Mary Ellen Wiederwohl and the team at Accelerator for America, Virginia Mayer and the Democratic Mayors Association, Clarence Anthony and the National League of Cities, the Texas Municipal League, the U.S. Conference of Mayors, my Bloomberg-Harvard (BH-2) City Leadership partner mayors and the Bloomberg Philanthropies team, the passionate network of Sister Cities International, the Mayors Migration Council, the NewDEAL Leaders Network, Rev. Diana Phillips, Noel Poyo, Lourdes Castro Ramírez, Mike Ramsey, Colleen Bridger, Nelson and Tracy Wolff, Henry and Mary Alice Cisneros, Howard Peak, Julián Castro, Ed Whitacre, John Montford, Jane and Larry Macon, Sylvester Turner, Mary Dennis, Greg Fischer, Berto Guerra, the Lawton family, the Starr family, Amy Hardberger, Charlie Conner, Bill Clover, Yonghun Kim, Rico Izaguirre, Carey Latimore, Juan Sepulveda, Oliver Lee, Tim Maloney, Justin Hill, Alberto Garza, Gary Slutkin, Steve Seidner, Cesar Cantu, Gen. John and Carolyn Evans, Erik Alva, Daniel Graney, David Kinder, Jorge Elizondo and his late husband Steve Trevino, Jeff Traylor, Gregg Popovich, Eric Cooper, Mario Obledo, the Mayor's Fitness Council, the Asian American Alliance of San Antonio, Marianne Kestenbaum, María and Manuel Berriozábal, Pastor Don Guthrie, Pastor Dan Harrington, Rev. Herman Price, Father David Garcia, Rev. Tom Heger, Rev. Kenneth Kemp, Rev. Raymond Judd, Rabbi Mara Nathan, Imam Omar Shakir, Robert Huesca, William Christ, Jennifer Henderson, Don Van Eynde, Kathleen Hall Jamieson, Carolyn Marvin, Larry Gross, Anne

Cowan, my LSA team and Class 37, Michelle Martinez, Francisco Gonima, Lisa Andrade, Lorraine Pulido, Melissa Sorola, Lisa Bombin, Stephen and Lena Delgado, Mark and Denise Hernandez, Ramiro Cavasos, Richard Perez, A. J. Rodriguez, Raul Lomeli, Wes Baerga, Kory Cook, JJ Lopez, Johnny Hernandez, Rudy Rodriguez, Clif Douglas, Walter Serna, Carri Baker, Will Long, Cherise Rohr-Allegrini, Steve and Jody Newman, Chris Victoria, Joe Litvin, Jeff and Lee Niederdeppe, and Brett and Heather Mueller.

Finally I will be forever indebted to the beautiful, diverse, compassionate people of San Antonio. I did not imagine this life when growing up, but I asked for their trust and promised to make them proud. Thank you for the privilege of serving you.

INDEX

CREDITS

Images on pages 15, 18, 39, 43, 239, 243, from the author's collection
Image on page 51, courtesy of the Annenberg School for Communication, University of Pennsylvania
Image on page 67, courtesy of Trinity University and KRTU-FM
Images on pages 68, 118, 158, 170, 182, 193, 198, courtesy of the *San Antonio Express-News*
Images on pages 81, 86, 121, 134, 142, 251, courtesy of Jonathan Alonzo
Image on page 108, courtesy of the *San Antonio Report*
Image on page 128, Getty Images
Images on page 202, courtesy of the United States Air Force
Image on page 223, courtesy of the Joseph R. Biden Jr. Presidential Library
Image on page 227, courtesy of Texas Public Radio
Image on page 237, courtesy of the City of San Antonio
Image on page 249, courtesy of Gobierno de Ciudad de México

pages 98–99, "Paradoxical Commandments" found on the wall of Shishu Bhavan likely adapted from text in chapter 2 of Kent M. Keith's pamphlet *The Silent Revolution: Dynamic Leadership in the Student Council* (Harvard Student Agencies, 1968; repr. 2003)

Ron Nirenberg served as the mayor of San Antonio, the seventh largest city in the United States, from 2017 to 2025. He previously served on the San Antonio City Council and worked in civic media and public policy at the Annenberg Public Policy Center. He is the Calgaard Distinguished Professor of Practice in the communication department at Trinity University and lives in San Antonio, Texas.

David W. Lesch is the Ewing Halsell Distinguished Professor of History at Trinity University and has had eighteen books published, including *A History of the Middle East since the Rise of Islam*, *Syria: A Modern History*, and *The Arab-Israeli Conflict: A History*. He lives in San Antonio, Texas.